Edit Like a Pro with iMc

Leverage Apple's free editor for iOS, iPadOS 3.0.1, and macOS 10.3.5 and enrich videos with Keynote animations

Regit

BIRMINGHAM—MUMBAI

Edit Like a Pro with iMovie

Copyright © 2023 Packt Publishing

All rights reserved. No part of this book may be reproduced, stored in a retrieval system, or transmitted in any form or by any means, without the prior written permission of the publisher, except in the case of brief quotations embedded in critical articles or reviews.

Every effort has been made in the preparation of this book to ensure the accuracy of the information presented. However, the information contained in this book is sold without warranty, either express or implied. Neither the author, nor Packt Publishing or its dealers and distributors, will be held liable for any damages caused or alleged to have been caused directly or indirectly by this book.

Packt Publishing has endeavored to provide trademark information about all of the companies and products mentioned in this book by the appropriate use of capitals. However, Packt Publishing cannot guarantee the accuracy of this information.

Group Product Manager: Rohit Rajkumar
Publishing Product Manager: Kaustubh Manglurkar
Senior Editor: Divya Anne Selvaraj
Technical Editor: Simran Haresh Udasi
Copy Editor: Safis Editing
Project Coordinator: Aishwarya Mohan
Proofreader: Safis Editing
Indexer: Manju Arasan
Production Designer: Ponraj Dhandapani
Marketing Coordinator: Nivedita Pandey

First published: March 2023

Production reference: 2130423

Published by Packt Publishing Ltd.
Livery Place
35 Livery Street
Birmingham
B3 2PB, UK.

978-1-80323-890-6

www.packtpub.com

To everyone who told me I could write, and to Packt, for letting me prove it.

- Regit

Contributors

About the author

Regit is a British YouTuber who, since buying a Mac in 2013, has used iMovie to edit everything from gaming videos to university film and TV projects. Regit holds a BSc Hons. degree in film and television production, and has academic interest in broadcast TV and its economics. Back in the real world, Regit is a keen advocate for consumer rights and sustainability issues.

Thanks to my editors, Keagan and Divya, for accommodating me in this unfamiliar authoring process, and letting me write on Google Docs. Thank you Chayan for asking on `r/iMovie` *whether someone wanted to write a book – and saying yes to me!*

Credit is due to forum stalwarts such as Rich839 and Kurt Papke, for their iMovie wisdom; Michael Kinney for his videos on QuickTime editing and Keynote as 'After Effects-lite'; and to Bruce for moving clip connections!

Thanks to Mrs. GG for teaching me that "English is a confidence game," and for the guidance of my mother, a former technical author.

On that note, I want to say a special thank you to my parents, for tolerating me longer than anyone else could and for giving me an unconditional place in a loving home.

About the reviewer

Bruce G. Macbryde is an independent trainer for iMovie and Final Cut Pro with over 20 years of experience gained from the various versions of both software packages. Bruce gained a marketing certificate from NSW TAFE in 1984. After obtaining this qualification, he continued with TAFE as a tutor in marketing and market research courses for several years. During a 7-year spell in Wellington, New Zealand, he established an Apple resellership, ECONET, while also teaching courses in Adobe Photoshop, PageMaker, Illustrator, and commercial Microsoft software packages within the New Zealand Polytechnic system. On his return to Sydney, he was employed as a sales manager by the Australian Authorized Apple distributors from 1998 to 2004. He was later employed by Apple-authorized resellers as a training manager for iMovie, Final Cut Pro, and other Apple-developed software from 2004 to 2009. In 2004, he established Wedding Media Productions as a wedding video business in Sydney, Australia. He is a YouTube creator for the `VideoTutors` channel, with over 500 published video tutorials.

Table of Contents

Preface   xiii

Part 1 – Get to Know Video Editing

1

Why and How We Edit Videos   3

Technical requirements	4
The importance of the editing process	4
The principles of editing	5
Coherence – making your video easy to follow	6
Conciseness – getting to the point quicker	7
Adding meaning – creating a richer, smoother viewing experience	7

In-file editing with QuickTime Player on macOS	8
Using Trim mode	8
Using Clips mode	9
Saving your finished video	14
Why choose QuickTime Player to make edits?	14
What about iOS and iPadOS?	15
Summary	**16**

2

Automatic and Template Editing with Magic Movie and Storyboards   17

Technical requirements	18
Understanding the pros and cons of automatic editing	18
Why isn't all editing simple like this?	19
When does automatic editing help?	19
Creating a movie with Magic Movie	20
Adding photos and videos in Magic Movie	23
Changing graphics styles with the Styles menu	24
Customizing music in Magic Movie	25

Using the Edit menu in Magic Movie	25
Using the Edit menu toolbar	26
Combining videos with Magic Movie	31
Exporting a Magic Movie	33
Using Storyboard mode	33
Creating a Storyboard mode project	34
Using the Storyboard editing menu	36
Using the Storyboard Edit mode	38

Limitations of Magic Movie and Storyboard mode	39	Summary	39

3

Using Movie Mode in iOS and iPadOS — 41

Technical requirements	41	**Editing videos in Movie mode**	53
Creating and setting up a Movie mode project	42	Edit actions in Movie mode	54
		Customizing clips in Movie mode	55
Why use Movie mode?	42	**Using cuts and other transitions**	60
Creating a project in Movie mode	42	Editing transitions in Movie mode	61
The Movie mode interface	44	Using the Precision Editor	62
Using the Movie mode Media Browser	45		
Adding video in Movie mode	46	**Editing audio in Movie mode**	64
Movie mode project settings	46	Limitations of background audio	65
Assembly editing in Movie mode	49	Layering sounds in Movie mode	66
Using keyboard shortcuts on iOS and iPadOS	49	Fading audio for better video	67
Rearranging clips in Movie mode	50	Making smooth audio transitions with J- and L-cuts	68
Editing photos in Movie mode	51	**Quality control and exporting**	70
Using photo animations – the Ken Burns effect	51	**Summary**	72

Part 2 – iMovie for macOS

4

Understanding iMovie for macOS – Keyboard Shortcuts and the Magnetic Timeline — 75

Technical requirements	76	Using the Project Media tab	80
Understanding iMovie for macOS – libraries and events	76	Adding media from the Photos library	80
		Navigating iMovie with keyboard shortcuts	81
The iMovie Library	77		
Creating multiple iMovie Libraries	78	File and project actions	81
Creating Events in the iMovie Library	78	Timeline and menu navigation	82
What are events used for?	79	Editing tools	84

Clip connections and the magnetic timeline	87	Working with connected media	90
		Working with connected audio	91
Timelines – tracks versus connections	87	Background audio in iMovie for macOS	92
Understanding the magnetic timeline	89	**Summary**	**94**

5

iMovie Editing Workflow – Import, Edit, and Export — 95

Import – preparing media for editing in iMovie	95	Using maps	117
		Using backgrounds	119
How to import directly from devices	96	Using transitions	120
Using and customizing the iMovie import menu	98	**Editing using the toolbar**	**122**
Marking media as favorited or rejected	101	Color balance	122
Customizing Media Browser settings	102	Color correction	124
iMovie project settings	**104**	Crop	125
Deciding your project settings	104	Creating Ken Burns animations that settle	128
Checking the project's frame rate – counting frames	106	Other Crop actions	132
		Stabilization	134
What frame rate should I choose?	106	Volume, noise reduction, and equalizer	136
The assembly edit	**108**	Speed	139
Using the Precision Editor	109	Filters and audio effects	139
Using the Clip Trimmer	110	Information, Enhance, and Reset All	140
		Copy and paste toolbar edits	141
Using iMovie media	**111**	**Exporting a project**	**142**
Using the Audio & Video tab	111	**Summary**	**144**
Adding titles	115		

6

Using iMovie Effects – Overlays and Keyframing — 145

Cutaways – introducing overlays in iMovie	146	Multi-camera editing with cutaways and opacity effects	151
Using cutaways to hide jump cuts	147	Syncing multi-camera footage	153
Adding fade transitions to overlays	148	Editing multi-camera footage	156
Creating Opacity effects	150	**Split screen and blue/green screen effects**	**157**

Using Green/Blue Screen effects	160	Using audio keyframes	168
Using Picture in Picture effects in iMovie	162	Using transition effects – speed and color ramping	170
Using Zoom and Swap transitions with PiP	164	Combining effects – creating compound clips	172
Using keyframe animations on macOS	166	Summary	175

Part 3 – Customizing Your Videos

7

Integrating Keynote – Titles and Animations — 179

Technical requirements	180	Exporting, importing, and adjusting multi-stage animations	195
Creating custom titles with Keynote	180		
Exporting Keynote titles	183	Creating path animations with Keynote	196
Importing Keynote files into iMovie	185		
Creating animated titles in Keynote	186	Using Magic Move animations	202
Exporting animated titles from Keynote	188	Custom transitions using overlays	204
		Creating simple transitions with Magic Move	204
Creating multi-stage animations with Build Order	189	Exporting and importing multi-stage Magic Move animations	205
Building out animations	192	Dead easy animation with Dynamic Backgrounds	206
		Summary	208

8

Custom Export Formats, ft. Handbrake — 209

Technical requirements	210	How to install and run Handbrake	219
Why all this video jargon?	210	Adding a source to Handbrake	220
Working with aspect ratio	210	Changing video cropping in Handbrake	221
Changing aspect ratio with Keynote	212	Exporting from Handbrake	222
Exporting sideways from iMovie	215	Transcoding multiple files with Handbrake	223
		Using presets in Handbrake	223

Creating presets in Handbrake	224	Creating a ProRes export from a mobile project	229
Batch-transcoding a folder of videos	225	Compressing a master video with Handbrake	230
Using Handbrake to compress files	**226**	Compressing to a specific size with bitrate controls	232
What is ProRes?	227	Disadvantages of using Average Bitrate	233
Compressing video with Handbrake	228	**Summary**	**233**

9

Common iMovie Problems and Their Solutions — 235

Technical requirements	**236**	**Problem – editing on iMovie is slow or choppy**	**242**
Problem – iMovie won't accept your video format	**236**	Solution 1 – change the project settings	243
Solution – transcoding video that iMovie won't accept	237	Solution 2 – compound your effects	243
Problem – clips don't play properly	**238**	Solution 3 – split the project into multiple timelines	244
Solution – "reminding" iMovie of the clips in the project	238	**Problem – iMovie constantly fills hard drive space**	**245**
Problem – iCloud videos are still "downloading"	**238**	Solution – delete render files	245
Solution – tidy up your iCloud storage	239	**Problem – iMovie export has failed**	**246**
Long-term solution – remove project media from iCloud libraries	240	Solution 1 – find and delete the problem frame	246
Problem – audio and video drift out of sync	**241**	Solution 2 – screen-record the project	247
Solution – change the speed of the audio clip	241	**What if my editing issue isn't listed here?**	**249**
		General solutions for general problems	249
		Summary	**251**

Index — 253

Other Books You May Enjoy — 262

Preface

Master iMovie for iOS, iPadOS, and macOS to create effective and engaging videos from import to export. It's not about your tools but what you do with them. By teaching you the foundational principles of editing, this book will help you to edit impressive and engaging videos that are uniquely yours.

Who this book is for

Suitable even for absolute beginners, this book includes simple, progressive guides to help you master editing principles. You'll then build toward a full editing workflow, using iMovie to create simple but effective videos to inform, educate, and entertain your colleagues, friends, and family. For more advanced users such as YouTubers and other online content creators, this book contains valuable tips on stamping your unique identity and brand onto your videos; and customizing them for exporting anywhere.

What this book covers

Chapter 1, Why and How We Edit Videos, explains the importance of the post-production process: creating and refining meaning. We'll also dip our toes into editing by looking at the basic trimming and splitting tools available in the macOS QuickTime Player.

Chapter 2, Automatic and Template Editing with Magic Movie and Storyboards, starts our journey with iMovie for iOS and iPadOS. We'll look at how Magic Movie and Storyboard mode can teach you parts of the editing process and even make videos for you.

Chapter 3, Using Movie Mode in iOS and iPadOS, explains the workflow for editing video and sound in a traditional timeline. We'll start to look at changing what's seen within the video frame and work with the Precision Editor to help you make your videos better with sound.

Chapter 4, Understanding iMovie for macOS – Keyboard Shortcuts and the Magnetic Timeline, will explain how iMovie's system of Libraries and Events works on the Mac, as well as running through useful keyboard shortcuts for navigating the app. We'll also develop an understanding of Apple's Magnetic Timeline and the idea of connected media.

Chapter 5, iMovie Editing Workflow – Import, Edit, and Export, goes into depth on the video creation process in iMovie for MacOS. We'll look at best practices for importing footage; using iMovie's stock media (and where not to); cropping and Ken Burns animations; and how to export a high-quality master file of your video.

Chapter 6, *Using iMovie Effects – Overlays and Keyframing*, follows on from *Chapter 5* by introducing iMovie's connected video layer. The chapter will explain how to use iMovie's overlay settings to introduce cutaways and green-screen effects, as well as add and animate pictures in picture. We'll also make use of cutaways and opacity to create visual effects and edit multi-camera footage.

Chapter 7, *Integrating Keynote – Titles and Animations*, will teach you to use Keynote to create and export highly-customized titles and animations that will help you put a unique stamp on your videos.

Chapter 8, *Custom Export Formats, ft. HandBrake*, is all about optimizing your video exports for different websites and maybe even clients. You'll learn to change the aspect ratio of your videos, rotate videos in iMovie to make portrait videos, and use HandBrake presets to compress multiple videos to the size you need them.

Chapter 9, *Common iMovie Problems and Their Solutions*, addresses a certainty in editing: things going wrong. This chapter runs through some of the most common issues for iMovie users. We'll look at how to solve and work around these problems and learn how to avoid them in the future.

To get the most out of this book

This book assumes that you're familiar with macOS, its basic commands, Finder navigation, and downloading apps through the App Store and files from the internet. There are plenty of guides online for getting used to the *Mac*. *MacMost.com* (`https://macmost.com/mac-basics`) is a long-standing fan favorite.

It will also be beneficial if you are familiar with using *iOS/iPadOS*, mostly in terms of using the *Photos* and *Files* apps. As for *iMovie*, no prior knowledge is assumed at all – it is what this book is all about, after all.

To follow along, you'll need to download a `.zip` file from `https://packt.link/hT570` that contains all of this book's interactive resources. Then, on both mobile devices and Mac, just type the link into your browser's search bar, then tap or click **Download**. Make sure to keep the materials in a place you'll remember so that you can keep coming back to them while you work through the exercises in the book.

Software/hardware covered in the book	Operating system requirements
QuickTime Player	macOS 10.15 (Catalina) or later
iMovie for iOS/iPadOS version 3.0	iOS/iPadOS 15 or later
iMovie for macOS version 10.3.5	macOS 12 (Monterey) or later
Keynote version 12.1	macOS 12 (Monterey) or later
HandBrake version 1.6	macOS 12 (Monterey) or later
Existential Audio Blackhole 2Ch	macOS 10.10 (Yosemite) or later

Notes (for the more advanced reader)

There is one iMovie feature, in particular, this book does not cover: **Cinematic mode**. Cinematic mode allows you to change what areas of your shot are in focus during the edit. It's certainly powerful and allows you to draw the audience's attention to certain people or objects without having to reframe. Unfortunately, it's only available using iPhone 13 and later – something I don't have access to. However, if you can access it, do! The following links are Apple's official guides for editing Cinematic mode clips on *iOS/iPadOS* (`https://support.apple.com/en-gb/guide/imovie-iphone/kna09b78e8dc/ios`) and *macOS* (`https://support.apple.com/en-gb/guide/imovie/movafa5244eb/mac`).

One wider topic that's absent from this book is production advice. This is because I'm not a videographer, and I'm never going to pretend to be. I use my iPhone camera because it's foolproof, but I wouldn't say that my shots are particularly artistic. If you want to learn how to shoot something beautiful – as well as how to frame, balance, and adjust using more advanced cameras – there are plenty of great resources online. Examples include *No Film School* (`https://nofilmschool.com/rules-of-cinematic-framing-and-composition`) and *Studio Binder* (`https://www.studiobinder.com/category/directing/cinematography/`). However, I will suggest a couple of rules to live by during production to make the editing process more flexible:

- Film more than you need – a wider-framed shot, filmed for much longer than you think you need to
- Film in a higher resolution than you need so that even if you reframe or compound effects together on your clip, the end quality of your video will still be high

Finally, know that the websites and resources I suggest in this book are not prescriptive – they're just examples to get you started. I watch and enjoy far more YouTubers than I refer to, and there are many alternatives to programs such as *HandBrake* and *Blackhole*, which you will see in *Chapter 8* and *Chapter 9*, respectively.

If you come out of this book with a passion for editing, fantastic! Going forward, have a look at channels such as *This Guy Edits* (https://www.youtube.com/user/svenpape) and the work of Walter Murch for guidance on editing fiction narratives. Telling a convincing story – while also convincing an audience it's real – requires you to juggle loads more considerations when editing: emotion, story continuity, and even tracking how your audience's eyes will move from one shot to the next.

If what I've just said sounds like gobbledygook, please don't be alarmed. Give the book a read before coming back to these notes. If this book has done its job right, it will make a lot more sense when you read it for the second time.

Download the color images

We also provide a PDF file that has color images of the screenshots and diagrams used in this book. You can download it here: https://packt.link/BNvrS.

Conventions used

There are some text conventions used throughout this book.

Bold: Indicates a new term, an important word, or words that you see onscreen. For instance, words in menus or dialog boxes appear in bold. Here is an example: "Select **System info** from the **Administration** panel."

> **Tips or important notes**
> Appear like this.

Get in touch

Feedback from our readers is always welcome.

General feedback: If you have questions about any aspect of this book, email us at customercare@packtpub.com and mention the book title in the subject of your message.

Errata: Although we have taken every care to ensure the accuracy of our content, mistakes do happen. If you have found a mistake in this book, we would be grateful if you would report this to us. Please visit www.packtpub.com/support/errata and fill in the form.

Piracy: If you come across any illegal copies of our works in any form on the internet, we would be grateful if you would provide us with the location address or website name. Please contact us at copyright@packt.com with a link to the material.

If you are interested in becoming an author: If there is a topic that you have expertise in and you are interested in either writing or contributing to a book, please visit authors.packtpub.com.

Share Your Thoughts

Once you've read *Edit Like a Pro with iMovie*, we'd love to hear your thoughts! Scan the QR code below to go straight to the Amazon review page for this book and share your feedback.

https://packt.link/r/1-803-23890-9

Your review is important to us and the tech community and will help us make sure we're delivering excellent quality content.

Download a free PDF copy of this book

Thanks for purchasing this book!

Do you like to read on the go but are unable to carry your print books everywhere?

Is your eBook purchase not compatible with the device of your choice?

Don't worry, now with every Packt book you get a DRM-free PDF version of that book at no cost.

Read anywhere, any place, on any device. Search, copy, and paste code from your favorite technical books directly into your application.

The perks don't stop there, you can get exclusive access to discounts, newsletters, and great free content in your inbox daily

Follow these simple steps to get the benefits:

1. Scan the QR code or visit the link below

`https://packt.link/free-ebook/9781803238906`

2. Submit your proof of purchase
3. That's it! We'll send your free PDF and other benefits to your email directly

Part 1 – Get to Know Video Editing

We are going to start our editing journey by first understanding the point of editing. Without knowing what we're editing for, the post-production process can seem vague, yet overwhelming.

The tools we'll use in this part of the book are aimed to introduce editing concepts gradually: we'll start with the most simple of actions using a program more simple than iMovie. Then, we'll move on to the entry-level version of iMovie, for iOS and iPadOS. First, we'll look at tools that do some of the work of editing for you, before using them as inspiration to create our own project.

While editing your own project, you'll begin to appreciate the importance of taking creative charge of the project, rather than trusting iMovie to create a video for you. You'll also be gradually introduced to the importance of sound, starting with adding sound to your project, before refining it to smooth out the cuts and other transitions in your video.

This part of the book comprises the following chapters:

- *Chapter 1, Why and How We Edit Videos*
- *Chapter 2, Automatic and Template Editing with Magic Movie and Storyboards*
- *Chapter 3, Using Movie Mode in iOS and iPadOS*

1
Why and How We Edit Videos

Welcome to a book all about iMovie, an editing program that I love and love to tell people about. This book will take you on an editing journey, starting with the basics in the iMovie app for iOS and iPadOS, where you will learn the fundamental actions involved in editing, before using those actions to tell your own stories in simple videos. Underpinning everything will be a focus on the principles of editing – why we edit and what we're trying to achieve by editing. Knowing what you're trying to achieve will help you save time and avoid feeling overwhelmed when you edit. In this first chapter, we'll look at what we try to achieve through editing, and master some basic editing techniques. You'll also learn how to save time editing on the Mac by performing basic editing within a file using QuickTime Player.

This chapter will start by discussing why editing is a necessary part of the production process, and cannot be avoided. We'll also look at the principles of editing: establishing coherence (getting clips in the correct order); making the video concise (removing unnecessary parts); and then adding meaning (through titles, animations, and graphics). Editing principles are really important to keep in mind because without them, there is no clear starting point in editing. Without a purpose to center on when editing, the unfamiliar world of an editing program can quickly become stressful and confusing. Knowing and being guided by simple principles will help you to make creative changes that make your video say what it intends to more successfully.

In this chapter, we will learn about the basic actions of editing by using a program that's simpler than iMovie but still very capable. QuickTime Player is a pre-installed macOS application, and we will use it to make an unfinished, jumbled-up video coherent and concise. We will use QuickTime Player's Trim and Clips modes to split and remove unnecessary bits of the video, as well as add extra video and an audio track that adds meaning through a voiceover. All of this editing will be done within a file, which is great for saving space and time on your computer. We are not jumping straight into iMovie because, for basic editing, even this comparably simple editing program is more complex than necessary. There is one golden rule in this book, which is to use the simplest tool that gets the job done!

The main topics we'll cover in this chapter are as follows:

- The importance of the editing process
- The principles of editing
- In-file editing with QuickTime Player on macOS

Technical requirements

To edit with QuickTime Player, you'll need a Mac computer running macOS Catalina (10.15) or later. QuickTime Player is the macOS default video player that comes pre-installed on your Mac. If you have any file with the `.mp4` or `.mov` extension (which you will if you use the Camera app on an Apple device), it will open automatically in QuickTime when you double-click the file.

> **Important note**
> You shouldn't need to download QuickTime Player. It's not on the App Store, and you should avoid looking for it on the web. It's part of the macOS operating system and will be on every Mac. There used to be a version (QuickTime 7) that was available for Windows, but this became unsupported as of 2016. QuickTime downloads advertised online could be scams or viruses, so be careful.

We'll also be using resources hosted on GitHub. The interactive exercise in this chapter involves putting together different parts of a video called *The Timeline*. The materials you need for that can be found within the `Chapter 1_The Timeline` folder within the `.zip` file provided to you through a download link in the *To get the most out of this book* section in the *Preface*. I'd recommend dragging all the files onto your desktop for easy access: when using QuickTime Player, you'll be doing all of your edits on the desktop. With that, let's get started on our journey toward editing like a pro.

The importance of the editing process

Why do we need to edit? Can't we just film something and be done with it? In a word, no. **Post-production** is a process that's integral to any video, TV, or film production. A video won't make it to its intended destination (YouTube, Vimeo, or maybe even a film festival) without some kind of input after it's been shot. Even if the sum total of your off-camera effort is clicking **upload**, that's still a post-production process.

You cannot avoid the post-production process. Film has always been synonymous with editing, but ever since television first arrived, production methods have been developed to reduce the need for tinkering with footage and create almost ready-packaged shows. But editors and post-production houses are still employed to apply finishing touches or make a recorded program fit to a time slot. Live programs still have edited clips played within them. A *Tom Scott* video impressively recorded in one take still benefits from audio adjustments and captions. Quite simply, editing is everywhere.

But if you can minimize the post-production process to simply clicking **upload** on what you recorded, why not do that? Well, without editing, you won't be able to fix any mistakes you made when the video was recorded. Secondly, the video is likely to be full of gaps and hesitations that make the video look unprofessional. Thirdly, an unedited video is unlikely to make its intended point very quickly, or it won't give the audience enough information. Finally, an unedited video is very likely to be boring, confusing, or both.

They say time is money, but a little bit of time spent editing can make a world of difference to how well your video is perceived. Moreover, editing doesn't have to be a waste of time if you're focused and deliberate. To help you focus on editing the most important bits of a video, entry-level editing programs such as iMovie have stripped-down interfaces that help you to prioritize the most important tasks.

iMovie was the first editing app I found, and I stuck with it for three reasons: it's free, unintimidating, and – unlike most basic software – it grows with you. Once you've learned the ropes, there are a lot of avenues available to expand your creativity and begin editing like a pro without the outlay of *pro* software. Before we jump into using iMovie, though, it's important to understand why we edit in the first place. Accordingly, this chapter is going to cover the most basic principles of editing. Keeping them in mind will make your video (and by "video," I mean anything audiovisual – a social media teaser, a tutorial, or a feature film) more engaging and effective.

The principles of editing

Fundamentally, editing creates meaning. Regardless of the type of project, editors start with a load of clips that, although they may look nice, don't yet tell a coherent story. A video won't make any sense or carry any meaning until the relevant clips are placed next to each other and in order. The idea of creating meaning can be broken down into these three purposes of editing:

- Coherence
- Conciseness
- Adding meaning

As a heads-up, in this section, we will discuss general tools and key terms that are associated with editing and how they link to each of the three principles. Don't worry if these terms feel vague or disconnected at the moment, as we'll get the opportunity to put them into practice throughout this book.

Coherence – making your video easy to follow

Putting everything in the right place and in the right order will make your video coherent. It's easy to appreciate that if you have a random jumble of clips, no one will understand what the video is trying to say. Assembling clips in the right order is a crucial first step, and that's why in professional post-production, the first stage of editing is called the **assembly edit**: making sure the whole story is present and in the intended order, for it to then be trimmed down, and added to, to make the video more engaging.

To get all these clips into sequence and play one after another, you're going to need a space where they can all be placed initially. It's no use having them as separate files that the viewer needs to close before opening the next one to watch. That'd make for a very tiresome viewing experience! In an editing program, all the clips are placed next to each other in a **timeline**. The timeline is a blank horizontal canvas. From left to right, it charts increasing time as your video plays. You can add as many clips as you like, and the end of the last clip is where the video ends.

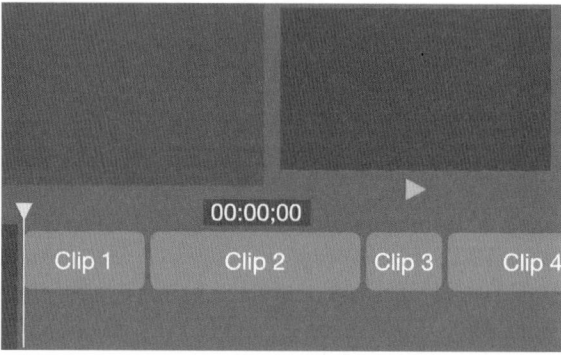

Figure 1.1 – An illustration of the timeline paradigm: the general structure of timeline-based editing programs

In the timeline **paradigm** (illustrated in *Figure 1.1*), the structure most editing programs are built around, the timeline sits at the bottom, with a preview window above it. The preview window shows a frame from the video based on where you click with your cursor on the timeline. That cursor location is marked by the **playhead**, a vertical line running down through the timeline. The **timecode** tells you how far through the timeline the playhead is. Phew, a lot of key terms in one paragraph. But never fear, we'll be reviewing these when we put our *The Timeline* video together in the *In-file editing with QuickTime Player on macOS* section!

Conciseness – getting to the point quicker

Director Alfred Hitchcock is credited with saying that `drama is life with the dull bits cut out`, and that's what editing does: it turns life, which is continuous (and drags in places), into a collection of the most interesting and relevant bits. That's what makes drama – the edited version of life – exciting and engaging.

You may have clips in your timeline that are in the right order but don't add anything to the video. Maybe they go over something that was already explained; maybe you trip over your words; maybe it's footage of something that isn't really relevant at all. You should always be asking yourself: does this clip really help my video to tell its story? If the answer is "no," remove the clip.

In the early days of editing, removing clips meant physically cutting them from a reel of film and throwing them away. Fortunately, in this digital world, you can rearrange and remove clips without degrading their quality or permanently deleting them. If a clip seems better somewhere else, you can move it. If you'd rather it wasn't there at all, you can delete it. If you change your mind, you can undo your actions. Not having to work *in order* in editing software is why iMovie and its fellow editing programs are called **non-linear editing** (**NLE**) programs: you can go back and make whatever changes you like, whenever you like.

However, it is possible to lose perspective and be a bit too ruthless with removing clips. If you cut too much out, you may find that your storyline or narrative (all videos have a narrative, even factual videos!) becomes confusing because there's not enough information to connect one bit of the story to the next. In this case, the video is not coherent. You may have deleted too many clips or moved them about too much. You should never fulfill one principle of editing at the expense of another – we need all three!

Adding meaning – creating a richer, smoother viewing experience

After you have a coherent timeline with unnecessary parts removed, you can consider how editing can add meaning to the video. It's important that you leave this stage till last because coherence and conciseness are like a strong foundation that you need in order to build your video further. Added meaning often comes in the form of information in captions and titles (the ones on news programs or talk shows telling you people's names and professions, for example, are called **lower thirds**). You can also add effects to the video or **reframe** shots to emphasize something in particular. But meaning can also be added through the way that you edit – the rhythm of the video and the way that you cut says a lot about the video's tone and intended meaning. More discussion on that can be found in the *Using cuts and other transitions* section of *Chapter 3*. To learn about reframing, check out the *Crop* subsection in *Chapter 5*.

A word to the wise – be careful about being rash and over-enthusiastic when adding *stuff* to your video. Remember that the core of what you're trying to do with editing is to make a few effective changes that will make your video better. Once you go past a certain point, each element you add loses its uniqueness and usefulness. Like everything in editing, this point is subjective; some people like more graphics than others. But a good technique is to ask yourself whether something really needs adding. If you can't think of a good reason, don't add it. Editing at its purest is simple, purposeful, and instinctive. There's no need to overcomplicate it.

That was a brief summary of the principles of editing. To put all of this into practice, the next section is going to guide you through making a video coherent and concise, as well as adding meaning through voiceovers, music, and extra context. This can be done entirely within a video file. You don't even need iMovie!

In-file editing with QuickTime Player on macOS

On macOS, it's possible to make quite a lot of edits within a video file – meaning that if you just need to (re)move a few sections of your video to tidy it up, you don't need to go through the much longer *import, edit, export* workflow that we'll cover in later chapters.

Using Trim mode

Trimming is the first editing action we're going to look at. Like most editing terms, it comes from the days of physically cutting bits of film and refers to what you might do with a pair of scissors. Because you're cutting bits off of a clip, the action of trimming is all about removing the parts of a video you don't need. Follow these steps to trim a video file in QuickTime Player:

1. Double-click to open the video file (`Chapter-One_the-timeline.mov` if you're following along) and use ⌘ + *T* to open Trim mode (to access this through the menu bar, it's **Edit | Trim…**). Trim mode will bring up a video strip – a basic timeline – that shows your whole video. There is a border highlighting the strip and **trim handles** at either end. In editing, a handle is something on the timeline you can select and move by dragging left or right.

2. In Trim mode, you can drag the trim handles inward as far as you like to make the video start later or end sooner. When you drag the handle, a tooltip appears above the handle showing the timecode at which you have trimmed the video start or end. If you're following along with the *The Timeline* video, drag the trim handle so that the video starts at the **title card**, as shown in *Figure 1.2*, not at the color bars before it.

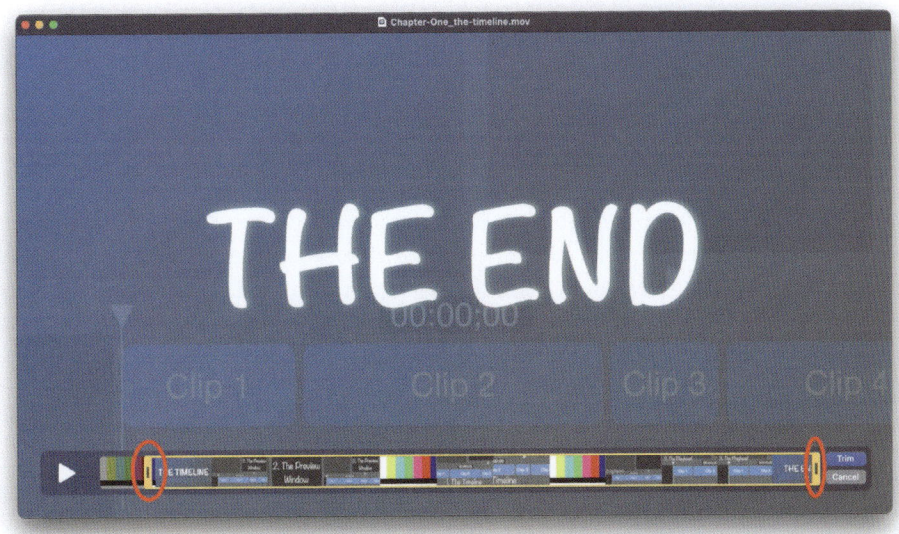

Figure 1.2 – The Timeline video with the trim handles (circled) in the correct place

3. To make more precise edits in Trim mode, drag a trim handle slowly until the video strip shows a zoomed-in section of the video. Unfortunately, this feature isn't very well-realized in macOS; it can be difficult to prompt the zoom change because there is no menu command to activate it. If you need to make edits that require you to be pinpoint accurate, you should use Clips mode. We will discuss Clips mode in the next section.

4. When you're happy, click **Trim** or press *Enter* to save the trim changes you've made.

Using Clips mode

The other command you can use to make edits in QuickTime, ⌘ + E, allows you to do even more than in Trim mode. Clips mode shows a translucent border around the clip. Instead of using trim handles, the tool used to make changes in this mode is the playhead, shown as a thin, red, vertical line. Take the following steps to see how Clips mode works:

1. When you play the video (which you can do by pressing the *L* key or the space bar), the playhead moves along the timeline as the video plays.

2. To stop the playhead, press the space bar again or the *K* key. It's good to get into the habit of using the letter keys, because the three main shortcut keys, *J* (play in reverse), *K,* and *L,* allow you to edit more efficiently.

3. To make fine adjustments to the playhead's position, make sure the video is paused. Click on the video strip and use the keyboard arrow keys (← and →) to move left and right. One key press moves the playhead one frame at a time, which can help you to make very precise edits.

4. Alternatively, if you need to move the playhead a larger distance, move your cursor to hover over the thin red line, and its shape will change to that shown in *Figure 1.3*. You can then click and drag the playhead to your desired location on the video strip.

5. If the playhead ever disappears, press the space bar or *L* again, and it should reappear.

Figure 1.3 – The playhead adjustment cursor icon

> **Extra tip – frames**
> A frame is the smallest unit of time in a video: each second of a video is usually made up of between 24 and 60 frames. In *Chapter 5*, we'll look at frame rates and how to check them in an iMovie project on the Mac.

Splitting clips

The main advantage of Clips mode is that it also allows you to **split** clips. Splitting cuts a clip into two separate pieces, at the playhead's position. Here's how to do that in Clips mode:

1. The ⌘ + *Y* keyboard shortcut will split the clip at the playhead's position. If you're following along, use ⌘ + *Y* twice to cut out one of the color bar sections from the middle of the video.

2. When a split has been made you can select the two pieces of video separately by clicking on either of them. Selected clips are highlighted with a border, as seen in *Figure 1.4*.

Figure 1.4 – Two splits have been made on either side of the color bars, isolating the bars into their own clip. That clip has been selected

3. You can delete a clip with the *backspace* key. If you're following along, do that for the color bars.
4. If you're following along, use steps 1-3 again to remove the other section of the video that's just color bars.

So why use splitting instead of trimming? Trimming only lets you manipulate the **in and out points** of the video – where the edited version of the video will start and end. Splitting allows you to cut out sections in the middle of your video, like the trick you learn where folding a piece of paper lets you cut a shape out of the middle. Splitting can be helpful if, for example, you misspeak and have to repeat something in the middle of a clip.

Adding video and audio

You thought Clips mode stopped there? Oh no. Not only can you split and reorder your original video, but you can even add other videos and an additional audio track. This is what makes the QuickTime Player genuinely capable as a basic NLE. If you're following along, you've made your *The Timeline* video coherent and concise; now, you can add meaning with an extra video clip and a voiceover:

1. To add clips, make sure you're in Clips mode (⌘ + *E*). If you're following along, get the extra clip (`extra-clip_part-4_The-Media-Bin.mov`) ready next to the QuickTime window (this is why I suggest having the file on your desktop).

2. To add the file to your video, click and drag the file over the video strip. The strip will move to make space for that file on the right or left of the clip, depending on which side you hover the video. Hover the extra clip between the third and fourth clips, as shown in *Figure 1.5*.

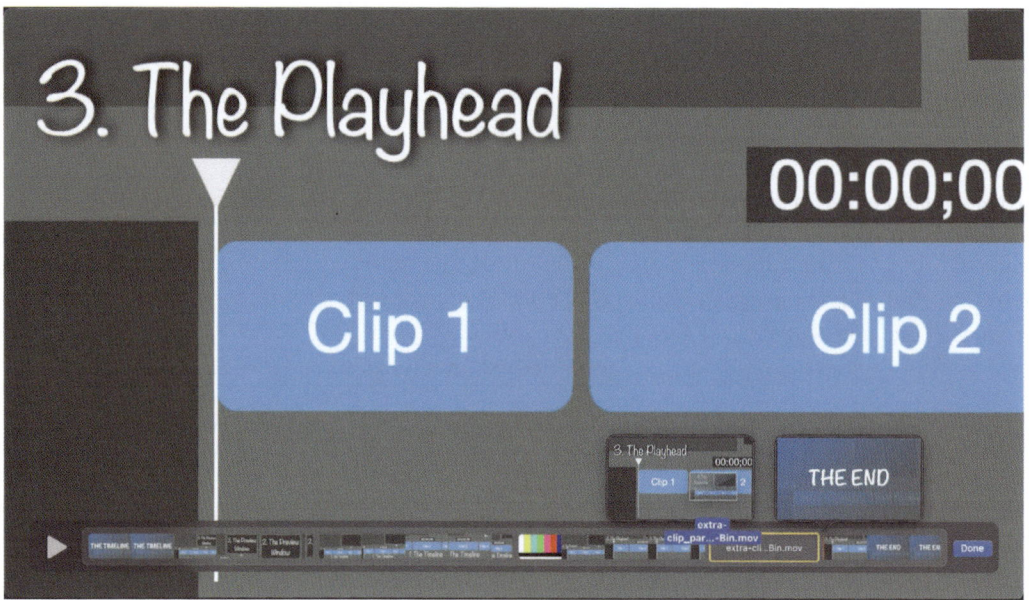

Figure 1.5 – If you hover the clip for long enough, little preview windows will show what's in the clips on either side

3. Simply drop the file to place the video – it's now been added.

As promised, you can also add your own audio track underneath the video. You might do this to complement a vlog with music or to enhance a tutorial with a how-to explanation. Let's finish off the interactive task by adding this audio:

1. Drag an audio file (`The-Timeline_Audio.mp3` if you're following along) over the video strip. A new space will appear underneath the video for the audio to go into.
2. Drop the file: you now have an audio track underneath your video that will play at the same time. *Figure 1.6* shows how this should look.

Figure 1.6 – Audio added below the QuickTime video strip

When you add the audio, it shows up as a **waveform**, which is how the clip's loudness changes over time. Big, relatively consistent waveforms usually mean human speech or loud environmental noise. That's what you can see in the waveform in *Figure 1.6*.

Do be aware that if your audio file is longer than the video, it will not stay at its original length; audio will always fit the size of the video in QuickTime by trimming off part of the end. Fear not, though, because you can trim audio files in the same way as video files:

1. Right-click or ^ + click on an audio file and select **Open With** | **QuickTime Player**.
2. Type ⌘ + *T* and use the trim handles to change the in and out points of the clip.
3. Click **Done** when you're happy.
4. Save your changes by going to **File** | **Export As** | **Audio only…**.
5. Add the new audio clip to the original video.

> **Check how you've done**
>
> If you're following along and have removed the right sections, you don't need to worry about trimming the audio with QuickTime Player. The *The Timeline* audio (a mix of voiceover and music) will fit snugly from the beginning to the end of the video.
>
> When you're done, check `The-Timeline_correct-video-audio` to see how the final video is intended to look. Remember, editing isn't an exact science – it's about making audiences informed and entertained. So don't worry if your video looks a little different!

Saving your finished video

When you make any changes to a video file, the name of the file will change to `Untitled`. This is because macOS likes to preserve the original file; your changes automatically become a new file. When you're happy with your changes and additions, here's how to save them:

1. Click **Trim** (Trim mode), **Done** (Clips mode), or press *Enter* to save your changes.
2. Save the new file by going to **File | Export As | 1080p...** in the menu bar, or save via the prompt when you click the red circle to close the QuickTime Player window.

If you want to only save the audio portion of the video, or remove the audio from a video, you can do this with QuickTime too, by going to **Edit | Remove Video** (or **Audio**) in the toolbar. You might want to do this if you have a screen recording with background noise that you don't want to share.

Why choose QuickTime Player to make edits?

So why would you choose this limited set of tools instead of going straight into iMovie? Well, quite simply, the simpler the system, the smoother it is, and the less that can go wrong. When you make changes as part of QuickTime Player, you can save the file and – usually within a few seconds – have a finished, edited video.

When you edit in an NLE, the process is a lot more complex. First, you need to import footage, which will fill up extra space on your Mac's hard drive. When you finish editing, you then have to **render** your changes, which is the process of the NLE turning your timeline into a playable video file. That process can take anywhere from minutes to hours, exponentially longer than just saving changes to a file. So if you're only planning on making simple changes such as cutting out mistakes and adding audio, or you have to make small edits to tens or hundreds of individual videos, editing within a file via QuickTime Player can save you a huge amount of time.

But, of course, not all edits are going to be that simple. You'll often need to add extra information through titles or graphics or direct the audience's attention by zooming into a specific part of the video frame to effectively tell the story you want to. You may have noticed that this happens in the *The Timeline* video you followed along with. For these kinds of changes, you'll need to use a proper NLE workflow, which we'll cover starting in *Chapter 3* through to *Chapter 6*.

What about iOS and iPadOS?

Because QuickTime Player is only available on macOS, unfortunately, you can't split and combine videos using iOS or iPadOS as you would with QuickTime Player. However, you can trim media in the Photos app. The following steps show you how:

1. Open the Photos app on your device.
2. Tap a video and select **Edit** at the top right. There you can move the trim handles to change the in and out points of the video, as shown in *Figure 1.7*.

Figure 1.7 – Trimming video using the Edit menu in the iOS/iPadOS Photos app

3. Tap **Done**, and you are given two options: **Save Video** or **Save Video as New Clip**. Here's a bit about each to help you choose:

   - Saving the video lets you play your shortened video in Photos and exports the shortened version if you share the video, but keeps the whole video preserved in case you go back into the `Edit` menu later or you want to import the whole video to iMovie.
   - Saving the video as a new clip permanently removes the grayed-out footage beyond the trim handles in the new video. The original is saved separately with no changes.

Unfortunately, there is no Clips mode in Photos, meaning that you can't cut out a section in the middle of your video. Although in-file splitting and combining of clips aren't possible on mobile devices, there are convenient alternatives within iMovie for iOS and iPadOS. Splitting and combining clips using Magic Movie (which we'll look at in *Chapter 2*) is a reasonably quick and easy alternative.

Summary

This chapter has hopefully helped you to see editing in a new light – as a necessary process that is integral to the whole world of video production, from amateur to professional. Fundamentally, editing creates meaning.

To narrow down what is most important to focus on when editing your video, we covered the three key purposes of editing. These are to make a video coherent, so the story it tells makes sense; to make the video concise, so it tells its story efficiently; and to add meaning so that your story becomes richer and has more context. It's important to ignore anything that doesn't help you fulfill these principles. That way, you shouldn't get waylaid or distracted when editing, which is especially important if you're working toward a deadline.

We also learned about how clips are arranged in the timeline and how the timecode and playhead tell you what part of the video you are looking at. We edited a simple video using QuickTime Player, using trimming and splitting to remove unwanted sections, added new video and audio to the original file, and saved a new file with the edits completed. I hope you'll now agree that every video tells a story. Thinking about how your narrative is communicated can help make your videos clearer and more impactful. In the next chapter, we will delve further into the idea of storytelling and video structure by looking at Magic Movie and Storyboards mode on iMovie for iOS and iPadOS.

2
Automatic and Template Editing with Magic Movie and Storyboards

Welcome to the second chapter, which is all about the tools in **iMovie** for iOS and iPadOS that make the job of editing easier. These *automatic* tools are designed to expand your creativity without overwhelming you with tools and functions that you need to learn about. The magic, as it were, happens behind the scenes.

In the first chapter, we established that editing is all about creating meaning. To tell a story effectively, you first need to build an assembly edit that keeps the basic principles of coherence and conciseness in mind. Now that we have created meaning by making our video coherent and concise, we are able to add meaning. This chapter will introduce you to Magic Movie, which does the job of assembling your videos for you, ready to add meaning instantly. Accompanying Magic Movie is Storyboard mode, which offers you a suggested video structure into which you can add your own videos – a kind of fill-in-the-gaps exercise. If the first chapter didn't light a video editing fire in your soul, seeing what you can make with Magic Movie and Storyboard mode will hopefully spark your interest in the creative aspect of editing!

In this chapter, we'll cover the following main topics:

- Understanding the pros and cons of *automatic* editing
- Creating simple videos with Magic Movie
- Using the more advanced tools in Magic Movie's Edit mode
- Creating themed videos with the guidance of Storyboard mode

Technical requirements

This chapter requires an iPhone or iPad, as we will be using the mobile iMovie app. For the best experience following along, you'll want iMovie version 3.0.1, which requires iOS/iPadOS 16.1 or later. However, Magic Movie and Storyboards were introduced with iMovie version 3.0, which runs on iOS 15.3. So, if you have an Apple device that can't run iOS 16 but already has iMovie installed, you will get a similar experience with iMovie 3.0.

We'll also be using stock footage downloaded from the internet. For Magic Movie, the interactive resources are available in the `Chapter 2` folder in the `.zip` file provided to you, and for Storyboard mode, we will download footage from a free stock footage website. Therefore, you'll need an internet connection and plenty of space on your device. Mind you, it's always important to have space to spare when editing! The steps for downloading videos on an iOS/iPadOS device can be found in the *Creating a Storyboard mode project* section of this chapter.

Understanding the pros and cons of automatic editing

In the first chapter, we looked at the timeline paradigm. It's the standard layout for NLEs, in which clips are laid out horizontally, from left to right. However, other models and structures do exist. In Magic Movie and Storyboard mode, clips are laid out in a vertical list. Each clip looks like a banner, separated from the other clips. This can feel a lot less intimidating than a blank timeline.

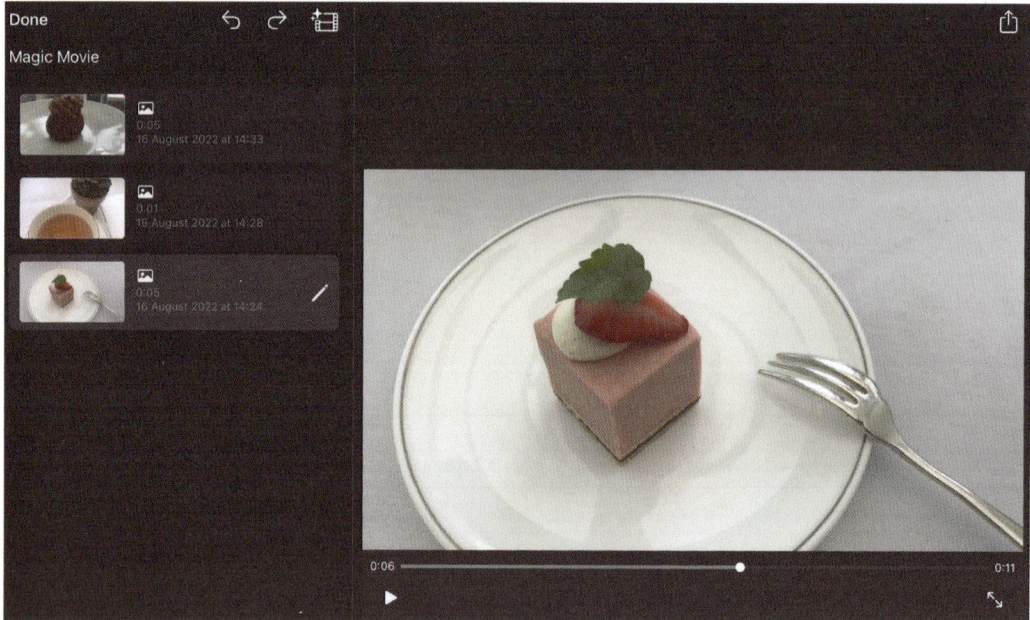

Figure 2.1 – The Magic Movie interface in which the clips, a tasty selection of tea and cakes, are shown as separate banners

Another advantage of this structure is that by having separate banners, less can go wrong off the back of a single action. In a timeline, clips sit on or below other clips and are often influenced by one another. For example, if you deleted one clip, several other clips could be deleted with it, and the video could fall out of sync with the sound. By making clips into separate banners, Magic Movie ensures that one edit going wrong won't cause problems for other clips. Think of each clip as a rung on a ladder: if one rung breaks, the ladder remains intact.

Why isn't all editing simple like this?

So, if this ladder-like structure is easier to understand and is less prone to mistakes rippling out and causing more trouble, why doesn't everyone use it? Firstly, there's history – the timeline paradigm aimed to emulate the look and feel of physical editing that took place with scissors and developed film. Editors are also creatures of habit, so the timeline paradigm has remained popular. Perhaps more importantly, though, simpler models – although they're easy to get to grips with – aren't catching on in professional circles because they miss part of the point of editing.

Professional editors want as much control as possible over how clips fit together. That's because the whole theory of editing is based on the idea that the nature of the first clip affects how we feel about the clip after it (a phenomenon called the **Kuleshov effect** if you want to find out more). Because clips exist in such a close relationship, a pro editor must be able to see and manage that relationship closely. Automatic editing tools reduce the interaction between clips. This reduces the creative options available to you because these tools make decisions on interactions and transitions for you. They don't eliminate the need for transitions and interactions, they just leave you out of the process. This is a complete no-no for professional editors, who have to make videos that fit exactly with what paying clients (advertisers, TV execs, or film directors) want to see.

When does automatic editing help?

Despite their limitations, automatic editing programs do a couple of things very well:

- Combine clips (whereas you can't do this in the Photos app, for instance)
- Add meaning and context to simple videos and sequences

Since we're right at the beginning of our editing journey on the iPhone and iPad, starting with Magic Movie and Storyboard mode can help to build confidence before we work on projects with greater creative scope and complexity. These tools are great for inspiring creativity, and also provide very simple ways of adding meaning to the video through on-screen graphics and titles. If your project doesn't require a great deal of creative freedom, they can make editing quicker and let you skip to the good bit.

Creating a movie with Magic Movie

Apple has understood that creative storytelling is a more jazzy prospect than stringing clips together and is, therefore, a more popular starting point for editors. Accordingly, they've developed Magic Movie and Storyboard mode, both of which take some of the effort and guesswork out of creating a coherent and concise project. Magic Movie promises to "create a video for you – no video editing required," taking the photos and videos in your Photos app and using machine learning to cut them to music it selects. With this as a foundation, you're free to begin adding more meaning and context to your video with titles and filters.

To make it easier to follow along with this chapter, we will be using the `Chapter 2: Berlin Album` files within the `Chapter 2` folder in the `.zip` file, which you can use to create a Magic Movie – a folder of photos and videos from a trip to Berlin. Magic Movie is built for exactly this kind of video, so let's create a simple video memory of our trip. To start, you'll need to get the media you're using into your Photos app. Here's how to do that:

1. Download the photos and videos book resources from the link given in the preface. Tapping **Download** will save them to your downloads.
2. In the **Downloads** section of your Files app, tap on the `.zip` file. It will expand into the folder `iMovie-Book_Video-Materials`.
3. Tap on the folder and select the `Chapter 2` subfolder, then `Chapter 2_Berlin Album` within that.
4. In the toolbar at the top of the Files app, tap **Select** and then **Select All** (as in *Figure 2.2*).

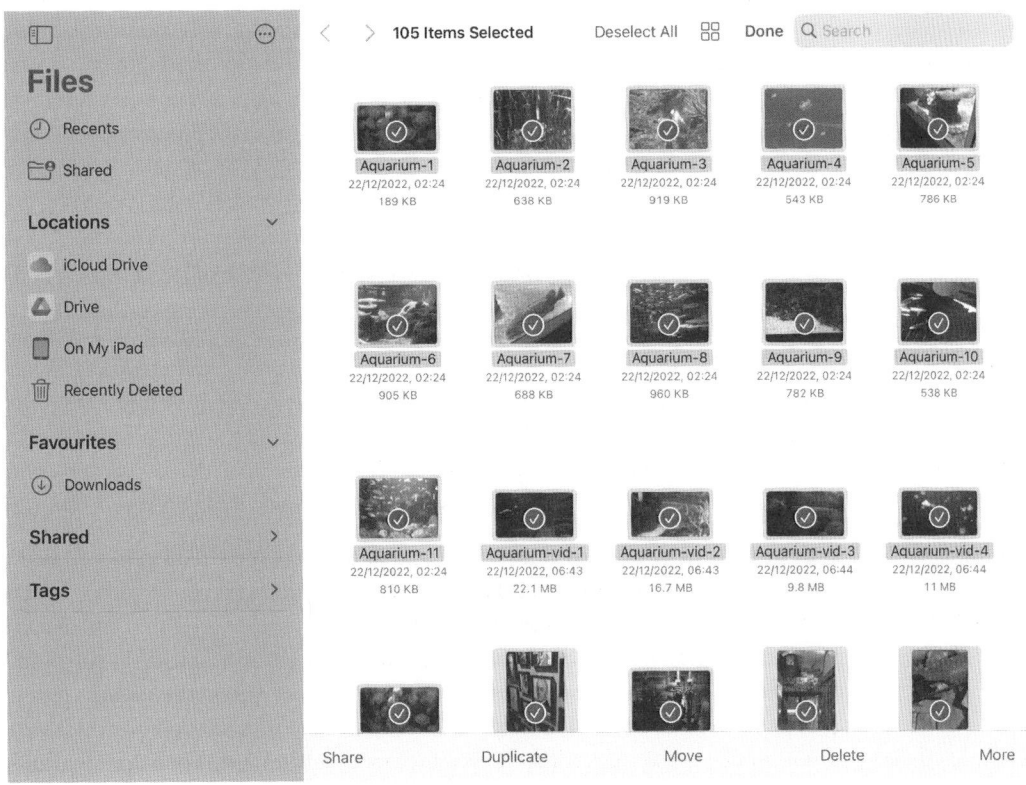

Figure 2.2 – Selecting all items in the file app

5. Tap **Share** at the bottom of the app window.
6. On the *share sheet* that then comes up, tap the **Save Images** option, with a download icon next to it.
7. In your Photos app, create an Album just for the Berlin photos and videos.
8. To add your photos to that Album, tap **Select** at the top of the Photos app and drag a finger along and up so you can select all the Berlin materials quickly.
9. Now tap the *Share* icon at the bottom left, then **Add to Album** on the share sheet.

Now that your media is in place, you can create the Magic Movie:

1. Open the iMovie app, and you'll be taken to the main Projects screen.
2. Select **Magic Movie** from the **Start New Project** banner at the bottom of the Projects screen.
3. When you start a project, the **Choose your Media** menu will come up with a view of your photos and videos. Scroll left and right to look through your different Albums and Memories.

4. When you select an album or memory, you can choose individual photos and videos to use, or you can use them all by tapping **Create Magic Movie from this Album / Memory**.

Figure 2.3 – The Album selection menu on iPadOS

If you're following along…

I'd suggest selecting from your Album instead of creating the Magic Movie from everything inside it. Not all of the photos and videos provided for this exercise will tell the audience much about the trip or be very entertaining or clear to look at. I'm not going to tell you which ones to use: as an editor, it's up to you to decide what's good enough to make it into your video and what gets left on the cutting room floor.

5. After tapping **Create Magic Movie**, iMovie will place the photos and/or videos you selected in separate banners, in chronological order, from top to bottom.

6. To change the order of the videos in your project, you can hold and drag each banner upward or downward. Dragging one banner on top of another creates a group, which can be expanded to show the videos in it. This can be useful if your Magic Movie is made up of so many clips that it would be annoying to scroll down through to the end.

Figure 2.4 – A group made within the Berlin project (tap on the name of a group to rename it)

If you've put photos into the Magic Movie, iMovie will use an effect called **Ken Burns** animation (named after a documentary maker who used the effect), where it will either zoom into or out of the photo or **pan** across it. This creates a sense of movement that makes the video more engaging than if the audience had to look at a static photo. In later chapters, we'll look at how to add and edit our own Ken Burns effects, but in Magic Movie and Storyboard mode, these effects can't be changed or removed. The only way to avoid animations is by only using landscape videos in your Magic Movie.

Adding photos and videos in Magic Movie

Once the magic movie has been created, you can add new photos or videos by tapping **+ Add** at the bottom left of the screen. The video/photo you've recorded will be placed underneath the banner you last selected.

You can also tap on a banner to shoot a new photo or video that will take the place of the old clip. This can be helpful if you're at the location where you want to make your movie and a recording doesn't go to plan. If you choose to **Use Video**, your re-recorded clip will overwrite the original, taking its place on the same banner.

Figure 2.5 – The Retake menu video strip (the menu also contains a full-size video preview, cut out of this figure)

That's pretty much it for what you can do on Magic Movie's main banner-style menu. As discussed, it's a simple model intended to be intuitive and not too wide in terms of creative scope. However, there are two other menus you can use to customize your Magic Movie. First, let's look at the **Styles** menu.

Changing graphics styles with the Styles menu

The **Styles** menu is represented by a filmstrip with two stars, and it sits at the top of the interface above the clip banners.

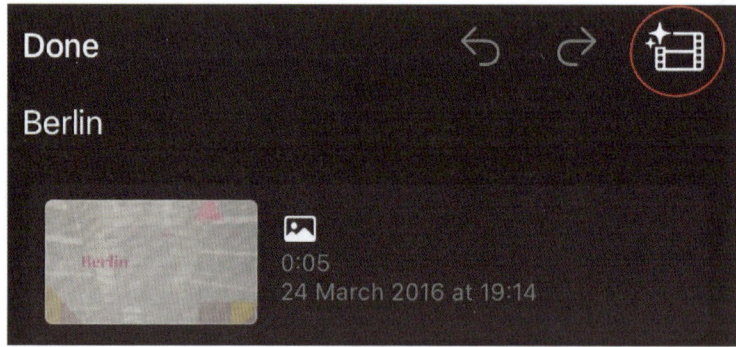

Figure 2.6 – The Styles menu icon (circled)

This menu allows you to change certain details that affect the whole project. These are demonstrated in the following list:

- Title styles (**Choose a Style**)

Then under **Options**, you can change the following:

- The Magic Movie's soundtrack (♪)
- Title font (**Aa**)
- The style of graphics that come with titles (*eyedropper* icon)
- A visual *filter* that changes how all clips in the project look

> **Filters in iMovie**
>
> Filters can be seen throughout all versions and modes of iMovie, but they're very visually striking, so much so that they can make it hard to see what's in the clip. So, be careful when using filters so that you're not distracting from the story your video is trying to tell.

Any style changes you make will only be applied to the automatic title generated on the first clip of your Magic Movie. But if we add any titles later (see the *Titles and text* section), they will follow the **Style**, **Font**, and **Color** settings you choose for the project. These aren't the only kind of project-wide changes you can make, however.

Customizing music in Magic Movie

As well as changing how the text looks on screen, you can use the Styles menu to make some simple changes to the music in your project. Within the Styles menu, the **Music** interface changes the soundtrack that is used throughout the Magic Movie. If you want to remove audio or change the music that iMovie chose, you can use the following steps:

1. Tap on the *music* (♪) banner under **Options**.
2. In the **Music** interface, you can choose the soundtrack for the project by tapping **Soundtracks**. The music within this menu is split into different musical moods to help you choose appropriately for our project.
3. You can also choose your own music and sound files through the **My Music** and **Files** menus. Do be aware, though, that if your music isn't as long as the Magic Movie, iMovie will just play it twice in a row. It's best to avoid repeating music like that if you can.
4. If you don't want music in your project at all, tap **None**. When you're happy, tap **Done** to save your changes.

We can reverse all of the changes we made to the soundtrack, font, color, and filters by tapping **Reset**. However, an overall style (**Charm**, for example) needs to be in use at all times. That concludes the style settings that bridge the whole of your Magic Movie. If you want to edit individual clips in closer detail, you will need to use the **Edit** menu.

Using the Edit menu in Magic Movie

The **Edit** menu gives you a lot more functionality than the main menu in Magic Movie. If you want to add custom titles and voiceover to your Magic Movie, it's the place to go. Here's how to access it:

1. Select a clip banner by tapping on it.
2. Tap the *pencil* icon on the right of the banner.
3. From the hover box that appears, tap **Edit Clip**.

Figure 2.7 – The pencil icon (circled) lets you retake, replace, or edit the clip

Using the Edit menu toolbar

In **Edit** mode, clips are represented in a timeline format, with a preview window showing what the video looks like at the playhead position. Apple calls this window the **Viewer**. Below the timeline is a toolbar containing different options for customizing the clips. Let's have a look at what they do.

Edit

When you tap **Edit** on a video, three options hover below the playhead. The middle option splits the clip in the same way we looked at in *Chapter 1* (⌘ + *Y* in QuickTime Player). The other two options show an edit known as **trim to playhead**. This splits the clip at the playhead position and deletes the clip to the left or right of the playhead, depending on which option you choose. In effect, this performs two actions in one, speeding up the editing process.

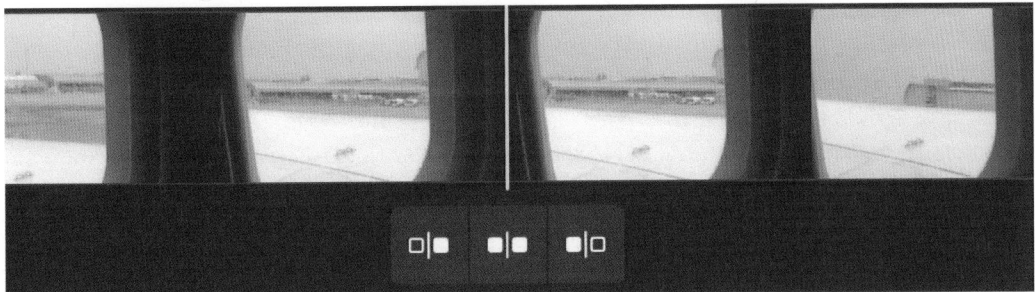

Figure 2.8 – The edit actions for videos: some may be grayed out if the playhead is near one end of the clip

Titles and text

On the right side of the **Edit** actions, **Titles** allow you to add information and meaning to clips in a number of formats. There is a choice of different title styles that place text in different areas of the screen, allowing you to choose a title that fits the video well. They are as follows:

- **Full Screen**: This removes any title that was in place and shows no title
- **Mortise**: This pinches your video in so the title looks like a caption on a picture
- **Lower third**: This is a small title at the bottom, useful for writing names, roles, locations, and other information
- **Title over footage**: This is a standard title you might like to use for a title card
- **Sidebar** and **List**: These are useful if most of the action in a shot is on one side
- **Text over footage**: This removes the graphics that come with most titles, allowing you to just have text over the clips (however, with some font styles, it will be quite small compared to the video)

Now for putting one of these titles over a clip in your project. Here's how to create and edit a title using the **Edit** menu in Magic Movie:

1. Select the clip you want to add a title to by tapping it.
2. Tap **Titles** on the toolbar: a series of title layouts appear, as shown in *Figure 2.9*.

Figure 2.9 – The title layouts available in Magic Movie and Storyboard mode

3. Scroll up and down the list and tap to select the title layout you'd like.

4. Tap **X** in the top right of the title layouts menu to return to the **Edit** menu. In the timeline, the clip will have a **T** symbol in the top left, showing that there is a title on the clip.

5. Look in the Viewer and tap **Title Text Here** to edit the text. A keyboard comes up, and you can edit text like you normally would in iOS/iPadOS.

6. Write your title, then tap **Done** in the top left of the keyboard menu to stop editing and save the title. To come back and edit the text later, select the clip in the timeline and tap **Text** on the toolbar.

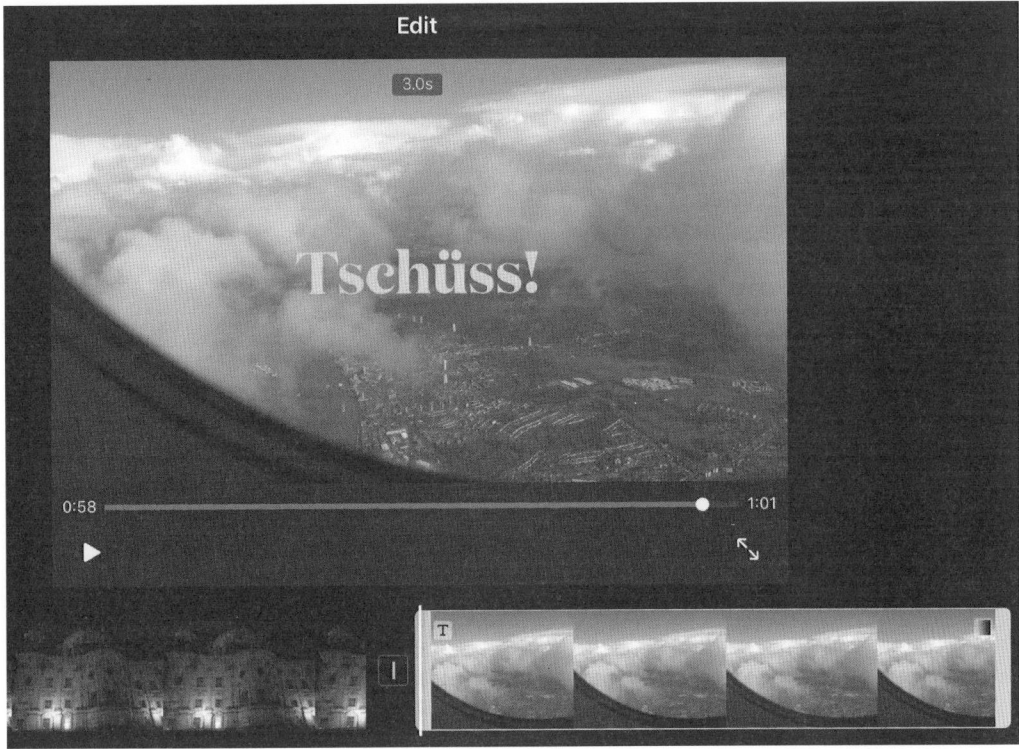

Figure 2.10 – A Charm style title in the Title over footage format (translation: "Bye!")

Do remember that the font and color are chosen according to the title style you selected when creating the project. If you want to change that, go back out into the main editing menu and select the **Styles** menu again. There, you can change the title style and font used for titles.

Music and voiceover

Tapping **Music** allows you to make the same changes to the overall soundtrack that you can in the **Styles** menu. You can choose from iMovie's curated soundtracks, your own music and files, or nothing. Do be aware that unlike in QuickTime Player, where audio appears in its own track and can be edited, soundtrack audio is never represented visually in Storyboard mode. This is because you can only choose one audio file, and it will be faded out when the project ends or be repeated if it doesn't fill the project. For that reason, it's probably best to stick with iMovie's suggested soundtracks because they are designed to fit with the rhythm of its automatic editing. Editing clips to fit the rhythm of music draws attention to the visuals, often making them more striking and engaging – we'll look into this further in the *Using cuts and other transitions* section of *Chapter 3*.

Choosing **None** in the **Music** menu can be a good idea if you plan to add a voiceover to your project. The **Voiceover** button allows you to record your audio directly underneath a clip. Here's how to do that:

1. Move the playhead to where you want the voiceover to start.
2. Tap the **Voiceover** button, then **Start New Voiceover**.
3. Check that the microphone can hear you: when you speak, most or all of the green bars should illuminate, as seen in *Figure 2.11*.

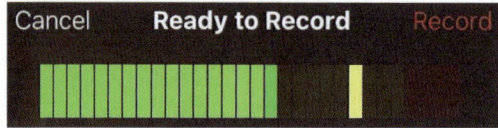

Figure 2.11 – An ideal loudness for recording your voiceover

4. Look at the furthest bar that lights up: if a red bar is illuminated, move further away from the device's microphone.

> **Extra tip**
> The bars in the **Ready to Record** menu tell us two things:
> > The main group of lit-up bars shows your average loudness
> > The single bar to the right of that shows **peak loudness** – the loudest volume the sound reached, even if for a very short time

When you record, you want your average loudness to stay in the upper end of the green bars, and when you're at your loudest, you want an average loudness in the yellow range. This will make voices clear against the background noise of the room. You shouldn't be hitting the red bars because they signal **clipping**. This means your audio is too loud for the microphone in your device to interpret it properly.

When you're ready, tap **Record**. You'll be given a 3-second countdown, and then a red overlay will move with the playhead to show you what area of the timeline you've recorded over:

1. Tap **Stop** when you're done (leave a second after you finish speaking so you don't cut yourself off). You can listen to, retake, or accept the recording you just made.

    You want your voiceover to flow smoothly after you start speaking. Anything that goes wrong before you start and after you finish can be trimmed out afterward.

2. When you accept a recording, a purple audio banner will be highlighted beneath the video clip in the timeline. You can then perform the following actions:

    - Drag the trim handles to trim out sections you don't want.
    - Hold and drag the clip to move the voiceover.

3. With the voiceover clip selected, you can adjust the loudness of your voiceover by tapping **Volume** at the bottom of the screen. The audio starts at 100% and can be magnified up to 500% or silenced at 0%. Tap **Volume** again to return to the **Edit** menu.

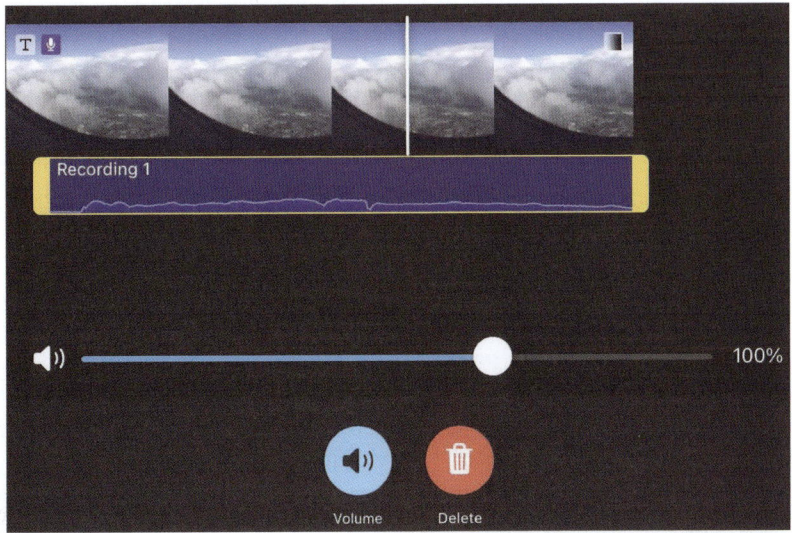

Figure 2.12 – Editing the voiceover clip

Speed and Replace

Speed and Replace are controls for clips that you have already added to the project. For videos, **Speed** brings up a control similar to the volume control, allowing you to speed your clips up to x2 speed or down to ⅛ the speed of the original (0.125x speed). **Replace** simply gives you the option to retake a video or replace a photo from your Photos library. This is the same as the option from the main Magic Movie menu.

That's the **Edit** menu covered; now let's use it to do what QuickTime Player worked so well for on the Mac: combining multiple clips into one.

Combining videos with Magic Movie

Although combining and splitting clips isn't possible in the Photos app, it is possible to do this within Magic Movie's **Edit** mode. To give you some practice at this, I've split the *The Timeline* video from *Chapter 1* into two parts. If you'd like to follow along, download the footage from the `Chapter 2: 'The Timeline' for Magic` subfolder and follow these steps:

1. Create a new Magic Movie project.
2. Choose the two *The Timeline* clips from the **Videos** Album in the **Choose Your Media** menu.

3. Tap **Create Magic Movie**.

4. Now, in the main Magic Movie menu, make sure the clips are in the right order – if they're not, reorder them by dragging and dropping the first banner below the second.

5. Use the pencil icon on either banner to go into the **Edit** menu.

6. Drag the trim handles as far to the left and right as you can on both clips so that all the video you need is there in the timeline.

Now we have both clips in the timeline, in full, but there may be automatic edits applied that we want to remove. At the top of each clip, there may be a **T** and a speaker symbol, meaning that there are titles applied and the volume has been changed. Here's how to reverse those changes:

1. Select a clip with titles by tapping on it. On the toolbar at the bottom, tap **Titles** and select **Full Screen**. This removes any automatic titles. Repeat this for the other clip if you need to.

2. Tap on the **Volume** button on the toolbar. Two different sliders will come up, as in *Figure 2.13*. The bottom slider is for the soundtrack, and the top slider is for the video you added.

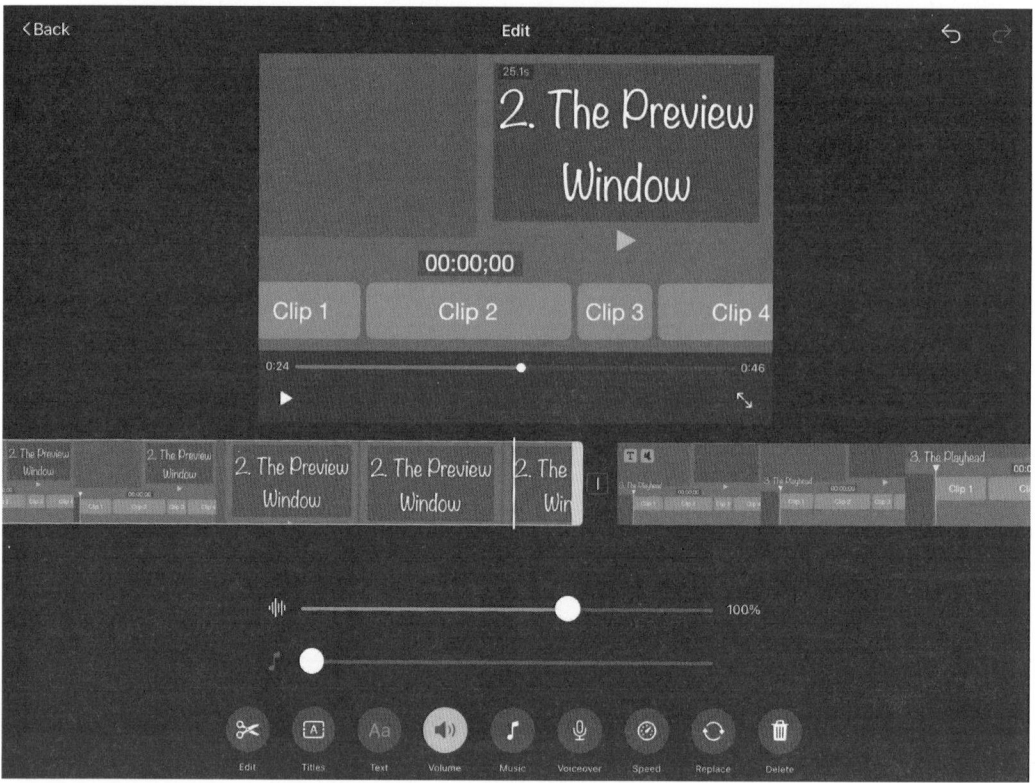

Figure 2.13 – The correct position for the volume sliders when combining videos

3. To restore the sound to how it was in the original video, slide the bottom slider to 0%, and the top slider to 100%. Then, repeat this for the other clip.
4. Export the Magic Movie – see the next section for how to do that.

What we've done here really is work against the whole purpose of Magic Movie to 'un-edit' video. We achieved something we wanted to do, but not in an efficient way. When we look at Movie mode in *Chapter 3*, you may find that this same process is easier there because fewer automatic effects are applied. It's never a good idea to work against the way something's designed because that causes friction in your workflow and slows you down.

Exporting a Magic Movie

When you're happy with your Magic Movie, it's time to export it. Here's how to do that:

1. Access the main menu for Magic Movie, where the clips are shown as banners.
   - If you're in the **Edit** mode, tap **< Back** on the top left of the screen.
   - If you're in the **Styles** menu, tap **Done** on the top right to save changes or **Cancel** on the top left to leave without saving style changes.
2. Tap the icon at the top right of the screen, the **Share** button. This takes you to the standard **share sheet** menu for iOS and iPadOS.
3. To save to your Photos library, tap **Save Video**, or to save to the Files app, select **Save to Files**. In the share sheet, you can also AirDrop the project to another Apple device or send the video via social media apps.

And that's it for Magic Movie. If this seems like a lot, don't worry because the other automatic editing mode in iMovie, Storyboard mode, shares almost all of the same features, including the export process. Let's look at what makes it different from Magic Movie and why you may want to use it.

Using Storyboard mode

Storyboard mode takes a different approach to Magic Movie, using templates to give you a starting point for making your own video. It offers ready-made video formats, which use short descriptions and concept-drawing-style art to tell you what kinds of clips to put in certain places.

In iMovie, Storyboard mode used to be called Trailer mode. Still available in iMovie for macOS, Trailer mode was what got me really excited about editing. It offered different genres of film trailers that you could put your own clips into, allowing you to make your life into a Hollywood-style trailer. It was simple, not to mention really exciting – being able to create totally different stories with the same random selection of clips. Storyboard mode is even better. Not only does it offer the same trailer formats as Trailer mode but it also has templates for many different types of full-length *popular videos*, as iMovie puts it.

Storyboard mode categories include **Cooking** and **Product Review**, and – especially helpful for if you're in school and tasked with creating a video – **Science Experiment** and **Book Report**. Storyboard mode even offers a structure for a full short film – though perhaps the current length of 1:09 isn't quite long enough to create a narrative with a satisfying beginning, middle, and end. Don't let me discourage you from trying, but for most intents and purposes, Storyboard mode is best used to create short, simple, factual videos.

Creating a Storyboard mode project

Storyboard mode relies on you having the right kind of clips to fit the style of video you're making. When you get into filling out the project, you'll notice just how many clips it takes to fill the whole video – it's a huge amount for such short videos, but that's how video production always goes! To create your Storyboard video, I'm going to suggest making a cooking video: how to make pizza.

To help you find relevant clips for your Storyboard, I'd recommend using Pexels (`https://www.pexels.com/videos/`). It's a website full of free-to-use stock photos and videos. Here's how to download footage from there and get it ready for use in Storyboard mode:

1. Go to `https://www.pexels.com/videos/` in your preferred browser app. For this example, I'm using Safari.
2. Search for the kind of stock footage you want. If you're following along, `Pizza` is a good start!
3. Scroll to find the footage you'd like to use. When you've found a clip you like, tap on it once, then tap on the **Free Download** button.
4. After a few seconds, an Apple banner should appear in the foreground of the screen, asking whether you want to download the file. Tap **Download**.

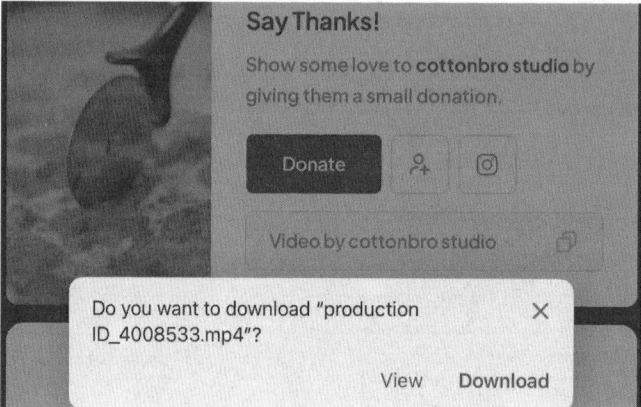

Figure 2.14 – Make sure you're downloading the intended file – tap View if you're unsure

5. A download progress bar will appear in the top right of Safari next to the website's URL. Tap on the *Downloads* (↓) icon when the download is finished, then tap on the file.

6. In the top right of the new screen, tap the *Share* icon. Then tap **Save Video** in the share sheet – this saves the video to your Photos app, which is where you need it to be for Storyboard mode to access.

> **If you're following along…**
>
> When looking up stock footage for making pizza, think of other search terms for footage you'll need to illustrate the whole process. Consider the ingredients you'll need to show, the process of making and kneading dough, and how you're going to cook the pizza.
>
> If you're not sure where to start with using stock footage, the YouTube channel *Half as Interesting* (www.youtube.com/@halfasinteresting) is good for inspiration. They make creative use of all sorts of stock footage in both informative and tongue-in-cheek ways!

With your footage downloaded and added to your Photos app, it's time to create your Storyboard mode project. You can – and should – go back to download more stock footage whenever you need to, but for now, here are the steps for creating a Storyboard project:

1. Tap **Storyboard** on the **Start New Project** menu. You'll be shown a selection of video formats to choose from (as shown in *Figure 2.15*).

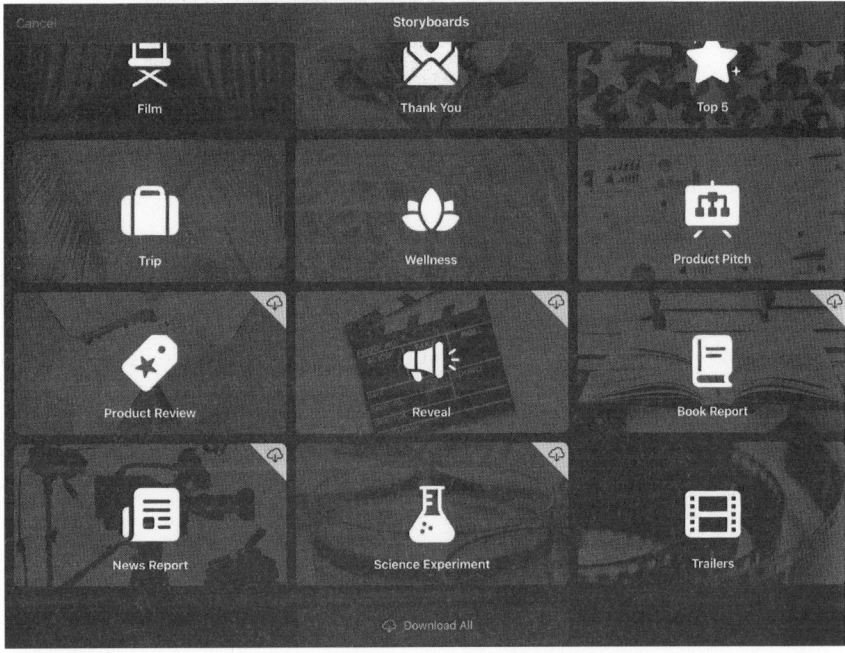

Figure 2.15 – Some of the Storyboard formats on offer

2. A cloud icon means the item needs to be downloaded to your device before it can be used. To download all the Storyboard formats, scroll to the bottom and tap **Download All**.

3. Choose a video format by tapping on it. If you're following along, choose **Cooking**.

4. You'll first be taken to the **Styles** menu that you're familiar with from Magic Movie. A compatible style will be selected. You don't have to use it, but make sure the **Style** and **Editorial Options** settings you choose work well together and suit the tone and feel of your video.

5. When you're happy with the chosen style, font, and color, tap **Create**. You'll be taken to the main editing menu for Storyboard mode.

Using the Storyboard editing menu

The Storyboard editing menu is very similar to Magic Movie: it uses banners that hold your own photos and videos. However, there is a bit more detail. You'll see the following functionality:

- Ready-made banners with diagrams showing how the shot might look
- Descriptions in the banners giving information about what should be in a shot
- Clips placed in ready-made groups that represent different parts of the video

Figure 2.16 – The main editing menu for Storyboard mode, with pizza footage added

Diagrams of people and objects help to explain the different shot sizes used in filming, from a wide shot to an extreme close-up. If you tap the **i** icon underneath the Viewer, the lower third shows you more shot information, such as how long the shot should be. This is also true in the **Edit** mode.

The focus on shot length is an important difference between Magic Movie and Storyboard mode. Magic Movie cuts your clips where iMovie's machine learning chooses to, and clips placed in storyboard banners remain their original length. More of the creative decisions are yours from the start, and more emphasis is placed on using videos rather than photos. Once you've read the shot descriptions and suggested shot lengths, it's time to choose footage to go in the banners:

1. Tap the **+** icon (at the top left of each banner) or the pencil icon (to the right when a banner is selected), and you will have the chance to do the following:

    - **Rename** the clip (e.g., from **Closeup** to something more descriptive, such as `Closeup Pineapple`).
    - **Take Video or Photo**.
    - **Select from library**.
    - **Retake** or **Replace** the clip already in a banner.

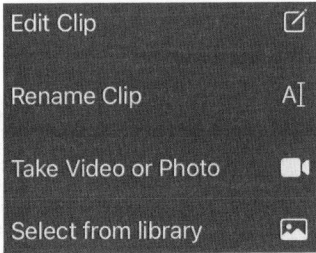

Figure 2.17 – The pencil icon menu for a blank Storyboard banner

2. Tap **Select from library**. This will open up a window showing the media from your Photos app. The pizza videos you downloaded should be there.
3. If you want to edit a clip in more detail, tap **Use Video**, then choose **Edit Clip** from the pencil icon menu to go into the **Edit** menu.

Using the Storyboard Edit mode

The **Edit** menu works almost exactly the same for Storyboard mode as it does for Magic Movie, so do refer to the *Using the Edit menu toolbar* section of this chapter for guidance on using those tools. Once the clips are in place, your job is to add meaning. You may want to try using the Voiceover tool in the toolbar to narrate the process of making the pizza:

1. Record **scratch** (practice) voiceovers describing what is in each clip – this will make it clear which clips are longer than they need to be, as those clips will continue playing after you've finished describing what's in them.
2. Trim those clips or increase their speed to fit your voiceovers with a little bit of overhang.
3. Delete and re-record any voiceovers you aren't happy with.

Once the voiceovers are complete, you can add titles to clips to give specifics such as weights, volumes, temperatures, and times. That way, the audience can note down instructions if they need to:

1. In the **Edit** mode, tap on a clip.
2. Tap **Titles**.
3. **Lower Third** and **List** are good for giving factual information or instructions beside the video.

Once you've added meaning with voiceover and titles, it's time to look back over the video to make sure it works as a whole. You may not be totally happy with the structure of the video – something may feel off when editing the project. If there's a banner that you feel doesn't help your video's narrative, it's possible to remove it:

1. Tap on the clip or placeholder you don't want in the project.
2. Tap **Delete** on the far right of the toolbar. If there is a clip filling the placeholder already, you'll be given two options:
   - **Delete Media** deletes the clip you recorded, keeping the placeholder.
   - **Delete Clip** deletes the whole placeholder/banner from the project.

With the tools available in the **Edit** mode, you should be able to fine-tune your pizza-cooking tutorial to be coherent, concise, and bursting with extra context and flavor too! When you're done, share the project using the steps in the *Export a Magic Movie* section.

Limitations of Magic Movie and Storyboard mode

We've seen that Magic Movie can effortlessly create a coherent and concise video out of a load of photos and videos, massively reducing the time we need to spend on assembly editing. Storyboard mode is a good teacher of some of the conventions for different types of video and gives you practice at telling all the important parts of your story in the most concise way possible. Both modes also allow you to add a lot of extra meaning and context with titles and voiceovers. However, we know that with convenience, there is compromise. In Magic Movie and Storyboard mode, you can't do the following things:

- Change how clips are shown in the frame
- Choose the transitions between clips
- Decide where the non-voiceover sound starts and ends

These modes' biggest limitation arguably lies in sound. Because soundtracks – or your choice of audio file – aren't shown as an audio track, it's impossible to customize music by trimming or splitting, or even adding different music at different points. To make sure that your voiceover audio can be heard over any music, storyboard mode uses **audio ducking**, which is where the software automatically lowers the volume of soundtrack audio when other audio clips are present. This usually works fairly well, but you can't change the level of ducking or turn it off.

Realistically, if you want significant control over the sound, you will need to use Movie mode, which we will cover starting in the next chapter. You'll notice that having different visual layers for video and audio really helps expand your creative scope.

Summary

In this chapter, we looked at the *automatic* editing mode of Magic Movie and the template format of Storyboard mode, which mostly share the same simple menus and controls. Firstly, you let Magic Movie automatically edit your chosen photos and videos of Berlin into a memory of the trip. You then used the **Edit** menu to change styles and add titles. We also used the **Edit** menu to combine two videos into one.

We then looked at Storyboard mode. This mode places banners in a ready-made layout that changes depending on the type of video you want to make. All you need to do is find or shoot the right clips to go in those gaps. You used footage downloaded from Pexels, and maybe some of your own footage, to create an instructional video for making pizza.

Finally, we looked at the limitations of Magic Movie and Storyboard mode. Simplicity in an editing program almost always reduces your creative scope, and you need to think about the needs of your video to work out whether a simple mode such as Magic Movie or Storyboard mode will be enough to do what you intend. If you want to change how video is shown in the frame, what transitions are used, or edit the audio in the timeline, Movie mode – which we are just a page away from looking at – is the tool for the job.

3
Using Movie Mode in iOS and iPadOS

Welcome to the third chapter, which is all about using Movie mode in iMovie for iOS and iPadOS. Movie mode is the third and final project type in the iMovie app, and it is the most advanced. It uses a blank timeline and offers more features and creative options than the timeline we saw in the **Edit** menu for Magic Movie and Storyboard mode.

The two previous chapters have hopefully helped you to understand not only the purposes of editing (coherence, conciseness, and adding meaning) but also the variety of different structures that help the user achieve them. Understanding the different layouts will help you when it comes to choosing the best platform for creating your video.

This chapter will outline how to create a video using Movie mode, from choosing your clips, to making changes to them, to exporting the final video. This is the most involved form of editing so far, with a lot more creative scope for editing sound and transitions. I'd encourage you to follow along using the `Chapter 2_Berlin Album` video materials you used in *Chapter 2* to recreate the same video in Movie mode. Also, don't be afraid to refer back to the previous chapters for a recap on the basics of splitting and cutting clips. The topics covered in this chapter include the following:

- Creating and setting up a Movie mode project
- Navigating the timeline and using Movie mode editing tools
- Using transitions and editing audio to make videos feel smoother

Technical requirements

Just as in the previous chapter, you will need the iMovie app to use Movie mode. The version used in this book is version 3.0.1, which requires iOS or iPadOS 16. However, this update did not add anything new to Movie mode. If your device cannot be updated, iMovie version 3.0, which runs on iOS and iPadOS 15, will give you an almost identical experience.

If you're following along and recreating the *Berlin* video from *Chapter 2*, make sure you still have the pictures and videos downloaded to your device. Instructions for downloading footage on mobile devices can be found in *Chapter 2, Creating a Movie with Magic Movie*. They don't need to be in a Photos app album this time, but if they're still in one, that's great.

Creating and setting up a Movie mode project

Movie mode is a blank canvas; an empty timeline that we have to make our own. That means choosing the clips you want, with the shot sizes you want, in the order you want. It's important to remember there's no right or wrong in deciding this, and if you're unsure, have a look at the Magic Movie that you made in the previous chapter, and try recreating that shot-for-shot. But before we decide what our story looks like, we need to set up the project and get it ready for adding our clips.

Why use Movie mode?

Before we start using Movie mode, we should be sure that this is the right mode for the project we're working on. Use the rule *Choose the simplest program that gets the job done* to help you decide whether it is. We have seen that for simple jobs such as combining videos and splitting clips, QuickTime Player on Mac or Magic Movie on iPhone and iPad serve the purpose perfectly well. But if we want to change what we see within the frame, or we want to edit transitions, these modes don't do what we need them to. Additionally, if we're looking to use multiple different soundtracks or music clips in our project, QuickTime Player and Magic Movie are again too limited for our needs. Therefore, if we need to do any of these things as part of our project, we will need to use Movie mode. It's a little more complex and less guided, but that gives you a lot more creative scope.

Creating a project in Movie mode

Now we're sure Movie mode is best suited to the job we need to do, the first step toward making a video with Movie mode is to create a project. Here's how to do that:

1. Select **Movie** from the **Start New Project** banner at the bottom of the **Projects** screen.
2. We're then taken to the Media Browser, where we select the clips we want to use in the project. The Media Browser is split into five sections:

    - **Moments**
    - **Video**
    - **Photos**
    - **Albums**
    - **Backgrounds**

Unfortunately, unlike in Magic Movie, we cannot select a whole album to bring into the project using Movie mode. Instead, we have to select photos and videos individually.

3. Tap **Albums**, then tap on your **Berlin** album.
4. Tap on the videos and photos you think will work best in the project (make sure to be picky, because there are a lot of videos and photos in there!). When we tap on the thumbnail of a clip, it will show that it has been selected with a *tick icon*:

Figure 3.1 – The album selection screen

5. The total number of clips you have selected (and their total length) is indicated at the bottom, below the **Create Movie** button. Once you've selected all the clips you want, tap **Create Movie**.

    The media you chose will be added to the timeline in the order you selected it, so if you have an idea for how you want to order your scenes (for example, town, TV tower, zoo), selecting your chosen clips in that order will save time you would otherwise spend rearranging clips.

6. If you want to get your project started but don't have any clips, or your clips are in the Files app, you can create a movie with nothing in it by just tapping **Create Movie**.

That covers the process of creating a project. Next, we're going to look at the editing interface and how to customize some project settings to your liking.

The Movie mode interface

After creating a movie from the media we selected in the Media Browser, you'll be taken to the Movie mode timeline, which is split into three sections:

- The Viewer (shows what's at the playhead position)
- The Media Browser (where we can select more media to add to the project)
- The timeline (which we use to edit our added media)

You can see an overview of this in the following screenshot:

Figure 3.2 – The Movie mode interface

If you did create a movie with no clips, you will be given the option, inside the Viewer, to record a clip. The clips will be placed directly onto the timeline after going through the same **Retake/Use Video** menu that we saw in the *Adding photos and videos in Magic Movie* section of *Chapter 2*.

Using the Movie mode Media Browser

When you're in the timeline view in Movie mode, you can still add clips using the Media Browser. If it isn't showing as a banner on screen, it can be accessed by tapping the + icon at the top right of the screen. This Media Browser is a little more sophisticated than the one used to create the project. Let's have a look at some of its best bits.

In the **Video** tab, we have the following:

- **All** shows every video you have in the Photos app (except for those in the **Recently Deleted** album).
- **Unused Media** shows all videos from your Photos app that aren't currently being used in the project. It's great, for example, if you need more clips to cover a voiceover you recorded but want to avoid repeating clips.

In the **Backgrounds** tab, we have the following:

- A load of different background images are available. These can be used as placeholders or for separating scenes with **intertitles** (see the *Titles* section later in the chapter).

The **Files** tab:

- This lets you access images and videos stored in your Files app, iCloud Drive, or a connected Google Drive. Do be aware that any videos you have saved in the Files app won't show up in the **Video** tab of the Media Browser.

Separately, the **Audio** menu (at the bottom of the Media Browser, as in *Figure 3.3*) contains stock sounds and soundtracks that come with iMovie:

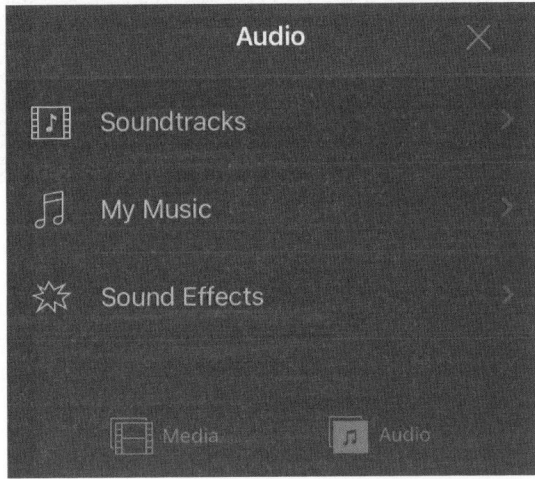

Figure 3.3 – The Audio menu

- **Soundtracks** contains a list of music that is also available in Magic Movie and Storyboard mode.
- **My Music** accesses the music library in the Music app, allowing you to use any songs from there that aren't copyright protected. The menu also allows you to search your Files app for audio files.
- **Sound Effects** contains a series of effects for everyday objects, animals, and some short jingles that can add meaning to your video. For more on using sound effects, take a look at *the Using the Audio & Video Tab in iMovie* section in *Chapter 5*.

Adding video in Movie mode

For Movie mode, video selection differs slightly from what you've seen in iMovie's other modes. Let's take a brief look at the process:

1. When you tap on a video, a border appears with trim handles at either end.
2. Press the play button by the video, and it will play in the Viewer while a playhead moves across the video strip:

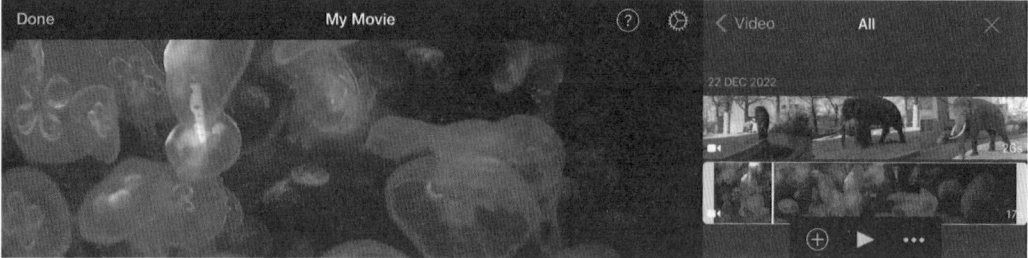

Figure 3.4 – The Movie mode video preview/selection menu

3. You can move the trim handles to decide the in and out points for each video you want in your project. When you're happy with the section you've chosen, tap the + icon, and it will be added to your project.
4. Now, in the Media Browser, the section of the video you've chosen will be underlined in orange.

Movie mode project settings

Above the Viewer, on the right, is a cog icon. This holds the **Project Settings** menu, which allows you to choose two extra settings for the project:

- A filter
- A theme

Filters change how all the clips in the timeline look by applying an effect to them. Although they're different from those in Storyboard mode, Movie mode's themes work in a similar way. Choosing a theme changes the style of titles available, and adds special transitions that play on the theme.

You can't choose to have no theme in Movie mode, but I'd suggest avoiding filters and choosing the **Simple** theme for most projects. This is because themes and filters can be quite distracting, and because they come with iMovie (and, therefore, everyone using iMovie has access to them), they're not likely to feel very unique to the audience. However, if you're creating a deliberately stylized video, themes can help to communicate that. **News** would be good for making a report-style video, and **Travel** can work well for making a recap of a trip or holiday. As we're creating a video recap of a trip to Berlin, let's select the **Travel** theme in the project settings.

Also in the **Project Settings** menu, you can choose whether to add a soundtrack associated with the theme. If you do, the audio of the soundtrack will be added as a track at the bottom of the timeline. We decided to use Movie mode to be more independent with how we edit sound, though, so I'd suggest keeping that toggled off:

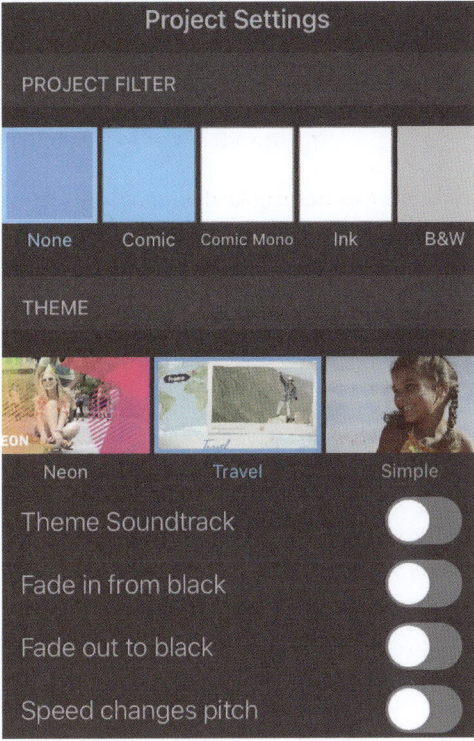

Figure 3.5 – The Project Settings menu

Also in the project settings are the options to fade in from, and out to, black. These options place transitions at the start and end of the project, and you can tell that they're in place as the first and/or last clip will have a little gradient icon at the top right. These fade-in/out transitions can only be turned on or off—unlike transitions between clips, you can't edit these in Movie mode:

Figure 3.6 – Fade-to-black icon

The last option in this settings menu, **Speed changes pitch**, is about how audio behaves when you change the speed of a clip. When a clip is faster, the audio will naturally sound higher pitched (voices become nasal and squeaky). If you deselect the option, you can increase the speed of a clip and keep it sounding mostly normal. That can be useful if you're making a small speed increase (of up to 5%) to a clip to speed up really slow talking, for example.

That's it for **project settings**, but there's one other useful icon at the top. Next to the cog icon is the **Help** icon. Tapping it gives tooltips for the different options in Movie mode. This is really helpful if you ever forget what something does, or you want to get a better idea of Movie mode's functionality. Tapping **Learn more >** at the bottom opens an in-app window showing Apple's *iMovie User Guide*. When you've found what you were looking for, press the **Help** icon again to hide the tips:

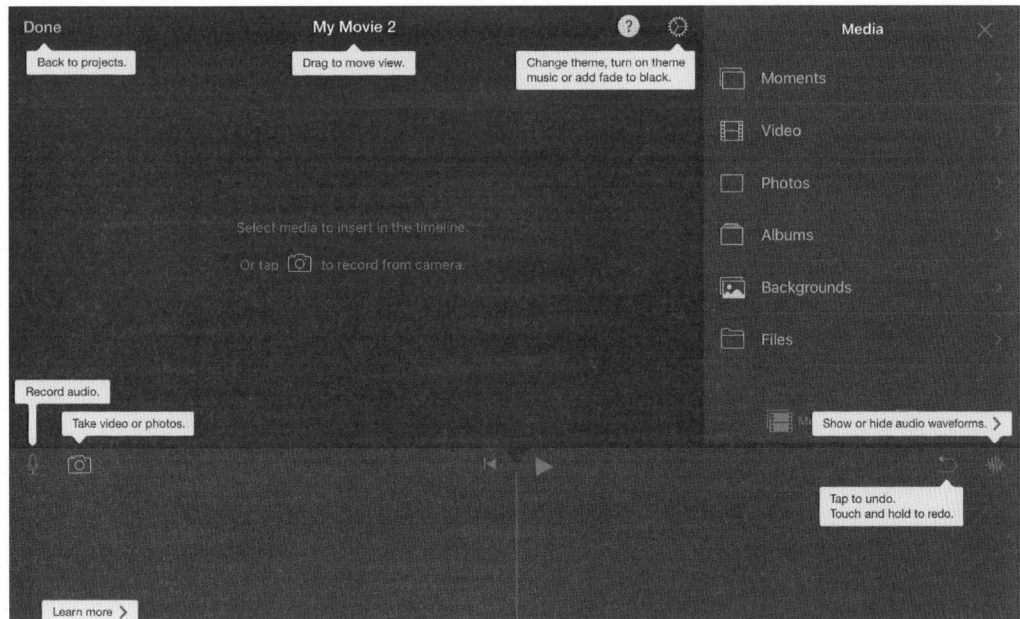

Figure 3.7 – The Help icon, toggled on

Now that we've chosen our media and set up the project, and the interface is a bit more familiar, it's time to start editing.

Assembly editing in Movie mode

Assembly editing is the first task for an editor after importing media. It's the process of adding all the relevant (parts of) clips to the timeline and making sure they're in the right order—in other words, making sure the story you're telling is coherent. Using a blank timeline opens up a lot of creative avenues that aren't open for Magic Movie/Storyboard mode or QuickTime Player. Although the editing task can seem quite daunting when there is just a blank timeline in front of you, the options allow you to tailor the interface to help you work faster. One key way of doing this is by utilizing keyboard shortcuts. If you use a keyboard with your mobile Apple device, there are a few shortcuts you can make use of.

Using keyboard shortcuts on iOS and iPadOS

Although iOS and iPadOS are mainly touch-based, it is possible to pair a Bluetooth keyboard with your device and use the keyboard shortcuts that are available. As we'll see in the *Navigating iMovie with keyboard shortcuts* section of *Chapter 4*, using a keyboard can make your editing quicker and more precise. Any Bluetooth keyboard will work with iMovie on iOS and iPadOS; you don't need an Apple-branded keyboard to make this work.

A full list of keyboard shortcuts is available at `https://support.apple.com/en-gb/guide/imovie-iphone/kna85e7ed58b/ios`, but here's a small selection for navigating the timeline and performing actions:

- **Left/right arrow keys**: Move one frame forward/back
- **^ + left/right arrow keys**: Move the playhead to the start/end of the project
- **⌘ + B**: Split clip at playhead position (this is different from QuickTime Player, where we use ⌘ + **Y**)

I'd encourage you to make use of these and other keyboard shortcuts if you have a Bluetooth keyboard, but for those who don't, we'll be working with the standard touchscreen actions and options available to everyone.

Rearranging clips in Movie mode

In Magic Movie, you have to use the main editing menu to rearrange clips. However, Movie mode lets you reorder clips within the timeline. This is crucial when assembly editing. To get the video you've always dreamed of, you'll need to rearrange a lot of clips. The first thing we should therefore do is master the art of the switcharoo:

1. Tap and hold onto a clip—it will shrink into a mini version of itself (as in *Figure 3.8*).
2. Drag that clip wherever you like along the timeline—other clips will move aside to let the clip in:

Figure 3.8 – Tapping and holding onto a clip allows you to move it

By default, each video clip will show the audio recorded with it as a waveform below the video strip. There is a setting to turn this off at the top right of the timeline, but I'd recommend keeping it on because it's always a good idea to have all the information you need in front of you when editing. Doing this means it's less likely something will take you by surprise when you later review your video for quality control. Those are the basics of navigating the timeline in Movie mode. Now, let's look at how to edit clips, starting with photos.

Editing photos in Movie mode

In the Movie mode timeline, photos are actually treated very differently from videos. Apart from having fewer editing options, the way you interact with photos on the timeline is different. The playhead can only be placed at the start or end of a photo—when you tap on a photo, the playhead will move to the left or right edge of the clip. For this reason, you cannot split photos in Movie mode: you can only trim them from either end. Photos also behave differently in the Viewer compared to most videos. This is all to do with their shape and how they fit the video frame.

Using photo animations – the Ken Burns effect

When you place a photo into the timeline, chances are that iMovie won't show the whole thing (especially if you used an iPad, or took a portrait photo). This is because the photo doesn't have the same **aspect ratio** as the video. The aspect ratio tells you how long a frame is compared to how tall it is, and if this ratio isn't the same as the Viewer's aspect ratio, the photo won't fit the whole screen. The photo will either be too tall or too wide to fit the frame fully; photos are usually too tall.

What iMovie does to solve this is zoom in on the photo so that it does fit the whole screen, a technique known as **crop to fill**. When crop to fill is in use, a smaller section of the photo takes up the whole frame. By default, iMovie then applies an animation to the photo, moving across or up and down the photo so that you can see as much of it as possible. You will have seen this kind of animation in Magic Movie—it's called the **Ken Burns effect**. Although in Magic Movie you cannot edit Ken Burns animations, you can change or turn off the animation in Movie mode. Here's how to do that:

1. Tap on a photo in the timeline—the lower-left corner will show the controls for the effect (as in *Figure 3.9*):

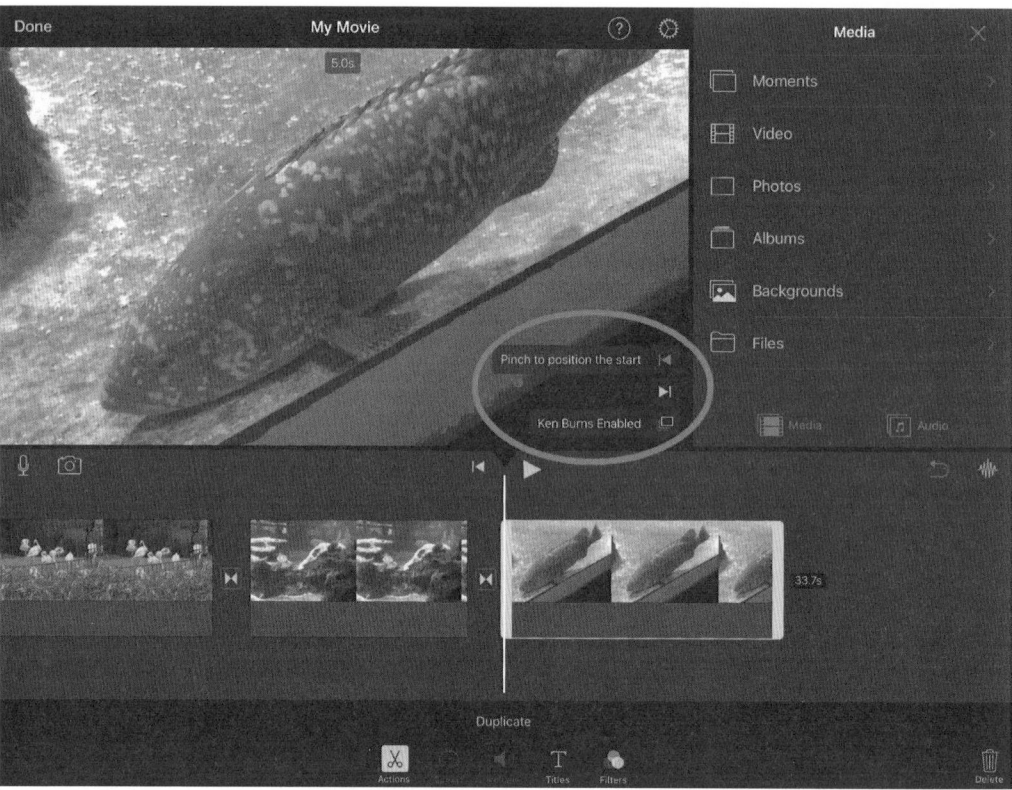

Figure 3.9 – The Ken Burns controls (circled)

2. In iMovie, a blue shade highlights the option or menu that's currently selected. In the Viewer, that's the **Pinch to position the start** option. The playhead's location will also hint at whether you're editing the start or end position of the animation.

3. If you pinch the Viewer when you're at the start of the clip, the start point of the animation will change. You can do the following:

    - Spread two fingers outward to zoom in
    - Pinch two fingers in to zoom outward
    - Drag with one finger to move the frame around

4. If you're moving the frame around and you see black at the edges, you've reached the edge of the image. iMovie will bounce the photo back so that the whole frame is filled.

5. When you're happy with your start position for the animation, tap the skip icon (triangle and vertical line) facing the other way to set the end position. **Pinch to position the end** will be shaded blue if it's selected.

6. When you're happy with both the start and end positions, move the playhead back to the start of the image and press the play icon at the top of the timeline. In the Viewer, the frame should move smoothly between your set start and end positions.

7. If you don't feel the Ken Burns effect works for your video, you can disable it by tapping on the bottom option: the **Ken Burns Enabled** toggle. The Viewer will confirm that Ken Burns is disabled.

If you do choose to disable Ken Burns, the problem is that the photo will still be cropped to fill the screen. If you want to see the whole photo, you will need to add the photo as an **overlay**. Overlaying a clip means placing it on top of a clip you already have in the project, so it appears higher on the timeline.

> Showing a whole photo using overlays
>
> To keep things simple, we won't be covering overlays in detail in this chapter. But because overlays are necessary for getting most photos to show without cropping in Movie mode, here's a brief guide on showing a whole photo using overlays:
>
> 1. Go to **Backgrounds** in the Media Browser and add a black solid background to the timeline.
>
> 2. Move the playhead back to the start of the background.
>
> 3. In the Media Browser, find the photo you want to add and tap the three dots next to the + icon.
>
> 4. Choose **Cutaway** from the options.

The whole photo will then be shown, with a black border around it. If you want to customize overlays, hold your horses! We'll look into these more complex effects in *Chapter 6*.

Do also be aware that with the Ken Burns effect, you can't set the start or end point for the animation. The animation will start immediately and only finish moving when the clip ends. This means you can't have the image stay static for a second, then start an animation. Being able to do so can make animations look a lot more natural and less jarring. There is a workaround for this in iMovie for macOS, which we'll look at in *Chapter 5*.

That covers photo editing in Movie mode—it's actually quite limited compared to the customization options for videos. For that reason, it's often best to use videos in your Movie mode projects where you can. In that spirit, let's look at how to edit videos in the timeline.

Editing videos in Movie mode

Under the previous *Rearranging clips in Movie mode* section, we looked at how to move clips around in your project to start your assembly edit. This section will go over the tools you can use in Movie mode to quickly trim down your clips so that you can make your assembly edit more concise. Then, we'll cover some tools for adding meaning.

Edit actions in Movie mode

Apart from trimming clips (simply by holding and dragging the edge of a clip in the timeline), the most common process for editing clips after rearranging them is splitting. These are editing actions that you'll be familiar with from our dabbling in QuickTime Player (see the *Using Clips mode* section of *Chapter 1*) and Magic Movie (see the *Using the Edit menu in Magic Movie* section of *Chapter 2*). In Movie mode, these tools are contained in the **Actions** section, which is the first menu on the bottom left of the toolbar. The toolbar appears below the timeline when you tap on a clip. **Actions** contains three options:

- **Split**: Splits the clip at the playhead position. There are no trim-to-playhead options like those seen in Magic Movie and Storyboard mode.
- **Detach audio**: Audio recorded as part of the video is moved below the video as a separate track. You can't do this in Magic Movie and Storyboard mode, or if the video has no audio.
- **Duplicate**: Duplicates the selected clip, placing it after that clip with a transition between them.

The options are shown in the following screenshot:

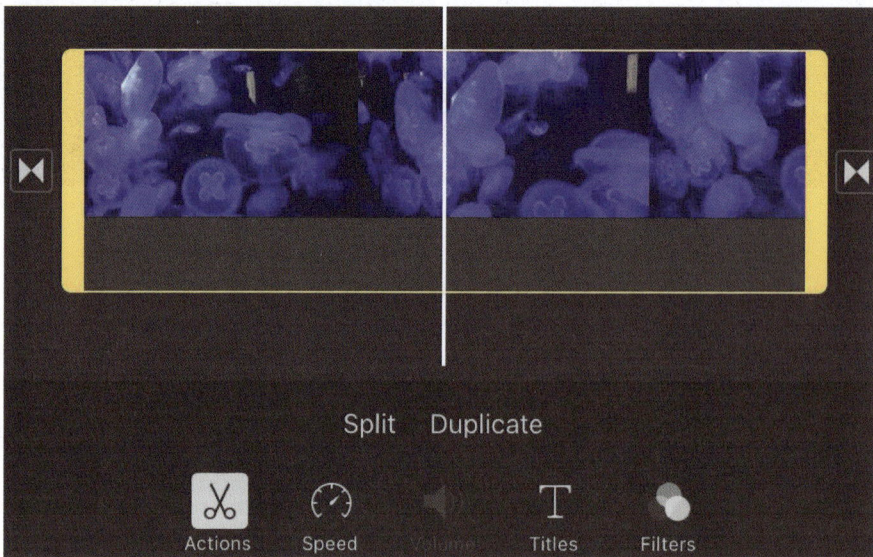

Figure 3.10 – The Actions menu for video clips

If you ever make a change you want to reverse, Movie mode has an undo option:

1. Tap the *undo* icon (an arrow pointing to the left) at the top of the timeline.
2. If you want to redo an action you've just undone, tap and hold onto the undo button.

Although they are relatively few, these edit actions make up most of the editing process. Trimming, splitting, and moving audio and video clips around will be key to creating a sense of flow in your video. There's no perfect recipe for success in this but bear in mind that editing is re-editing. There's nothing better than reviewing your work with a fresh pair of eyes. After a couple of iterations, it's time to add meaning to the video.

Customizing clips in Movie mode

The options for customizing clips, shown in the toolbar, are quite similar to Magic Movie and Storyboard mode. However, they were added to iMovie much earlier than those modes, and so there are a few differences: some features aren't as advanced, but with some, you can do more.

Speed

The **Speed** editor has the same sliding scale as Magic Movie and Storyboard mode, allowing you to change the speed between one-eighth of the original and 2x as fast. There's also a freeze-frame option:

1. Tapping **Freeze** stops the video where the playhead is, creating a freeze frame that's represented on the timeline with a thick horizontal bar.
2. You can use the handles around that bar to increase or decrease the length of the freeze frame.
3. Tap anywhere outside the bar if you want to edit the rest of the clip; a range will be highlighted in yellow showing the section you're editing (before or after the freeze frame). Tap the horizontal bar again to edit the freeze frame.
4. When a freeze frame is in place, the word **Freeze** below the timeline will be highlighted. Tapping **Freeze** again will remove the freeze frame you added. Tapping **Reset** does the same but also removes any other speed changes you made:

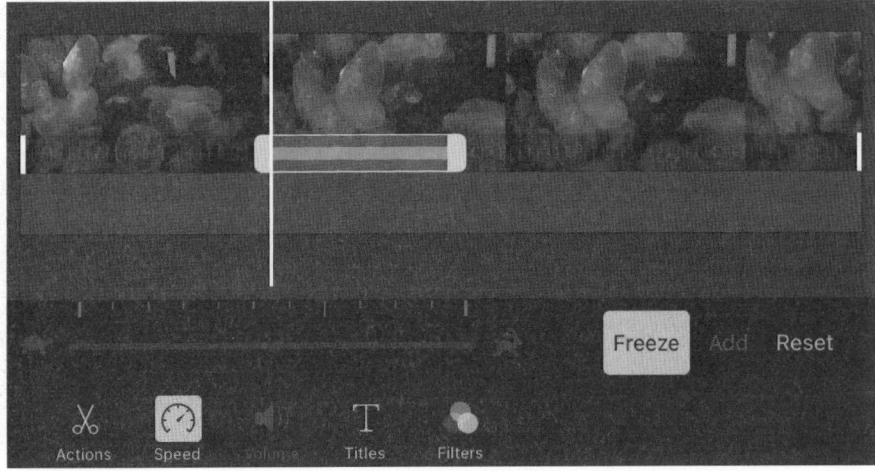

Figure 3.11 – A selected freeze-frame region

Next to **Freeze** is the **Add** option. This is a bit more tricky to use, but it helps you to make different parts of the clip go at different speeds without splitting the clip. Here's how to use it:

1. Tapping **Add** places a thicker vertical line at the playhead position.

   A new range is highlighted, between that line and the next line (if there's no other line, the range will last until the end of the clip).

2. You can change the speed of just this range with the slider in the toolbar.

So, in *Figure 3.12*, I tapped **Add** earlier in the clip where the first handle is, and the range extended to the start of the freeze frame in *Figure 3.11*. I then reduced the speed of the new range with the slider. This makes the clip slow down before stopping entirely:

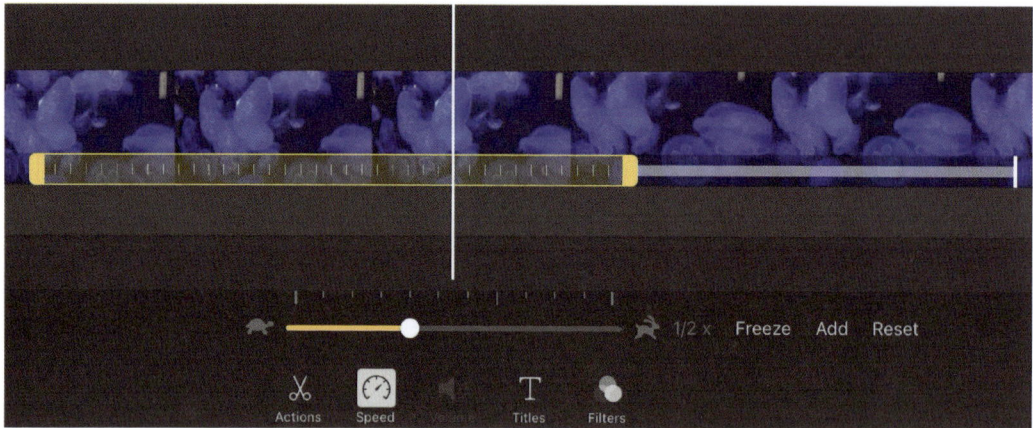

Figure 3.12 – Making changes with speed ranges

So, why would you want to use these speed changes? When changing the speed of the whole clip, you could create a slow-motion sequence, or a timelapse to show how something happened over time. Using regions, you could have a slow section within faster action to bring attention to something. Maybe try slowing down part of the water fountain at the Reichstag (`Reichstag-vid-6`) to draw attention to the water dancing around. Most of the time, speed changes don't help to add much context or meaning to videos; so, if you can't think of a good reason for making a speed change, don't make one.

Audio volume

The **Volume** option lets you change the clip's volume from 0 to 500% of its original volume. The 100% point is shifted toward the right of the scale because after you reach 200%, it's no longer possible to increase the volume by individual percentage points (that is, 201% to 202%). The smallest increase becomes 2%, rising to a 5% jump when going from 400% to 500% volume. This is a bit of a weird quirk, but for the most part, it shouldn't cause any problems; if you need to go as high as 400%, it would be because the audio is way too quiet. And if that's a voiceover, it might be a good idea to re-record it closer to your device's microphone (see the *Music and voiceover* section of *Chapter 2*).

Titles

Movie mode titles work a little differently from those in Magic Movie and Storyboard mode. Everything about them is edited through the timeline, instead of going to a separate **Style** menu. When it comes to titles, fortunately, you can add them to a photo in just the same way as a video. To add a title, take the following steps:

1. Tap on a clip and tap **Titles** in the toolbar.
2. Choose a title from the menu that comes up. For most of the titles, their animations are self-explanatory. The rightmost title is a theme title.
3. When you tap on a title, a **T** symbol appears on the clip in the timeline. A customization panel just below the timeline lets you change the font and color of the text (with an eyedrop tool so that you can get exact colors too).
4. There's also a further **Options** menu (...), with the following settings:

   - **Style** lets you choose between the default style that fills the screen and a less obstructive lower third.
   - Toggling **Text Shadow** on helps the title stand out against the background.
   - **Uppercase** allows you to toggle between mixed case and block capitals.
   - **Full Clip Duration** allows you to change the title length to fit the whole of a clip. Titles will always start at the beginning of the clip:

58 Using Movie Mode in iOS and iPadOS

Figure 3.13 – The title Options menu

5. When you've added a title in the style you like, tap on the text in the Viewer to edit it.

6. You can also edit the location and size of a title. Just hold and drag the words in the title, and you can move it anywhere in the frame you like. To make the title larger, spread outward with two fingers; to make it smaller, pinch in.

7. If you're using a background, you can also tap the color selector in the Viewer to change the shade of the background. I changed a light blue solid background to a darker blue shade to create an intertitle that marks the end of my "town" scene and the start of the "aquarium" scene:

Figure 3.14 – An intertitle made using backgrounds and a "Chromatic" title

Just a note on the rightmost title—the theme title. In the **Options** menu for that title, you can choose an **opening**, **middle**, or **closing** title. Opening and closing theme titles work like Mortise from Magic Movie, framing the video within a custom border. Also in the **Options** menu for theme titles is **Sound Effect**, which introduces the title with a short sound effect based on the theme:

Figure 3.15 – A closing title using the theme title

Titles are one of the main ways that meaning can be added to videos. It's a good idea to make use of them as they're helpful for signposting different parts of the video and explaining what the audience is seeing, especially if you choose not to use a voiceover.

Filters

Filters let you style a video very deliberately. As with titles, if you apply a filter, an icon will appear in the top left of that clip on the timeline. In the previous chapter, we discussed that filters aren't great to use if you're making a serious video, where subtlety is important. However, in Movie mode, you can tone down the strength of these filters using the slider that appears in the toolbar. Applying a Comic effect at 20% strength, for example, could give the video an interesting visual accent that isn't overbearing. Always think, though: is what I'm doing helping to tell my story more effectively?

Voiceover and Record

The **Voiceover** option in Movie mode sits just below the Viewer as a microphone icon. Apart from that, recording a voiceover is just the same process as it is in the **Edit** menu for Magic Movie and Storyboard mode. For guidance on how to use that, check out the *Music and Voiceover* section in *Chapter 2*.

And that's the editing tools covered. In this section, you have learned how to import clips and trim and cut them to size and how to add meaning with creative tools in the timeline. Now, it's time to look at some edit actions to refine your finished project, making it smoother and therefore more enjoyable to watch.

Using cuts and other transitions

In the *Understanding the pros and cons of automatic editing* section of *Chapter 2*, we learned that clips don't exist in a vacuum: they interact and interrelate in the timeline, and that's what gives them meaning. Now that we have more scope to change how clips interact in Movie mode, it's worth looking at this idea again.

One clip can interact with another by being overlaid (on top of a clip) or placed next to a clip. When clips are next to each other in the Movie mode timeline, there will be a visual indication of the transition between them:

Figure 3.16 – A cut transition between clips

The simplest transition is a **cut** (the transition in *Figure 3.16*). A cut is as simple as one clip ending and another starting. It's immediate and there's no animation—it's the same transition you created by splitting clips in QuickTime Player. The iMovie app represents a cut transition with a vertical line and calls it **None**. However, a cut isn't actually *no transition*. Every clip in a timeline transitions to the next, and the cut is still a valid transition to use. In fact, its simplicity makes it versatile: depending on the two clips you cut between, a cut can seem almost invisible or can draw attention to itself as a style point. The following are all types of cuts—the same transition, but in different contexts:

- **Jump cut**: Skips forward in time on the same or very similar shot. (This emphasizes time passing and feels abrupt. If you want your video to feel subtle, avoid these!)

- **Match on action**: When different shots show the same action, the most engaging time to cut between them is at a key point in the action. (If you had two shots of a door closing, for example, cutting when a hand touches the handle or when the door shuts fully would be good match points.)
- **Graphic match**: Cutting between two things that look similar. (This can imply a connection, or just make for a pretty transition!)
- **Rhythm cutting**: Cutting to the next clip on the beat of a piece of music emphasizes both the music and the visuals, drawing the audience's attention away from the narrative and toward the style of your video. It's often used as part of a montage (see next).
- **Montage**: Cutting back and forth between different people, different places, or different types of media such as live action and animation. (It emphasizes difference, but can also suggest that different things all contribute toward one idea.)

In all these cases, the transition is the same—a cut—with the clips on either side of the cut changing the effect it has on the audience. There aren't any hard and fast rules for using different types of cuts, so feel free to use the previous information as inspiration to add meaning to your edits in different ways.

Editing transitions in Movie mode

In the iMovie app, all transitions are represented by a symbol. When you tap on a symbol, a menu of transitions appears. If any of these transitions are grayed out for you, it means that one of the clips on either side of the transition is not long enough for the full animation of the transition to take place. To solve that, you'll need to increase the clip's length or place a longer clip after the transition. The transitions available are the following:

- **Theme**: A special transition based on the theme of the project. In the standard **Simple** theme, this transition is a fade.
- **Dissolve**: A cut that happens over time, creating a gradual transition from the old to the new clip that lets you see both at the same time. The iMovie app lets you increase the length of a dissolve in 0.5-second increments.
- **Slide**: The new clip moves from the left-hand side, over the old clip, replacing it.
- **Wipe**: Identical movement to the slide, but the clip "wipes" the old one out of the way instead of sliding over it (this makes the transition slightly more subtle).
- **Fade**: Often called a fade-to-black, this dissolves from the old clip to black, then from black to the new clip (this makes it good for transitioning to a new scene or section of your video):

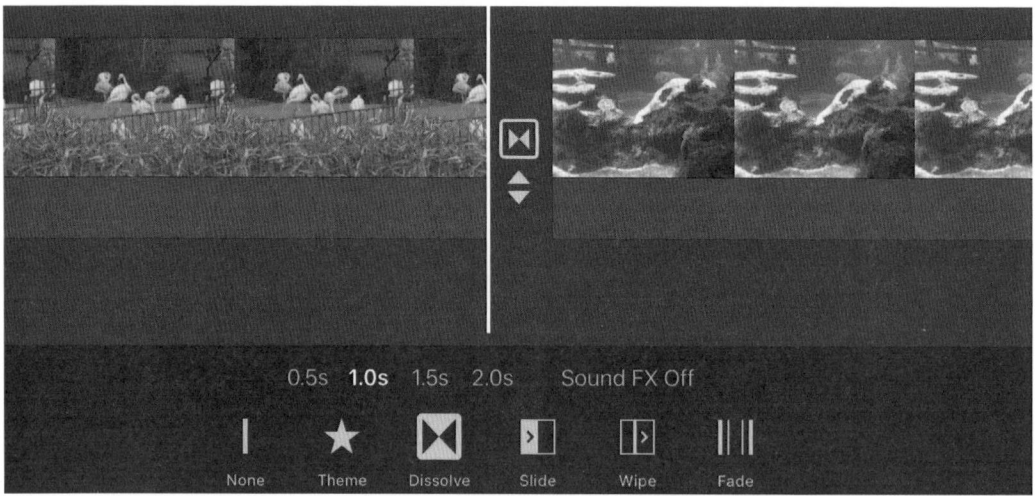

Figure 3.17 – The transitions menu

For every transition, including a cut, you can toggle **Sound FX** on. This is a *whoosh* sound effect—similar to the sound attached to the theme title—and its length changes depending on the length of the transition (a quick sound for a cut; slower for a dissolve or fade). That's the basics of transitions, but we're going to look at how to customize them further with a feature called the Precision Editor.

Using the Precision Editor

The Precision Editor shows all the workings of a transition, which are normally hidden on the timeline. The Precision Editor changes the layout of the timeline and can look intimidating at first, but once you're used to it, it's a powerful tool to use. Here's how to use it effectively:

1. When you select a transition symbol on the timeline, two arrows appear below it.
2. Tap on the two arrows to open the Precision Editor.
3. To get a better look at the Precision Editor, zoom in on the timeline by pushing outward with two fingers.
4. Tap the **?** icon to open the **Help** menu—its tooltips are helpful for explaining the many different handles and other features in the Precision Editor:

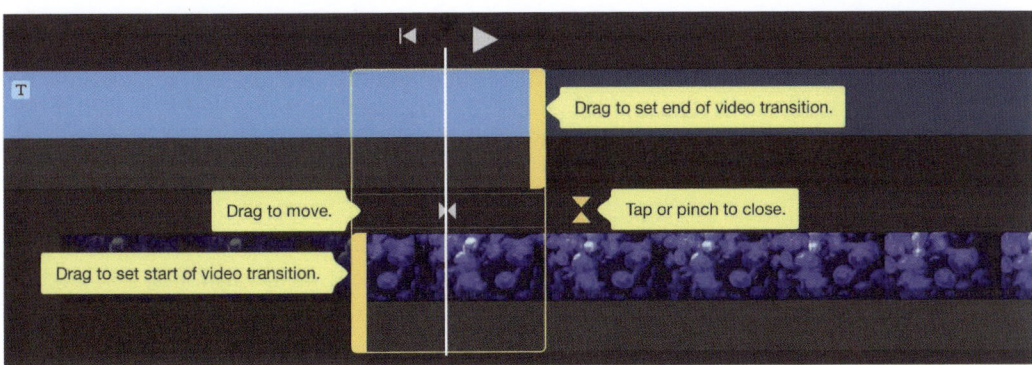

Figure 3.18 – The Precision Editor, with the Help menu open

Now, let's look at the features of the Precision Editor, as there are quite a few independent bits that you can change:

- A thin yellow border shows the area taken up by the transition. Hold and drag the middle icon (two triangles facing each other) to move the entire transition left or right:
  - Moving the transition to the left makes it start earlier on both clips
  - Moving the transition to the right makes it start later on both clips
- There are darker, grayed-out sections of the video strip for the clip. Those sections show the parts of the clip that aren't in use. For an image, this stretches out infinitely, because images don't have a particular length.
- Separate handles are available for fine-tuning the transition. Drag one of the thick yellow handles—it will move the transition's position on only one of the clips.

So, why would you want to use the Precision Editor? For one thing, it's the easiest way to relocate a whole transition earlier or later. Doing so in the timeline involves trial and error by adjusting the trim handles for both clips, before and after the transition. Moreover, moving the transition icon (but not the handles) is also a way to use different parts of video clips without trimming both sides of a clip. This is called a **slip edit**, and we'll look at those more in the *Using the clip trimmer* section of *Chapter 5*.

The Precision Editor is also very useful for working with sound. When you have a long transition such as a cross-dissolve, sound from both clips will end up playing at the same time (see *Figure 3.19*), competing, and causing confusion and cacophony. There are a couple of ways you can avoid this:

1. Drag the transition symbol to the right, or one of the yellow handles if there isn't room to move the whole transition. This will make it less likely that sounds will compete as we've moved to a later point in both clips.

2. If there is audio, you can use the thick blue handle to trim or extend where the audio starts and ends in the transition. Drag both blue handles so that they're in the same position vertically—that means one will start playing audio where the other stops and the sounds won't compete:

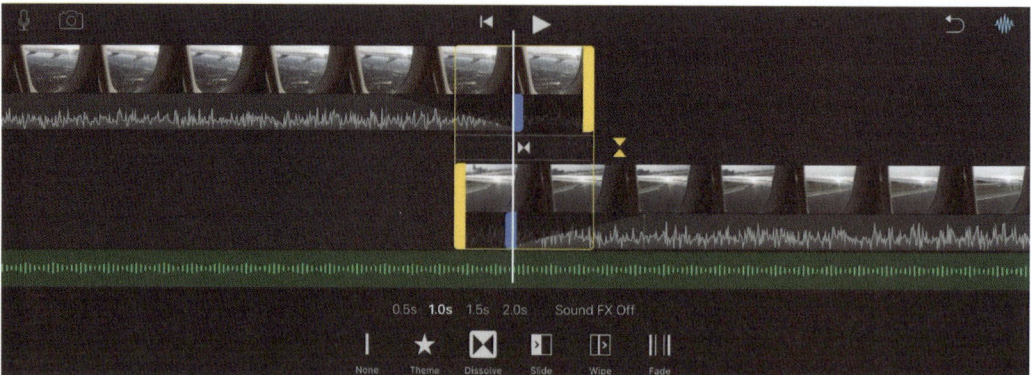

Figure 3.19 – Editing transition sound in the Precision Editor

3. When you tap on the timeline to exit the Precision Editor, arrow icons pointing in from the end of each clip show that the audio has been edited inside the transition.

With that introduction to closely editing audio, we're now going to focus on improving the audio in your project in general.

Editing audio in Movie mode

In a professional editing workflow, the video is normally edited first, and then the sound is edited after the **picture lock**, which means the video clips will always stay in the same position. That means no one has to worry about sound work falling out of sync if last-minute video changes are made. So, when you're editing, video first and sound second is a good order to keep.

In iMovie, there are two kinds of audio: foreground and background. In the mobile app, foreground audio is shaded blue and sits directly underneath the video. Background audio is shaded green and sits below all foreground audio. When you add audio to the project, iMovie will label it as one of these audio types. Broadly, the following can be used to help you decide which to select:

Foreground Audio	Background Audio
Voiceover recordings	Songs or music
iMovie sound effects	iMovie soundtracks

Whatever an audio clip is initially labeled as can be changed. You can move background audio to the foreground. To do that:

1. Tap on the audio clip.
2. Tap **Foreground**.
3. If the audio was a foreground clip, you can move it to the background by following the same steps and tapping **Background**:

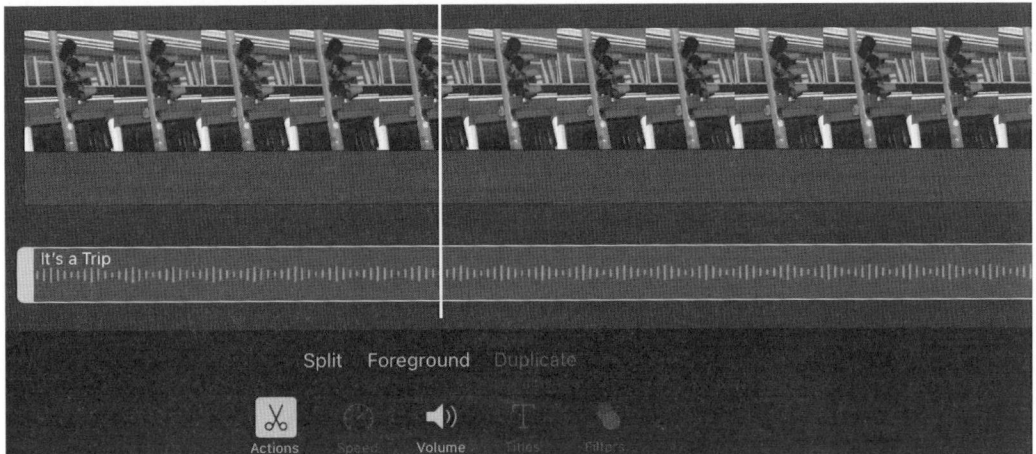

Figure 3.20 – The edit actions available for audio clips

Just as with video clips, foreground audio clips can be moved by holding and dragging. Do be aware, though, that you can only move clips horizontally. Although there can be audio clips stacked on top of one another, you can't move audio up or down in the app. Positions in the audio "stack" are decided by which audio clip was added first.

Limitations of background audio

iMovie allows a maximum of one background track. Any new track added as—or converted to—background audio will overwrite the track already in the background. Another limitation of background audio is that it will only last as long as there are clips in the timeline. For example, if you have 50 seconds of clips in the timeline, the background audio will cut off after 50 seconds. You also can't move background audio along the timeline—it will always snap back to the start of the project.

Moreover, although you can trim the end of the background track (just tap to select the audio clip and drag the trim handle at the end), you can't trim from the start. The only time you should really use background audio in Movie mode is if you already have three foreground audio tracks at the playhead position. Then, adding a background audio track allows you to have a fourth audio track, as in *Figure 3.21*:

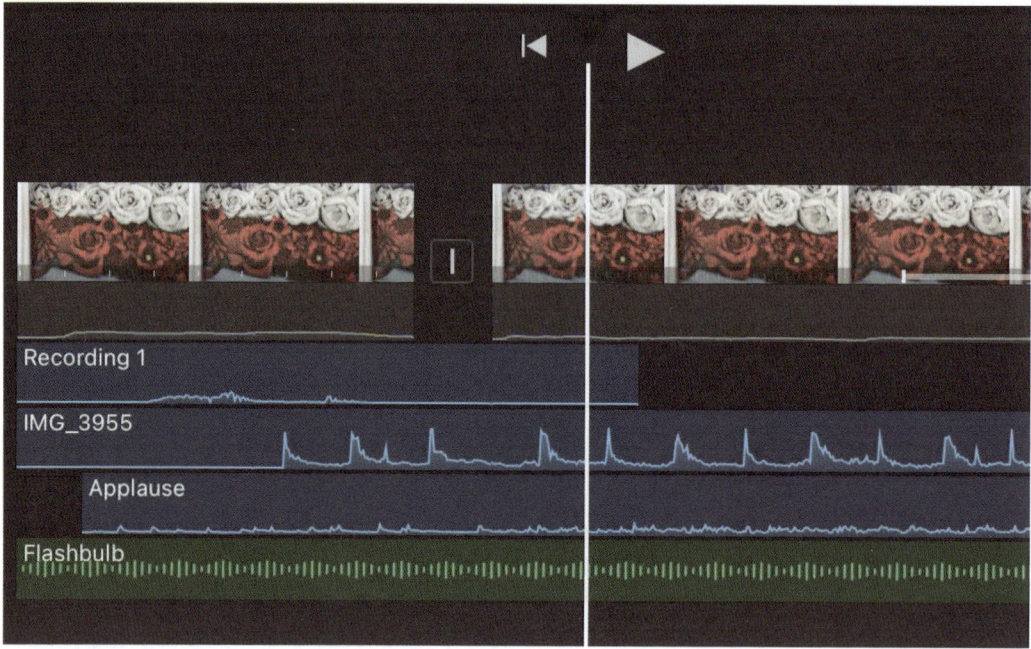

Figure 3.21 – Three foreground audio clips (blue) and a background clip below them (green)

Layering sounds in Movie mode

But why would you want multiple sounds going on at once? If we've edited transitions to avoid competing sounds, why are we putting them together below clips, deliberately? Well, whereas sounds competing in a transition are often unintended and tend to obscure what you want the audience to hear, putting sounds together deliberately can enhance the story you're telling.

Layering makes scenes feel more life-like because, in real life, there is no such thing as silence: multiple small sounds are always present in any situation. The sounds of the wind and breeze, the swaying of leaves, and the buzzing of bees would all sit below a clip of a meadow, for example. For the "town" scenes in your Berlin video, you may want to add the sounds of cars and crowds. However, neither are available in the iMovie Audio library; you'd need to check online on a website such as `https://freesound.org/`. We'll look at the different types of sound effects often used to layer sound in the *Using the Audio & Video Tab in iMovie* section in *Chapter 5*.

But even if you're not using sound effects, layering other sounds such as voiceover and music can make your video more engaging. For non-fiction videos, adding a quiet soundtrack underneath a voiceover is a simple way of indicating the mood of the video—thoughtful, serious, upbeat, or something else. Layering music also tends to drown out small glitches and microphone problems. If you're recording using the inbuilt microphone on your device, that audio can sound tinny and not so great to listen to on its own. Adding music underneath can help the audience to see—or hear—past that.

Another advantage of layering sound is that you can point out and draw attention to certain visual aspects of the video. Under the *Titles* and *Editing transitions in Movie mode* sections, we looked at the sound effects you can add to titles and transitions. Giving visual movements such as title and transition animations an audio accent can help emphasize their movement, adding meaning and making the video feel more deliberate and purposeful.

Do be aware, though, that if you have multiple tracks in any one place, you will need to consider how everything sounds together. Make sure to reduce the volume of the background track and any sound effects so that your main audio in the foreground—usually voice(s)—can be heard clearly. You also don't want all the sounds to make the project too loud overall. The best way to check everything's in balance is to listen back to the project; quality control is a crucial part of the editing process!

Fading audio for better video

Volume changes and listening back will be key to making all your sounds blend in well with one another, but Movie mode allows you to introduce gradual increases and decreases in volume to make audio clips start and end smoothly. Here's how:

1. Tap on an audio clip and enter the **Volume** menu.
2. Tap the word **Fade** on the right of the menu—a yellow triangle appears at the start of the clip. This triangle is another type of handle called a **fade handle**.
3. Drag the fade handle to the right, and a fade-in is created; the clip will reach its full volume wherever you set the triangle (*Figure 3.22*):

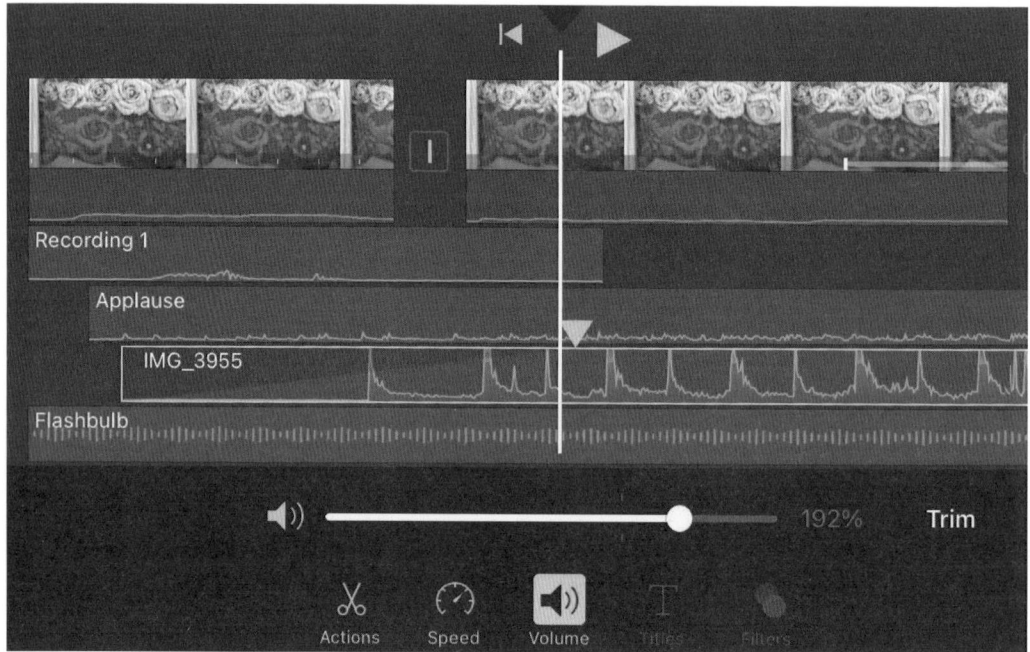

Figure 3.22 – Extending a fade handle

4. Repeat those steps at the end of the clip, and you can gradually fade the audio out.

5. When you're done, tap **Trim** to exit the **Fade** menu and bring the trim handles back.

Fades are useful to add because they make your video sound more natural, and audiences tend to like continuity (think of songs—how many times do you hear them cut out for a second, halfway through?). As humans, we like sound to flow gradually: unless you want to use abruptness to draw attention to something, smooth sound transitions help the different clips in your video combine into one continuous video more convincingly. That, in turn, improves the viewing experience for your audience.

Making smooth audio transitions with J- and L-cuts

Fades also appear in the Precision Editor. Using the blue handles to fade out the old audio while fading in the new audio creates a **crossfading** effect that gives you a smooth transition between different scenes in your video. Crossfading is nice and simple to see in practice when you have audio clips below video clips. However, there's another kind of crossfading that helps make videos feel smoother and more immersive, which uses the Precision Editor. Here's a recap on how to open that:

1. Tap on the transition between two clips.

2. Tap the two triangles next to the transition to open the Precision Editor.

When we last looked at the Precision Editor under the *Using the Precision Editor* section, we moved the blue (audio) trim handles to stop sounds from two different video clips from competing with one another. However, you can also use them to create a special kind of audio crossfade between clips, called a J- or L-cut.

But why are they called J- and L-cuts? It's all to do with the shape that the audio and video make together. If we extend the audio from the first clip to continue under the second clip, the audio will jut out to the right, creating a kind of L shape. If we were to extend the audio from the second clip back over the first, we would create a J shape, as you may be able to see in *Figure 3.23*:

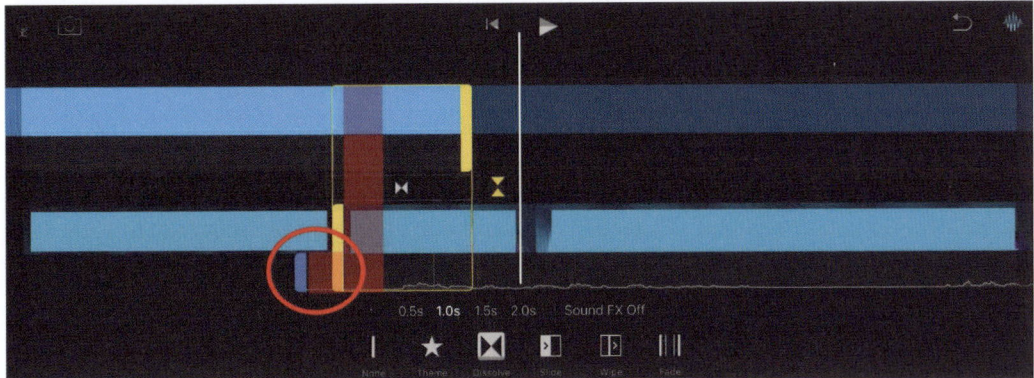

Figure 3.23 – A J-cut is formed by moving the audio from the second clip (circled) backward; to make the "J" shape clear, it's highlighted in red in this screenshot

By extending one clip's audio over the other (and therefore creating a J- or L-cut), we are crossfading the clips. Never underestimate the power of crossfading—it helps a huge amount to make transitions (especially cuts) feel smoother and more natural. Let's have a look at the general technique for making J- or L-cuts as you edit:

1. Open the Precision Editor on a transition (as described at the beginning of this subsection).
2. Check the audio waveforms that are grayed out beyond the edge of each clip (*Figure 3.24* shows an example):

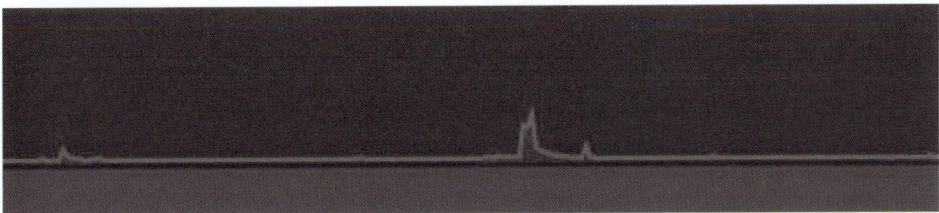

Figure 3.24 – An example grayed-out waveform; avoid areas with spikes in the waveform when making J- and L-cuts

3. We're looking for a space where the waveform is flat. This means that there are no unwanted sounds such as coughs or tapping; just the ambient sound, also known as **room tone**.

4. Find some room tone and extend it so that it can also be heard under the other clip. It doesn't matter whether you're extending to the left (a J-cut) or to the right (an L-cut): both act as an audio crossfade that smooths out the transition.

By extending the room tone underneath another clip, we smooth out the transition. Think of it like introducing the audience to the new clip in two stages: first by audio (if using a J-cut), and then by video; or the other way around for an L-cut. Doing the transition in two stages like this makes the change in the clip feel smoother and more natural.

Quality control and exporting

Now that we've looked at how to add and refine meaning in Movie mode, it's up to you to put this together to produce a finished video that tells the story of the Berlin trip coherently, concisely, and engagingly. Keep those main editing principles from *Chapter 1* in mind, but don't let them limit what you try. It's only through experimentation that you'll learn from mistakes and create timelines that make you sit back and smile. Practice will help you nail down the style of editing that helps you tell your stories the way you want to.

Before you export it, give your finished video a quality control watch-through to check there aren't any problems with the picture or sound. Fix any problems, make adjustments, and watch it again. We want a video that flows well and feels deliberate in the way it's put together. We also want its audio to sound smooth and balanced throughout the video. When you're happy, here's how to export the video:

1. Tap **Done** in the top-left corner of the timeline menu—the screen will go back to the project menu.
2. Tap the **Share** icon in the bottom middle of the next screen.
3. At the top of the **Share** window, tap **Options** (the menu is shown in *Figure 3.25*):

Figure 3.25 – The export options menu

4. You can choose to export the video or a project file (it's set to **Video** by default), and you can change the video resolution. Choose the maximum resolution you can if you have space on your device.
5. The best practice with video is to export a video file (in this case, it will be a .MOV QuickTime movie). Tap **Back**.
6. Now, tap **Save to Files** (this option should be near the top of your **Share** window).
7. When the progress bar is finished, name the file, choose the location in your Files app that you'd like, and tap **Save**.

The process of exporting to a file first makes backing up easier, and you'll have a valuable copy of your video that you wouldn't have had if you'd exported straight to a content-hosting app or website. If you don't have enough space on your device, saving to Google Drive or iCloud Drive can be a good alternative. Make sure you have enough storage on those cloud platforms too, though.

> **Project files**
>
> In the export options menu, you can export your project as a project file rather than a video. A project file saves the way the clips are arranged and edited in the timeline and allows you to pick up the project again on a different device. At the time of writing, you can only open iMovie for iOS/iPadOS projects in iMovie for macOS, not the other way around. You can export and open Magic Movie, Storyboard, and Movie Mode projects for editing further on the Mac.

Summary

In this chapter, we looked at Movie mode, the most advanced and flexible editing mode on the iMovie app for iOS and iPadOS. Using a timeline, Movie mode allows you to piece together videos, photos, and other files of your choice to create a video with a creative direction of your choosing.

Movie mode has a blank timeline for which we need to choose our own clips. There is no preset format or gaps to fill, but this lack of a helping hand gives us greater creative scope to tell the stories we want to. We learned that unlike in Magic Movie and Storyboard mode, Movie mode allows you to edit transitions as well as layering sound, using sound as a transition through crossfading. These techniques are important for creating a polished and enjoyable video because the transitions between clips help create and maintain rhythm, and layering and fading sounds make the video feel more continuous and make the scenes within it feel more believable.

In the next chapter, we will start looking at iMovie for macOS. But don't worry if you don't have a Mac—there's still plenty more in this book for iOS/iPadOS users. The next chapter will explain the logic behind the way that iMovie's timeline is built and show you how to navigate the timeline super-quickly with keyboard shortcuts.

Part 2 – iMovie for macOS

iMovie on the Mac is the flagship version of the app: it has more creative scope than the mobile version, and has a structure that more closely resembles other NLEs. So, this second part of the book is dedicated to using and understanding it.

We'll start by learning how to organize and import files with iMovie for macOS. We'll then take the time to understand the way that its timeline is structured, and what the effect of having "connected media" and a "magnetic timeline" is. We'll also go over some useful keyboard shortcuts for the app, because they are quite literally the shortcut to editing more quickly and confidently.

We'll then run through a whole video workflow in iMovie, similar to what we did in *Chapter 3*. This will give us an opportunity to look in depth at the Media Browser for iMovie, and the resources that it offers. We'll also look at the toolbar tools that allow us to edit color, cropping, and sound, as well as make corrections to the video. An important lesson we'll learn is not to let iMovie make creative decisions for us: your judgment on what looks good is better than a computer's.

Finally, we'll build on the video workflow we've looked at by learning how to add and use overlays in iMovie. Overlays are useful for all sorts of reasons, from subtly covering up cuts and jumps in your video, to creating special effects that can wow your audience. Overlays also help you to edit multiple perspectives at once, so we'll look at syncing, editing, and combining those too.

This part of the book comprises the following chapters:

- *Chapter 4, Understanding iMovie for macOS – Keyboard Shortcuts and the Magnetic Timeline*
- *Chapter 5, iMovie Editing Workflow – Import, Edit, Export*
- *Chapter 6, Using iMovie Effects – Overlays and Keyframing*

4
Understanding iMovie for macOS – Keyboard Shortcuts and the Magnetic Timeline

In this chapter, we're going to be taking a deep dive into the workings of iMovie for macOS. It's more versatile and capable than the mobile app, but because of that, there is more that you need to know about it in order to get the best out of it. Know your NLE as you know yourself, they say, and you'll have success in all editing jobs.

Although Movie mode for both iMovie for macOS and iOS/iPadOS use a timeline, editing on a computer-based NLE inevitably works differently from a mobile device. The biggest difference is that instead of tapping to undertake actions in the program, actions are now linked to menu commands, which means you can use keyboard shortcuts. For the initial time spent learning iMovie's keyboard shortcuts, you will save a huge amount of time when editing. One of the best ways to get to grips with a new program, I find, is to look at—and try out—all of the settings and the menu commands. You don't need to memorize all the keyboard shortcuts here or anything like that. But as you read through, try to give everything a go so that iMovie's Mac-based editing actions start to feel more normal.

The main topics we'll cover in this chapter are as follows:

- An introduction to iMovie for macOS and how to arrange projects and media
- Keyboard shortcuts for navigating the timeline and making edits in iMovie for macOS
- How Apple's "magnetic timeline" and "clip connections" affect editing in iMovie for macOS

Technical requirements

iMovie is a free default application on macOS, but it might not come pre-installed on your Mac. If it's not on your Mac, just head to the App Store and search for it. It's vanishingly unlikely that iMovie imitators will make it past App Store security, but just to be sure, check that the app you're downloading has Apple listed as the developer.

To have a consistent experience with this chapter (and going forward), you'll need iMovie version 10.3.2 or newer installed. That update allowed Magic Movie and Storyboard projects from the mobile app to be imported into the macOS version. You can check which version of iMovie you have by selecting **iMovie | About iMovie** in the menu bar at the top of the desktop. Do familiarize yourself with the menu bar (*Figure 4.1*) if you haven't already—we'll be using menu commands a lot in the rest of this book:

Figure 4.1 – The iMovie menu bar

Understanding iMovie for macOS – libraries and events

When you open iMovie for the first time, you'll be met with an empty projects screen. You can choose to create a trailer or movie by clicking on the large + icon. Trailer mode is the iMovie for macOS equivalent of Storyboard mode, which is available on iOS and iPadOS. For more information on Storyboard mode, check out the *Using Storyboard mode* section of *Chapter 2*.

If you don't have a mobile Apple device, iMovie for macOS will probably be your first foray into video editing. For that reason, you might be tempted to start with Trailer mode, using the templates to get to grips with clips and arranging media. However, the structure of filling in the gaps is very different from the timeline paradigm, and because the timeline paradigm is the dominant structure for NLEs, I'd recommend starting your learning journey on the Mac with its own Movie mode.

When you click to create a movie, you will be presented with a blank interface that should be quite recognizable by now (*Figure 4.2*). At the bottom is the timeline. Above it is the Media Browser (left) and Viewer (right). Above the Viewer is a toolbar with various features for editing clips—some of them are similar to the iOS/iPadOS Movie mode toolbar. We'll be going over what you can do with the macOS toolbar in the *Using iMovie media* section of *Chapter 5*:

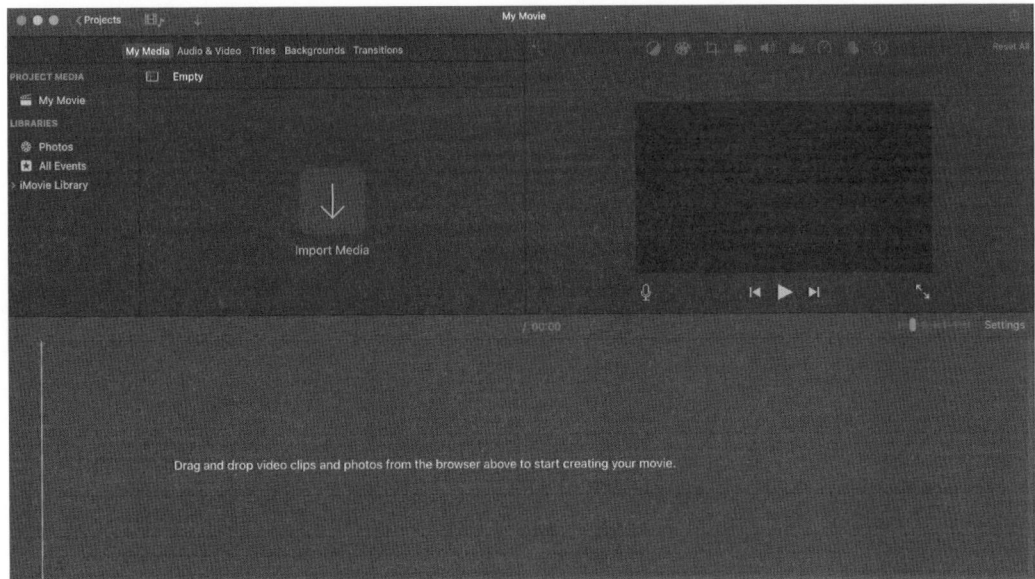

Figure 4.2 – A blank project interface for iMovie for macOS

With that brief overview of iMovie for macOS' overall layout complete, it's time to start looking at navigating the app. Our first job is getting to grips with the structure of the Media Browser because it's not as simple as the Media Browser on the mobile app. In iMovie for iOS and iPadOS, media is selected individually for each project from the whole Photos app and the whole Files app. When you select media, it's added straight into the timeline. In iMovie for macOS, the Media Browser acts as one **media bin** for all projects. In the next few subsections, we'll look into how this media storage system works in more depth.

The iMovie Library

In iMovie for macOS, all media is stored in the **iMovie Library**. If you don't know what a library is (I didn't when I first used iMovie) it's helpful to learn the definition so that you can appreciate what the iMovie Library does. A library is a special kind of folder that contains files from folders from different places in your filesystem but shows all the files in one place so that you can access them easily. In the same way, the iMovie Library contains media from all sorts of folders across your computer that you may have imported at different times, for different projects. If you look at the pane on the left-hand side of the interface (*Figure 4.2*), you'll find the iMovie Library.

> **Extra tip**
>
> You can find and look inside the iMovie Library in Finder, the macOS file explorer, as follows:
>
> 1. Type ⌘ + ⇧ + *G* (search for folder).
>
> 2. Now, type `~/Movies` (`~` means your user area, so `~/Movies` will take you to your `Movies` folder).
>
> 3. ^ + click or right-click on the **iMovie Library** folder and select **Show Package Contents**.
>
> There's no pressing need to do this, but checking out this folder can help you to understand how iMovie works with files. This process is most useful for checking which video files and projects are hogging space if your iMovie Library becomes excessively large.

Creating multiple iMovie Libraries

You can actually have more than one iMovie Library. To create a new one, do the following:

1. Go to **File** | **Open Library** | **New…**.
2. Give your new library a name that tells you clearly what will be in it—for example, `Finished_iMovie_Projects`.
3. Save that library in the `Movies` folder or to an external storage device.
4. You can then open this library in iMovie by going to **File** | **Open Library** | **Other…** (if it doesn't appear in that menu, use the **Locate** button to search your Finder for it).

Saying that, I wouldn't recommend creating new iMovie Libraries, even for a new project. For industry-level projects with hundreds of files to edit, having an iMovie Library dedicated to each project can be helpful. However, creating different libraries can make iMovie messy, causing confusion when you move between projects. If you have one iMovie Library, every clip you've ever imported will be there as soon as you open iMovie. With multiple libraries, you might not see all the projects and clips you expected to see because a library may not be open or it may not be stored on your device.

Personally, I have one iMovie Library that I use for my current projects and one that lives on an external SSD containing finished projects and their media files. That allows me to stay within my Mac's 256 GB storage limit (which for video editing is pretty tiny!) by keeping projects I don't need right now—but only those projects—off-device.

Creating Events in the iMovie Library

If you have multiple projects on the go, the iMovie Library will become like a huge list of files. This can make it cumbersome to search through. That's why iMovie lets you split your library into **Events**, sub-libraries that help you to sort the media in your iMovie Library. Events are shown in the iMovie Library drop-down menu, with their names indented. If you've started iMovie up for the first time and created a new project, the iMovie Library drop-down menu will show one event, named after the date you created the project:

Figure 4.3 – The iMovie Library and "today" event available on first opening iMovie

- To rename an event, click on it and press *Enter*.
- To create a new event, click on the iMovie Library and use the ⌥ + *N* shortcut (or go to **File | New Event**).

In case you have more events than the **Libraries and Events** pane can show at once, there is an **All Events** tab on the **Libraries** pane. This allows you to scroll through all the events in all your libraries.

What are events used for?

Events are yours to do what you want with. Their primary purpose is to split the iMovie Library up into smaller parts that are easier to manage. You can use an event for each project you make or use events for different types of media within a single project, such as:

- Videos
- Photos
- Audio

There is another way that you can structure your events—as different categories for resources that you can use for whichever project you're working on. Here are a few clip categories you might want to create events for:

- **Stock Sound Effects**
- **Background Music**
- **Stock Photos**
- **Stock Videos**
- **Custom Backgrounds/Animations** (more on that in *Chapter 7*!)

Do remember that this is just one of many ways you can arrange the events in your iMovie Library. I personally like to use events like folders of stock footage. I like this system because it's simple and doesn't need to be updated with every new project I start. Although this is the structure I will use in this book, that doesn't make it the only good structure. You may be wondering too: if I structure my events like this, where do I put the new videos, photos, and audio that form the majority of a particular video? This is where **Project Media** comes in.

Using the Project Media tab

When you import media, iMovie places it in its own area specific to that project: **Project Media**. This tab sits at the top of the **Libraries and Events** pane and works like a separate event that's dedicated just to the timeline you're currently editing on. This makes it a convenient place to put all the clips you have recorded for that project:

Figure 4.4 – Project Media for the "The Timeline" project from Chapter 1; other menu panes have been blanked out for clarity

There is a downside to storing all your project media in this section, though. The more clips you have, the more time-consuming it'll be to sort through them all. Luckily, marking and filtering media, which we'll look at in *Chapter 5*, can help to minimize this problem.

Adding media from the Photos library

Apart from the standard iMovie Library, your Photos library is also integrated within iMovie. Here's how to access that:

1. Click on **Photos**, just under the **Libraries** heading.
2. Give access to your Photos library if prompted.
3. The default view shows your Albums, but you can click the drop-down menu to view other sections.

4. To access your videos, go to **All Photos** in the drop-down menu. An additional drop-down menu on the right then lets you filter by **Photos**, **Videos**, and **Favorites** (*Figure 4.5*):

Figure 4.5 – Filtering by videos is a little fiddly and unintuitive

5. Click on the media in this section to select it. You can drag and drop it into the timeline (or press *E*—more on that later), an event, or the **Project Media** tab.

That covers the system of libraries and events in iMovie. You will hopefully now be a bit more confident knowing how to begin a project in iMovie for macOS. We'll look at importing clips to your `Project Media` folder and starting on an edit in *Chapter 5*. Now that we have looked at how you can arrange libraries and events in iMovie for macOS, it's time to look at how to navigate the program when you're editing.

Navigating iMovie with keyboard shortcuts

The fastest way to navigate any NLE is to learn and use the keyboard shortcuts for its menu commands. The sheer number of them might seem overwhelming at first, but when you've used them for a while, the process will begin to feel natural, and you'll be dancing over the keyboard like a virtuoso piano player. This section will go over some of the most useful shortcut commands in iMovie for macOS. The shortcuts are listed by what they do: file and project actions, timeline and menu navigation, and editing tools. Make sure to drag some clips into the timeline from your iMovie Library or events. Then, play along with each of these shortcuts; it's the best way to become familiar with them.

At any time, the ⇧ + ⌘ + / shortcut (think of this as command-question mark) brings up the iMovie help menu. Type any actions there if you can't find them, and macOS will show you which menu the command is in. The help menu also contains Apple's iMovie user guide (**iMovie Help**) and a full online list of keyboard shortcuts. So, with that, let's take a look at some of the most worthwhile ones to try out.

File and project actions

Earlier, we looked at ⌥ + *N*, which creates a new event. Similarly, there are a few useful shortcuts for quickly arranging files and projects:

- ⌘ + *I* brings up the menu for importing footage (we'll look at this in detail in *Chapter 5*)
- *2* (on the number row) takes you to that project's screen, out from the timeline

- ⌘ + N creates a new movie project when you're on the project's screen
- ⌘ + D duplicates a project (we'll see later how this helps for error-checking and more)

The Library actions (**Open Library**, **Copy to Library**, and **Move to Library**) are useful if you have multiple iMovie Libraries, but they can't be accessed through keyboard shortcuts. You'll need to click on the three dots next to the project's name or go via **File** | in the menu bar in order to access those.

Timeline and menu navigation

There are loads of shortcuts to help you navigate the timeline more quickly. Firstly, here are a few shortcuts for viewing the whole project:

- ⌘ + = zooms the timeline in toward the current playhead position
- ⌘ + - zooms out of the timeline
- ⇧ + Z zooms out of the timeline far as possible so that you can see as much of the project as possible

You'll want to use the zoom tools regularly while editing so that you can switch between checking that the project works as a whole and closely editing individual clips. Now for selecting clips and parts of clips. To select a clip, click on it, then drag it to wherever you'd like it to be. You can also use the following:

- Click + drag to draw a selection box. This allows you to select multiple clips without having to use ⇧ + click (selecting a range of clips) or ⌘ + click (selecting individual clips):

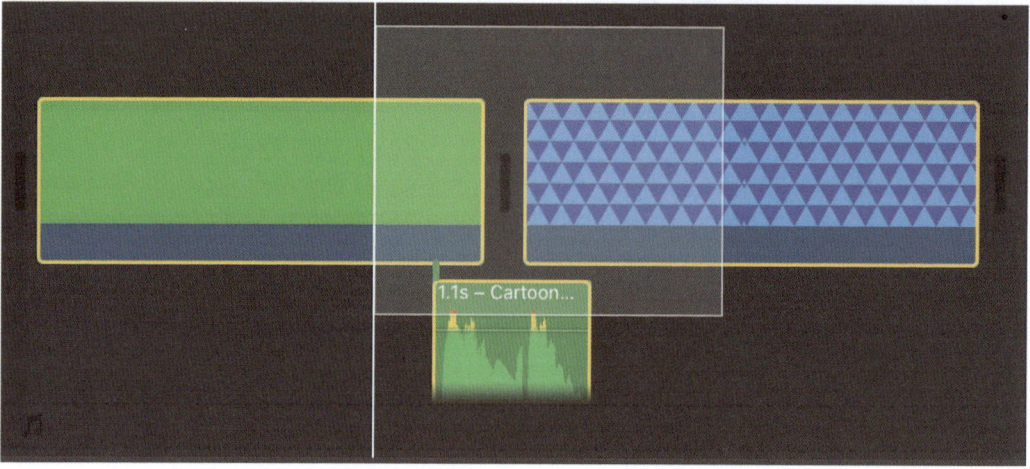

Figure 4.6 – Dragging a selection box just a short distance across and downward selects a lot of clips very quickly

- Hit *C* to select the clip at the playhead position (*X* does this too, but selects the entire clip you have imported, regardless of any trimming you did on the timeline).
- Hit *I* to set an in-point for a selection. By default, that selection goes to the end of the clip unless you use *O* to set an out point.
- Similarly, hold *R*, click, and drag over a clip to create a selection range of your choosing.

The following shortcuts give you keyboard controls for moving along the timeline and playing the project:

- *L* plays the project. Press again to go at 2x speed.
- *K* pauses the project, stopping the playhead.
- *J* plays the project backward. Press again to go backward at 2x speed.
- */* (forward slash) plays only the selected clip or range.
- *'* (apostrophe) or ↓ (down arrow) moves the playhead to the end of the current clip or the start of the next if you're already at the end of a clip.
- *;* (semicolon) or ↑ (up arrow) moves the playhead back to the nearest clip edge.

The following three shortcuts change how media plays, and whether you toggle them on is really a matter of preference:

- ⌘ + *L* loops playback. When the end of the timeline, range, or clip in the Media Browser is reached, it plays again from the start.
- *N* toggles *snapping*. When the playhead is near the edge of a clip or a marker in the timeline, it skips a few frames as it gets pulled to that edge. The playhead will turn yellow to show you that it has snapped.
- ⇧ + *S* toggles *audio skimming*. This means audio plays out when you move the playhead across the clip. The pitch changes based on how fast you move the playhead.

I like to keep snapping on as it generally makes trimming and other edits easier and avoids the accidental splitting of clips. With snapping on, you can still ensure you're moving frame by frame by using the left/right arrow keys (← and →). Audio skimming can be useful for identifying what part of the video you're at based on sound cues, but it does mean you'll constantly be bombarded with sound, and if you skim too fast, all you'll hear is high-pitched gibberish.

Finally, for menu navigation, these six shortcuts bring up the different iMovie media menus, which can be found just to the right of the **Project Media** tab (again, we'll look more closely at what they do in *Chapter 5*). The first five shortcuts change what is shown in the Media Browser:

- ⌘ + *1* shows **My Media**, which defaults to **Project Media** unless you have a library or event selected
- ⌘ + *2* shows iMovie's sound effects library

- ⌘ + 3 shows the stock titles you can drag onto the project
- ⌘ + 4 shows iMovie's stock backgrounds and world maps
- ⌘ + 5 shows the transitions available for dragging and dropping into your project
- ⌘ + 6 brings up the **Theme Chooser**, similar to the **Project Settings** sub-menu on iMovie for iOS/iPadOS

Editing tools

Now that you've learned the shortcuts for selecting clips and ranges within them, let's look at the keyboard shortcuts for adding clips and performing edit actions to those clips. Sometimes, the simplest shortcuts are the most useful—you may have expected these first few, being universal commands, but it's always useful to remind ourselves that we have them at our disposal:

- ⌘ + C copies the selected clip
- *Backspace* deletes the selected clip
- ⌘ + X cuts (copies then deletes) the selected clip
- ⌘ + V pastes the copied clip
- ⌘ + Z undoes an action (you can undo every action since you last opened iMovie)
- ⌘ + ⇧ + Z redoes the action you most recently undid

> **Using keyboard shortcuts to evaluate an edit**
>
> Bouncing back and forth between undo and redo can be helpful for testing out an edit you've made. Here's how you can do this:
>
> 1. Select the range you made the change in by holding *R* and dragging.
>
> 2. Play the range with the / key.
>
> 3. Switch back to the old version with ⌘ + ⇧ + Z.
>
> 4. Play again. Does the change make the video look or sound better, or was it better how it was originally?

These next shortcuts are for adding media at the playhead position:

- *W* inserts the clip selected in the Media Browser. One of two things will happen:
  - If the playhead is over a clip, iMovie splits the original clip at the playhead position and inserts the new clip in the gap.
  - If the playhead is in between clips, the clip will be inserted into the gap with no splits:

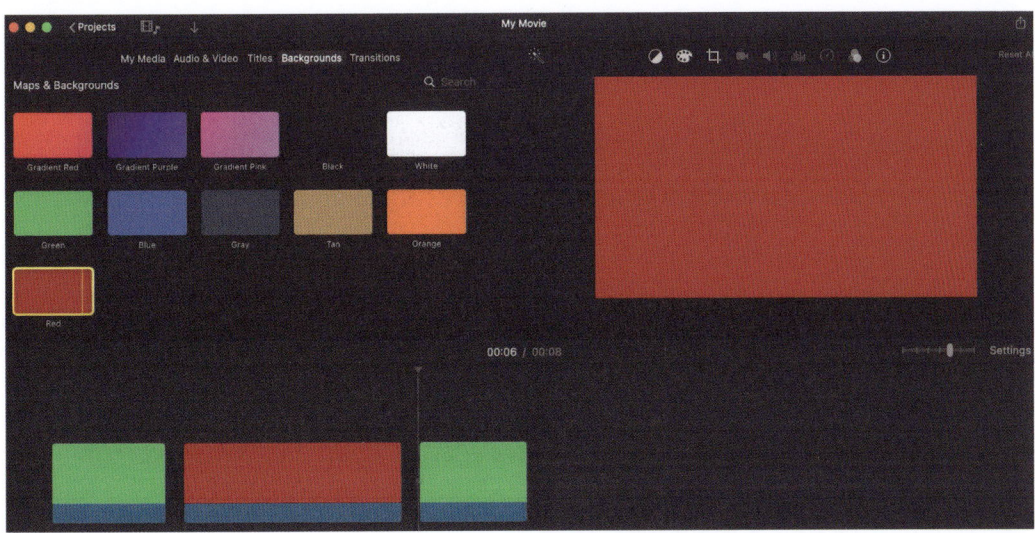

Figure 4.7 – A red background inserted at the playhead position (W) on a green background

- *Q* places the clip on top of the clip already in the timeline as an overlay (iMovie calls this connected media—we'll see why later).
- *E* appends the selected clip to the end of the project, after the last clip.

The following actions are shortcuts for widely used editing actions—splitting, trimming, changing speed, and adding and editing transitions:

- ⌘ + *B* splits the clip at the playhead position (not ⌘ + *Y* as in QuickTime Player).

  If you select multiple clips, either by dragging a selection box across them or by using ⇧ or ⌘ + click, edit actions such as split or trim to playhead (see next) will apply to all of those clips at once!

- ⌥ + / (option + forward slash) trims to the playhead, and can do so in two different ways:

  - By default, it trims a clip to the playhead position, from the clip edge that's nearest (like the trim-to-playhead tool we saw in the *Edit* section of *Chapter 2*).
  - If you select a range first, the shortcut will trim everything outside the range, so you're just left with the range you selected.

Because trimming to a playhead or range with ⌥ + / is basically two actions in one (split and delete), it's a much faster way to remove unwanted clips and ranges than using ⌘ + B and backspace. Definitely try it out for yourself to get to grips with it, both with and without a selected range. Practice makes perfect with this one, as it's quite difficult to explain on paper, but easier to get a feel for within iMovie! Next:

- When you click on the very edge of a clip, . (full stop) trims/extends the clip to the right by one frame. , (comma) trims/extends to the left.

Using a comma and a full stop to trim frame by frame can be really useful for getting the right feeling from a cut, especially if you're trying to make the timing of the cut comedic by lingering on the clip for just the right length of time. Moving on:

- ⌘ + ⇧ + B detaches the audio from the video, allowing you to move and work with the audio track separately from the video.
- ⌘ + R brings up the speed editor, allowing you to change the speed of a clip by adjusting a large circle next to the fade handles:

Figure 4.8 – The speed editor, circled in red

- ⌥ + ⇧ + R resets any speed changes on the clip and hides the speed editor.
- ⌥ + F adds a freeze frame at the playhead position, indicated by a hand symbol. When you click on the hand, the range of the freeze frame will be highlighted, and you can edit just that region:

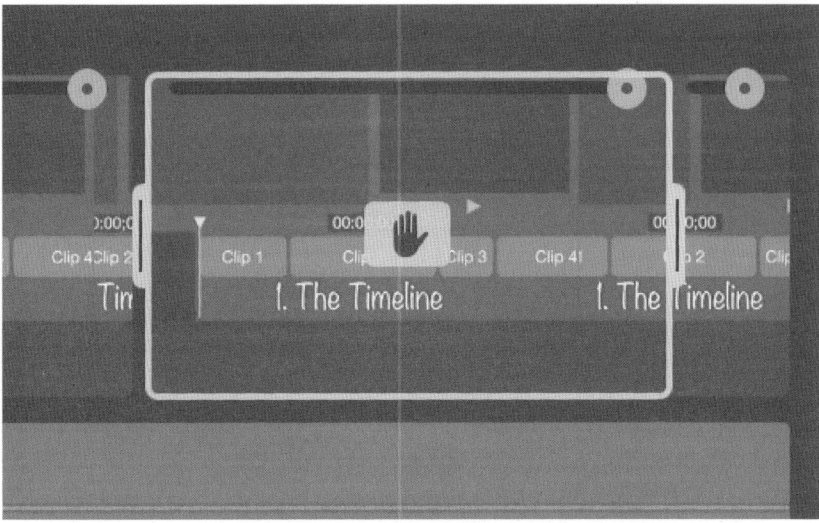

Figure 4.9 – A freeze-frame region

- When a clip is selected, ⌘ + T places cross-dissolve transitions on each side. If the playhead is in between two clips, ⌘ + T places one cross-dissolve in the gap.

That brings to an end our journey through some of the most useful keyboard shortcuts in iMovie. Wherever you can, try to use these shortcuts instead of the menu commands when editing. Getting used to the editor's dance around the keyboard is going to make the post-production process a whole lot faster and more efficient, even though it feels unnatural at first. Now that you know the best ways to navigate around the iMovie for macOS interface, it's time to look at how the timeline works. Apple's NLEs (iMovie and Final Cut Pro) are built differently from other NLEs, and this has been known to cause confusion and frustration. It's important to understand what's going on so that you can make your editing workflow frictionless.

Clip connections and the magnetic timeline

After the practical focus of the keyboard shortcuts earlier in the chapter, it's time to return to a little bit of editing theory to help you understand the intentions behind the way that iMovie is designed. In this section, we'll be looking at how Apple's timelines differ from other NLEs, and how its "connected media" works in practice.

Timelines – tracks versus connections

So far in this book, you may have noticed me talking about "tracks", often in the case of audio that we have added to a QuickTime movie, a Magic Movie project, or to the background of a Movie mode project. In editing, a **track** is a layer that isn't physically connected to anything above or below it—a track acts like a see-through shelf that media sits on.

You have already used a track-based editing program: QuickTime Player. There is one video track, rigidly set in place. If you add audio, it goes into an audio track, visually separated from the video track. The edits you make to one track do not affect the other. NLEs have always tended to be track-based. In most, tracks sit on top of one another, going up the timeline for video (Video 1, Video 2, and so on) and down the timeline for audio (Audio 1, Audio 2, and so on). *Figure 4.10* illustrates what a track-based timeline might look like:

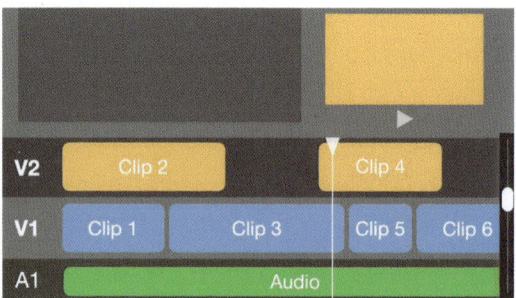

Figure 4.10 – An illustration of a track-based timeline; note how the clips are visually separated from one another

iMovie, however, works differently. Instead of giving you different tracks, Apple created a system of **connected media**. Clips above the main video layer and foreground audio below it *connect* to the main video layer (we'll call this layer **V1**, as in *Figure 4.10*), instead of having their own tracks:

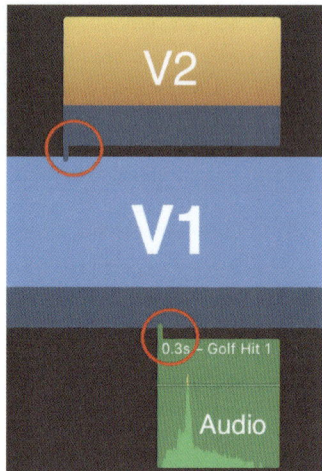

Figure 4.11 – Clip connections (circled) for video and audio

As you can see from *Figure 4.11*, the second video layer has a short leg coming out of the main clip. This is called a **clip connection**. Clip connections are how **V1** connects to the clips around it, and they form at the start of every connected clip. They make a kind of flagpole shape, looking like the letter *P* for clips above **V1**, and *L* for audio below it. Before we look more into working with connected media, there's another quirk of iMovie's timeline design that's worth keeping in mind.

Understanding the magnetic timeline

Apple's NLEs use what's called the **magnetic timeline**. It's designed to make sure no gaps are left in the timeline. When you delete a clip in the main video layer, the clip afterward will move left to fill the space that was previously occupied. Most of the time, this feels more intuitive than a gap being left. That's because if you delete a clip, you're likely to expect the timeline to act like that clip was never there, rather than leaving space for it.

However, you may be deleting a clip because you want to replace it with something else. In that case, you'd want to keep a gap. To get around this in iMovie, you need to directly replace the clip while it's still in the timeline. Here's how to do that:

1. Drag a new clip over the old one.
2. Wait for the old clip to be shaded white:

Figure 4.12 – Dragging a new video to replace part of the "The Timeline" video

3. Drop the new clip.
4. An Options menu will appear. Which option you choose depends on whether you want to fill exactly the same space the old clip occupied:

   - **Replace** puts the whole new clip in place of the old one, even if it's longer or shorter than the original.

- **Replace from Start** will fill the exact length of the old clip with your new clip, as long as the new clip is as long or longer. Choosing **Replace from Start** will trim part of the end of the clip if it's longer than the original, whereas **Replace from End** will trim from the start of the clip so that it ends at the end of the clip—a process called **backtiming**.

In *Figure 4.13*, I replaced a clip illustrating the timeline (7 seconds long) with a screen recording of an iMovie timeline (20 seconds long). By using **Replace from Start**, the new clip fits into the exact 7-second space the original clip occupied; that means the audio flows exactly as it did before. I detached the audio first because I don't want to replace that!

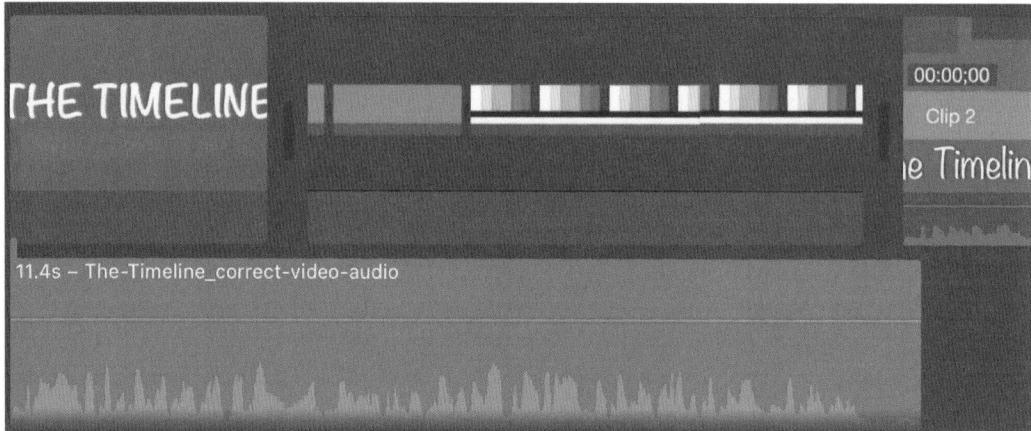

Figure 4.13 – Replacing a clip using Replace from Start

It's important to note that the magnetic timeline keeps **V1** attracted to the start of the project, but this doesn't apply to connected media. With this in mind, let's look at the best practices for using connected media.

Working with connected media

Because connected media doesn't occupy a track of its own, it moves wherever the **V1** clip it's connected to moves. The advantage of this system is that the connected media's relative position stays exactly the same: video and audio won't suddenly fall out of sync if you make a change to **V1**. The disadvantage is that it's possible to accidentally delete clips when you weren't intending to. When you delete a **V1** clip, the audio and video connected to it are deleted too.

The most important rule when working with connected media, then, is to check before you delete a clip: is there audio or video connected to it that you want to keep? If there is, you'll need to move the connection for the connected clip so that it doesn't get deleted too. Here's how you do that:

1. Hover the playhead (your cursor) over the connected clip at the point you want the connection to move to (as in *Figure 4.14*).

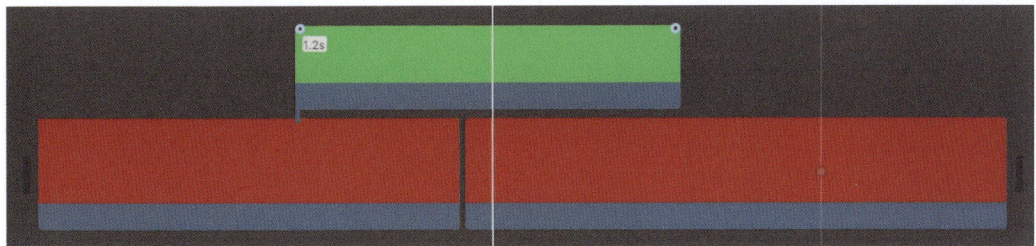

Figure 4.14 – When you hover over the playhead, the thicker line shows the hover position

2. Hold ⌥ + ⌘ and click on the connected media clip (you have to click directly on the clip). The clip connection should move the connection to the playhead position.

This is a great feature for when you come to work with overlays (more on that in *Chapter 6*). For now, there are a few other differences between **V1** and connected media/overlays to consider:

- Connected images and video aren't attached to the start of the project. If you delete one, the other connected clips will stay exactly where they are.
- Dragging a new video over connected media won't push it out of the way as it does for **V1**; it will just overwrite the clip.
- You can't have more than one connected video/image at any playhead position.
- You can't place transitions between connected media clips (all you can do is add fades—more on that in *Chapter 6*).
- You can't use the Precision Editor on connected media clips.

Working with connected audio

Audio comes under the banner of connected media, but it allows a bit more flexibility, which we'll look at making use of in this section. iMovie only allows one layer of connected video on top of **V1**, but you can have as many connected audio layers as you like. When you drag and drop audio in the same place as other audio, it will still form a connection to the **V1** layer, but it will sit below the other audio. To make it sit above other audio, click and drag the audio clip upward, and the other audio will be displaced (as in *Figure 4.15*):

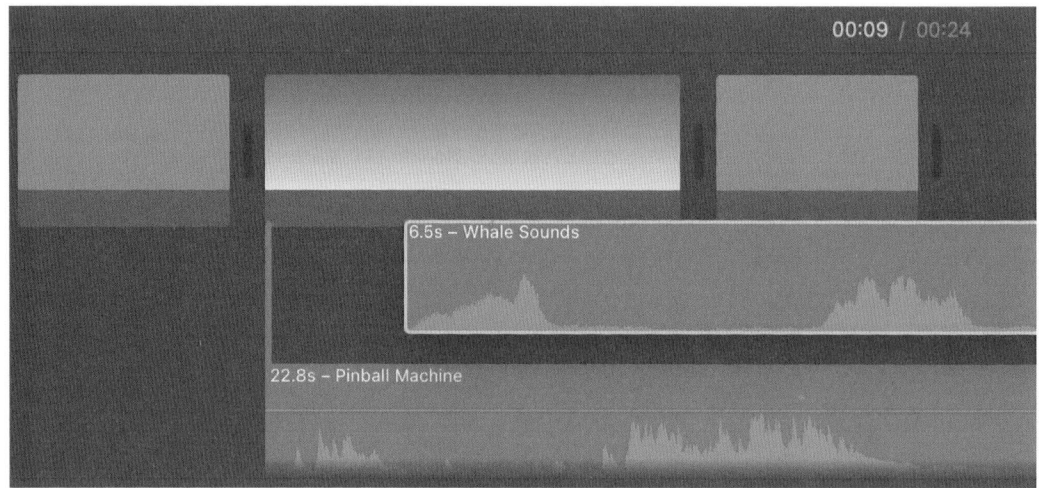

Figure 4.15 – A new audio track pushing the original downward; the original clip connection stretches taller to meet the V1 clip

How far away the audio clip is from **V1** doesn't affect its volume in any way, so why would you want to reorder audio clips? Well, it can be helpful to sort your audio from top to bottom based on what kind of audio it is so that your project is more clearly organized. If you have a clear idea of which layer is doing what in your project, it can help to make complex projects simpler to look at and work with. Here's an example of using your audio layers strategically:

- **Top**: Dialog/voiceover
- **Middle**: Sound effects
- **Bottom**: Music

Speaking of music, there is one part of the iMovie timeline (where music usually goes) that ignores clip connections entirely. You've seen it in *Chapter 3*: it's background audio. There is a track at the very bottom of the iMovie timeline in which the audio goes dark green. This can be an effective place to put music. Let's have a look at it, and its differences from connected audio.

Background audio in iMovie for macOS

The background audio track is marked out by a strip below the rest of the timeline—a dotted-line border around a musical note icon (🎵). It always sits locked at the bottom of the screen wherever you have scrolled to on the timeline. This means that if you have scrolled to the top of the timeline, the background audio track will hide some of the foreground audio that it actually sits below (as in *Figure 4.16*). Don't worry, though—all your audio is still there:

Figure 4.16 – The background audio track (below) hovers visually above other audio

Here's how to add audio to the background track:

1. Click and drag your audio clip below all other audio.
2. When it changes to a dark-green color, it's in the background track.

In the background track, the audio has no connection to the video layer. This freedom from clip connections makes a difference in what it's best to edit in that section. Because the foreground audio is connected to **V1**, you should always edit that *after* you've edited the video. This is the video-first, sound-second approach we talked about in the *Editing audio in Movie mode* section of *Chapter 3*.

The background audio—being a track, not a layer—is not connected to **V1**. This means that you can edit the video according to the sound. This is particularly useful if you're creating a montage or a music video, where sound dominates the storytelling and you probably want to use rhythm cutting (for more types of cuts, check out the *Using cuts and other transitions* section of *Chapter 3*.

Some final thoughts—there are another few quirks to the background track that are important to bear in mind:

- There is no background video track; all video is connected to **V1**
- Background audio isn't drawn toward the start of the timeline
- The background audio track applies an automatic fade-in and fade-out that you can't turn off
- The automatic fade comes at the start and end of every background clip, so it's best to avoid splitting the background clip into multiple clips

Because these automatic fades can be annoying and unpredictable, it's often best to use foreground audio as the first port of call. That way, you have more control over how your audio sounds in the project. Remember as well that clip connections are there to help you: if you spend your time in iMovie avoiding them, you're working against the way the program's designed. That's only going to make editing slower and more frustrating.

Summary

In this chapter, we looked at the structure of iMovie for macOS in order to build confidence working with it. We first looked at the media storage system on iMovie for macOS, which differs from the mobile version of the app because it allows you to create and populate your own iMovie Libraries, and smaller Events within them. We looked at what you might use Events for, and the possible risks of having more than one iMovie Library.

We then looked at some useful keyboard shortcuts and mouse/trackpad options for iMovie. Knowing your way around the interface and remembering keyboard shortcuts for actions will help speed up your editing flow, and will make editing feel easier and more natural. Remember to keep trying out the different actions and menu commands available to you so that you can get used to them!

Finally, we looked at the way iMovie's timeline works, and how that differs from track-based NLEs. The magnetic timeline removes gaps from the timeline, and connected media means that when you edit the main video layer, the relative position of clips above and below it stays the same. We also looked at the background audio track, which is free from clip connections. Understanding why clips act the way they do can help to avoid mistakes and frustration when editing.

In *Chapter 5*, we'll be focusing on an editing workflow from import to export using iMovie for macOS. The knowledge you gained in this chapter should help you to navigate the iMovie for macOS interface with confidence. Knowing the tools and the system should make the more mechanical part of editing—moving clips around—easier, helping you to focus more on telling your story coherently and concisely, with added meaning.

5
iMovie Editing Workflow – Import, Edit, and Export

In this chapter, we will go through the entire process of creating a video in iMovie for macOS. This will be similar to the process we used in *Chapter 3*; however, **iMovie for macOS** looks different and has more features available to you. Now that we have moved to a more fully-featured NLE, the way you choose to go about the edit becomes more important. This is because optimizing your process can make the whole edit go a lot faster and feel a lot smoother; but with more features available, an unstructured workflow will cause more friction and frustration than before.

With more ways to go about the process, your ability to customize your editing workflow also increases. Because of this, we are going to start from scratch again, creating our Berlin travelog video with iMovie for macOS. It is possible to share projects from the mobile app for editing directly on the Mac (see the *Creating a ProRes Export from a Mobile Project* section in *Chapter 8*), but I'd encourage you not to skip ahead. Repeating the import and assembly process can only be a good thing for learning.

The main topics we will focus on in this chapter include the following:

- The import and media marking process in iMovie for macOS
- Setting project resolution and frame rates
- The toolbar and media resources

Import – preparing media for editing in iMovie

In *Chapter 4*, we looked at Libraries and Events, which contain all of your media files. To recap, the iMovie Library contains every file that you have imported into iMovie, sorted into Events that you create. Each project also has a separate **Project Media** tab. When looking at the import process in this chapter, we're going to keep all the media for one video inside of Project Media, as this is a clean and simple way to arrange files, provided you don't have too many of them. When you're in the timeline, you can access the import menu in two ways:

- Click the downward-facing arrow in the Media Browser or at the top of the iMovie window
- Use the ⌘ + *I* keyboard shortcut

When you do, a file browser will open (*Figure 5.1*):

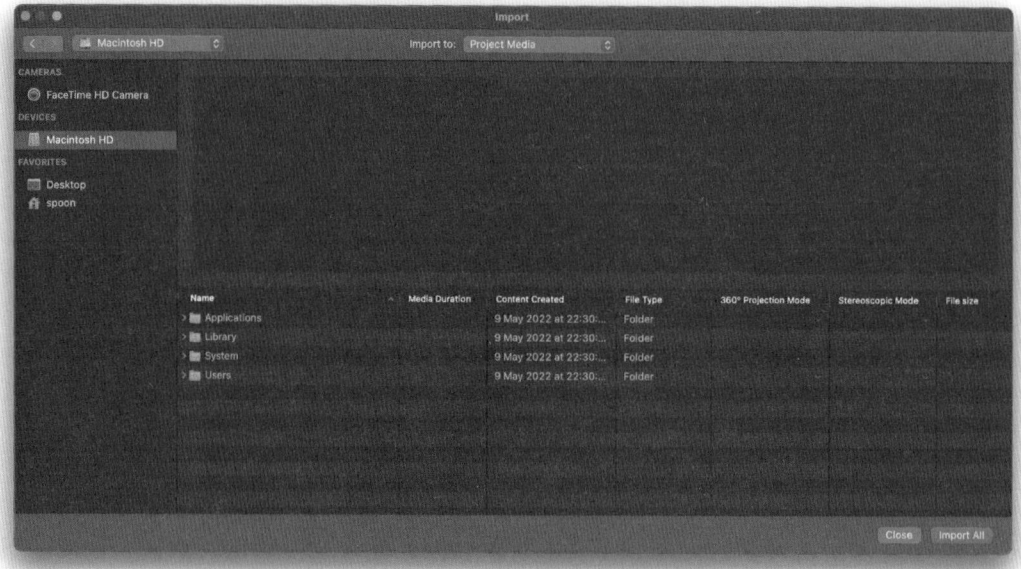

Figure 5.1 – The Import menu in iMovie for macOS

At the top middle of this window is the **Import to:** drop-down menu. This lets you decide where in the iMovie Library you're importing to. It defaults to **Project Media**, which is good for us, but if you want to import to a specific Event (or a new Event), choose that option from the drop-down menu. The list of files focuses on your Mac's filesystem. If we want to look inside a different device, such as a camera, we need to connect the device and use the side panel.

How to import directly from devices

If you've filmed or recorded something on a camera or phone, you might want to import it directly into iMovie. Here's how:

1. Check whether the device will be recognized by iMovie. If it's an iOS/iPadOS device, it definitely will be, but for a list of compatible cameras, check the support page: `http://support.apple.com/HT204202`.
2. Connect the device to your Mac, either by USB or an SD card slot (if your Mac has one).

3. The device will come up in the import menu, at the top left under **Devices**.

   Select the files you'd like to import. ⇧ + click to select a range of clips and ⌘ + click to select/deselect individual clips.

4. Click **Import Selected** at the bottom right of the menu.

The risks of importing directly from devices

Importing directly from devices can save space on your computer. iMovie creates a copy of every file you import, so if you import directly from a device, you'll only have files within the iMovie Library, so they won't clutter up your hard drive. However, this comes with its risks. If iMovie can't locate the file for whatever reason, it will display the media as missing. Your project could therefore be ruined a long way through the editing process if you've formatted the SD card the footage was on, or otherwise deleted the footage.

Therefore, another golden rule in editing is, where space allows, *always import to your filesystem first*. If you don't have space on your computer, try to use an external hard drive or SSD if it's available. You'll certainly thank yourself later. Here are some ways to import your footage safely.

Follow these steps for Apple devices:

1. Use AirDrop to import videos directly to your **Downloads** folder.
2. Move those files into a folder dedicated to your video; this is like mirroring the **Project Media** tab, but outside of iMovie. This is what I did for my own Berlin video (*Figure 5.2*):

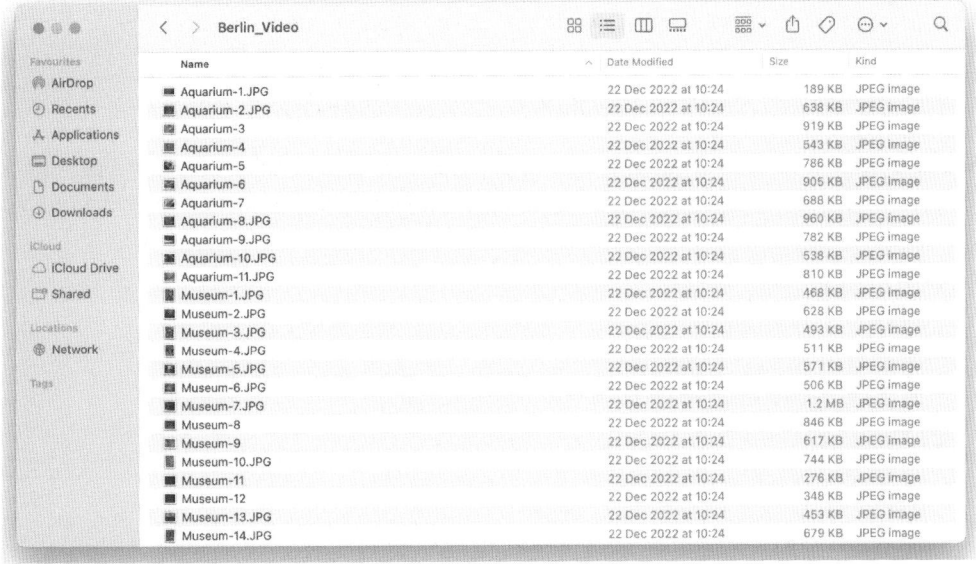

Figure 5.2 – A separate project folder in Finder that keeps safe copies of my "Berlin" files

Follow these steps for other devices and cameras:

1. Plug in an SD card or connect the device to your computer via USB.
2. Open Finder and click on the device on the sidebar on the left.
3. If you're low on space, check the media files on the device, selecting only the ones you need.
4. Drag the selected media files into a folder dedicated to your video.

Now that you have copies of your project media in Finder, we can import those copies using the iMovie import menu.

Using and customizing the iMovie import menu

With your media files – very sensibly – imported into your filesystem first, it's time to locate them and import them into your project. Here's how to find the files you need:

1. The sidebar on the left (under **Favorites**) shows which folder on the computer you're seeing in the file list – the main section of the Media Browser.
2. The **Favorites** section of the sidebar is pretty limited in the folder options it gives to start with, so it can be helpful to use the following macOS keyboard shortcuts to find what you're looking for:

    - ⌥ + ⌘ + *L*: **Downloads** (this will be where AirDropped files are first imported to)
    - ⌘ + ↑: Enclosing folder (the folder that contains the folder you're in. The enclosing folder of **Downloads** and **Documents** is the **Home** folder – that is, your user area)

3. There's no keyboard shortcut to access the **Movies** or **Pictures** folder, both of which tend to contain files you'll want to use in iMovie. To get there, use either of these methods:

    - Press ⇧ + ⌘ + *G* (go to folder) and type `movies` or `pictures` (as in *Figure 5.3*). Hit *Enter* or click **Go**:

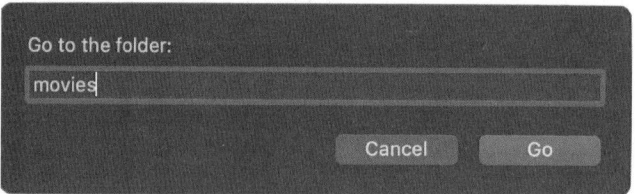

Figure 5.3 – The Go to folder: box in the iMovie import menu

    - Select **Desktop** from the sidebar and go to your **Home** folder with ⌘ + ↑. From there, you can see the **Movies** and **Pictures** folders.

When we can see folders such as Movies and Pictures, we can add them to the **Favourites** sidebar, to make the import menu easier to navigate in the future:

- Favorite the folders you'll return to so that they're just one click away on the sidebar. To favorite a folder, ^ + click or right-click on the folder and click **Favorite** (as in *Figure 5.4*). Permit iMovie to access the folders if prompted:

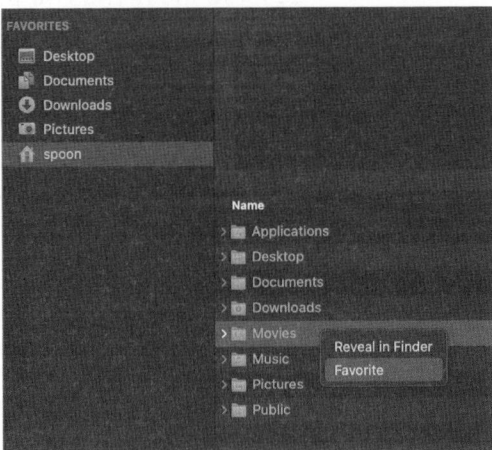

Figure 5.4 – Favoriting the Movies folder from the Home folder. I've already favorited Documents, Downloads, and Pictures

4. There's a lot of space on the sidebar, so really go mad with favoriting! This will make the menu quicker to navigate when you next want to import media. You can always remove a favorited folder later by right-clicking its panel and selecting **Remove from Sidebar**.

You can find almost any folder on your Mac using the **Import** menu and keyboard shortcuts, but there is one folder you may have media in that's very difficult to find: your iCloud Drive. The folder path is shown in *Figure 5.5*, and to get there, you need to do the following:

1. First, make sure that all the files in your iCloud Drive are downloaded to your Mac. You can do this by going to iCloud Drive in Finder and, in the **List** view, clicking all the cloud icons next to files.
2. Back in the iMovie import menu, click on the name of your user area – the bottom tab under **Favorites**.
3. In the file list, find **Library** and double-click on that.
4. Now, scroll to find the **Mobile Documents** folder and double-click on that.

5. Finally, in this folder, you'll find the **iCloud Drive** folder. Make sure to favorite the folder so it stays on your sidebar.

Figure 5.5 – The folder path for your iCloud Drive

If this seems too complex – and frankly, it is – don't worry. You can still drag and drop files from your iCloud Drive from Finder, into iMovie. That's fine for occasional use, and you might only want to use iCloud occasionally for storing video media.

> **Using iCloud Drive for media files**
>
> iCloud Drive has a very limited 5 GB space as standard, so it's not great for storing your videos. We'll also see in *Chapter 9* that iCloud downloads cause lots of headaches for iMovie users.
>
> However, iCloud Drive can be useful for keeping duplicates of small files; a kind of just-in-case. If I forget my external drive, I've got copies of all sorts of small images and iWork files (1 MB or less) in my cloud storage so that I'm less likely to be without something I need. Examples include:
>
> > Short sound files such as sound effects and common words and phrases I've recorded to fix gaps or mistakes in voiceovers
>
> > TextEdit files with video notes in them
>
> > Keynote projects (for graphics and animations)
>
> > Stock overlays and images that I regularly use
>
> Remember, though, if there's a video or image file you need to keep coming back to, it's best to store it in an Event in your Mac's iMovie Library.

That concludes our look at the import process. This may all seem like a lot of effort, but a lot of it was filling up our **Favorites** on the sidebar: that's a one-off task that will make all your future imports easier. With your files safely imported into iMovie, it's back to the timeline interface to view and sort them using the Media Browser.

Marking media as favorited or rejected

Once your media has been imported, iMovie allows you to mark your media as "favorite" or "rejected" and then filter the Media Browser by those tags. To mark media, follow these steps:

1. Go to the **Project Media** tab.
2. Select a clip and play it using the *J* and *K* play controls. The clip will show in the Viewer so you can see it properly.
3. Mark whether you want to use the clip or not:

   - *F* favorites the clip, showing a green line at the top
   - *Backspace* rejects the clip, showing a red line at the top
   - *U* unmarks the clip, allowing you to mark it in a different way

Marking media can be useful because it helps you to reduce clutter in your Project Media folder by only showing clips you like. You can even select and favorite a specific region of the clip:

1. Select your favorite range in a clip in the Media Browser by using the *I* and *O* keys to set in and out points, respectively.
2. With the range still selected, press *F* to favorite the range. A green bar will appear just in the favorited region, as shown in *Figure 5.6*:

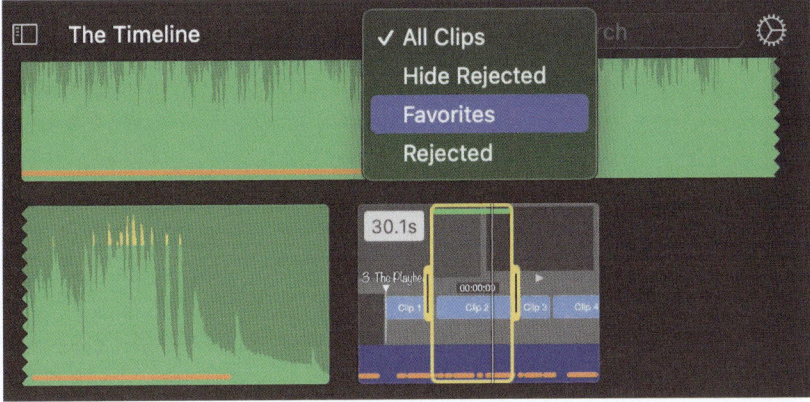

Figure 5.6 – Marking a favorite range

3. Now, you can filter your media by **Favorites** to only show that region of that clip. To do so, click on the drop-down menu at the top of the Media Browser (again, as shown in *Figure 5.6*) and select **Favorites**.

This is a great way to sort the media already in your Project Media, but it does beg a question: why have we bothered to import clips that we're not going to use? For the sake of saving time and space, I would suggest marking out media you don't want before you import a single file.

Don't reject – remove

When you reject a clip, it won't disappear from the iMovie Library. It – or rather the copy of the clip iMovie makes – will still be in the iMovie Library taking up space. Sorting through your project folder in Finder before you open iMovie has a couple of advantages:

- Importing fewer files means waiting less time before you start editing – especially if you're importing long, high-resolution files
- The iMovie Library takes up less space on your Mac because it's made fewer copies of files

If you have already imported all of the Berlin clips, or later decide a clip you imported is of no use to you, you can remove it from the iMovie Library:

1. Remove the clip from the timeline with *backspace* if it's in there.
2. Select the clip in the Media Browser.
3. Hit ⌘ + *backspace*.
4. Click **Delete** on the warning dialog (if the dialog doesn't come up, it means that the same clip is in a different Project or Event).

Don't worry about losing the original video when you do this. As we established earlier, iMovie makes a copy of every clip, and by removing a clip from the iMovie Library, you're only deleting the copy. You can always re-import clips from your Finder project folder later too.

Customizing Media Browser settings

When you're happy you've got just the clips you want, you can change how the Media Browser represents them ready for beginning your assembly edit. First of all, I'd suggest turning on **Skimmer info** with the ^ + Y shortcut. This adds a tooltip to the Media Browser that tells you the name of a clip when you click on it. It's really useful when you have similar-looking clips that need to go in a particular order.

You can also tweak the Media Browser to prioritize seeing all your clips at once or make the video/audio strip on each clip show more information. Here's how:

1. Click on the cog icon at the top right of the Media Browser (*Figure 5.7*):

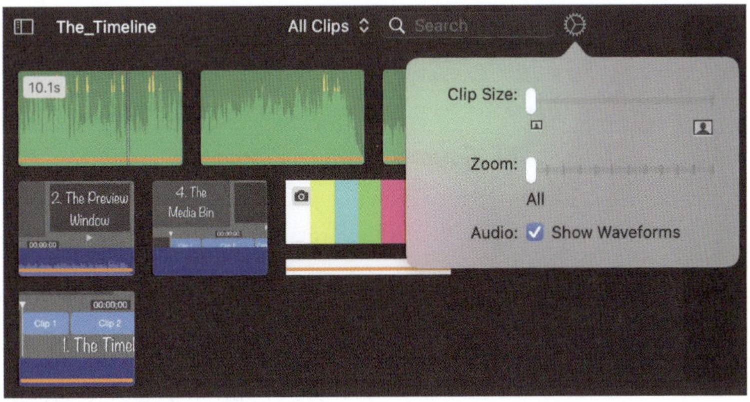

Figure 5.7 – Clips or ranges that are used in the timeline are underscored with an orange line

2. In that hover menu, the **Clip Size** slider changes the size of the clip thumbnails. I'd suggest starting with the slider near the smallest setting, as shown in *Figure 5.7*, so you can see more clips at once.
3. Tick the **Show Waveforms** box if it isn't already ticked. This displays the audio that's part of an imported video as a waveform at the bottom of the clip thumbnail.
4. Next up, the **Zoom** control makes clips that are longer take up more space in the Media Browser. All clip thumbnails will be a similar length unless a clip is longer than the time shown under **Zoom**.

To put this into context, in *Figure 5.8*, the first clip (10.2 s long) stays the same length as it was before we zoomed in. That's because we've set the **Zoom** setting to 10 s. The second clip (1.2 minutes long) has a longer audio strip that shows the waveforms in more detail:

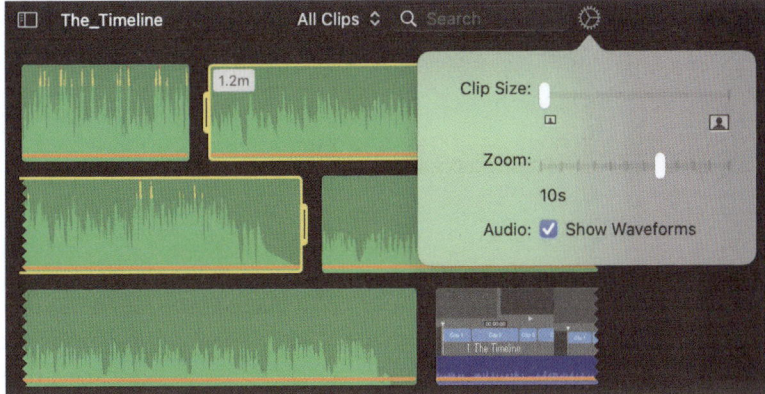

Figure 5.8 – The same media as before, but with a Zoom of 10 s

1. You can use the slider under the **Zoom** control to change the size of the clip thumbnails, or use the ⌘ + = and ⌘ + - keyboard shortcuts, just like you would to zoom into the timeline. Make sure you've clicked in the Media Browser first to be able to do this.
2. Expanding the **Zoom** control can clutter the Media Browser and make it difficult to navigate, but if you use ⇧ + Z (the same shortcut that shrinks the view of the timeline), the clip thumbnails will all return to their smallest size.

Using the **Zoom** tool can be helpful in the following ways:

- It allows you to select more precise ranges, especially on long video and audio clips such as podcast recordings or gameplay streams
- It more accurately shows how a clip changes over time, which is useful for pinpointing the right region to select
- It might show small gaps in the clip that haven't been used in the project
- It helps to further distinguish photos from videos (although photos are marked with a camera icon anyway)

Make sure to practice switching between zooming closely into clips and using ⇧ + Z to zoom out again. It's all part of the editor's dance and helps present clip information in just the way you need, at just the right time. Now that you have arranged and marked your media ready for the assembly edit, it's time to prepare the timeline.

iMovie project settings

Before you start the assembly edit, it's important to set your project settings so that they match what you intend to export. Most NLEs have a project settings menu included that allows you to set the resolution, frame rate, and more for your project. However, the **Settings** menu at the top right of the timeline in iMovie for macOS is mainly concerned with themes and automatic fades, only telling you what the project resolution already is. Therefore, it may seem like there's no way to change the resolution and frame rate of your project, but don't worry – there's a workaround. In iMovie, there's always a workaround.

Deciding your project settings

iMovie matches the project resolution of the first clip placed in the project. Do be aware that the "first clip" is not necessarily the leftmost clip in the timeline. The first clip is the one that's placed in the timeline when the timeline is blank. The following are some of the ground rules for determining your iMovie project format:

- iMovie offers 720p, 1080p, and 4K project formats

iMovie project settings

- iMovie offers 24 FPS, 25 FPS, and 30 FPS frame rates for all project resolutions (there's more on frame rates in the next section)
- 60 FPS is currently only available on up to 1080p projects, not on 4K projects
- Projects default to 1080p, 30 FPS before a clip is placed
- Photos can set project resolution, but only videos can affect project frame rate

The best way to be sure that you're getting the project settings you want is to have clips where you know exactly what frame rate and resolution they are. In the `Chapter 5: Project Format Clips` folder of the book resources are some I made earlier, in case you'd like to use them. Here's the process for deciding your project format:

1. Create a new Event (⌥ + N) for your project format clips.
2. Import your project format clips into the Event.
3. Add a particular format clip to your project according to what resolution and frame rate you need (as shown in *Figure 5.9*):

Figure 5.9 – Now, each time you open a new project, you can use your format clips

4. Add any clip from your Project Media to start your assembly edit.
5. Delete your project format clip and move on with the assembly edit.
6. Check the **Settings** area at the top right of the timeline to see whether your desired resolution and frame rate are in place. If they are, it's now perfectly safe to move on with the assembly edit.

Your project format has now been decided. I did promise more information on frame rates in projects though. We're going to build an understanding of frames in the next couple of sections so that you know what to look out for.

Checking the project's frame rate – counting frames

To recap, frames are the smallest unit of time in a video. Each frame is an image, and multiple are strung together each second to produce what we see as a moving image. However many frames there are in a second is known as the **frame rate**. However, it's not always the same number of frames that make up one second of video - it could be anywhere from 24 to 60 in iMovie projects. Fortunately, you can verify the frame rate of a project yourself. Here's how to do that:

1. Click to place the playhead in the timeline.
2. Use the arrow keys (← or →) to find the exact point where the timecode moves to the next second, such as from 1:03 to 1:04.
3. From that exact point, count the number of key presses you need to get to the next second (for example, from the first frame of 1:04 to the first frame of 1:05).
4. That number of presses should be either 24, 25, 30, or 60, and that is the frame rate of the project:

    - It is possible to have a 50 FPS timeline, but it will export to 25 FPS

That's how you calculate the frame rate in iMovie. But wait – it's all very well working out the frame rate of the timeline, but what's the *right* frame rate for your video? Let's take a look.

What frame rate should I choose?

Ideally, the frame rate you want to work in should be considered before you record clips for your project. Usually, you'll decide what frame rate you want to work in first, and then record clips to match that. Here are two factors to consider:

- The aesthetic, or "look," you want your project to have
- Whether there is a fast movement you want to follow clearly

First of all, you should consider what you want your project to look like. If you can't think of an answer, that's fine; go for 30 FPS. It's the default, it's standard, and it's rock solid. If you want your project to look *cinematic*, choose 24 FPS, the standard frame rate for cinema. 60 FPS tends to look slightly surreal because it makes movement much clearer and cleaner than our eyes see it in real life. The clarity and sharpness high frame rates give to movement make 60 FPS a good frame rate for sports or other clips where movement is tracked. Lower frame rates suffer (though it's not a bad thing if you want a more cinematic style) from a lack of sharpness known as **motion blur**.

If you haven't been able to consider frame rate choices before you recorded, the best rule to use is to *choose your frame rate based on what frame rate the majority of your recorded clips are.*

Choosing your frame rate from your recorded clips helps to avoid compatibility issues. If you make iMovie force all your clips into a different frame rate, the movement in them may end up looking jittery and stuttering – not because of an aesthetic, but because of an error. To check the frame rate of your recorded clips:

1. Locate the clip by searching with ⌘ + *F* in a Finder window or ⌘ + *spacebar* for Spotlight.
2. Right-click the file and select **Open with | QuickTime Player**.
3. Use the ⌘ + *I* shortcut to open the **Inspector** window.
4. Look for **Encoded FPS** in the **Video Details** drop-down menu (*Figure 5.10*):

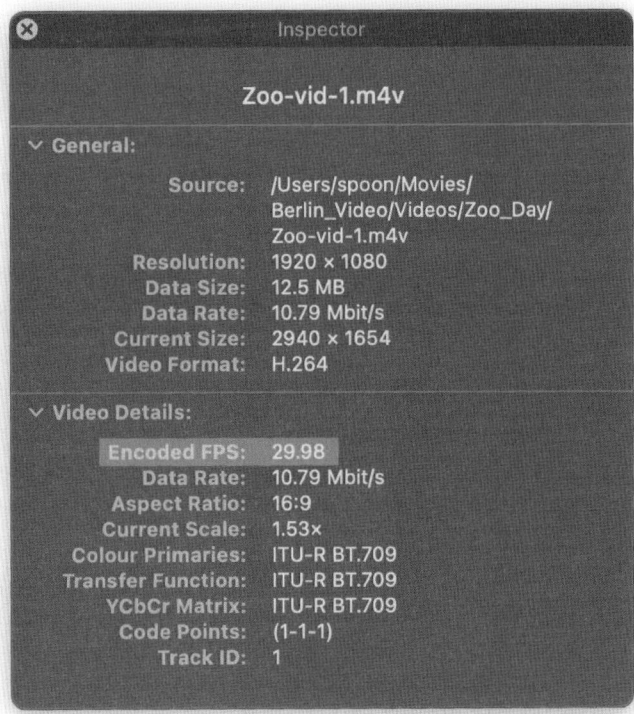

Figure 5.10 – The Inspector information for a Berlin trip video (frame rate highlighted)

In the case of the Berlin videos, they will say 29.98 FPS, which is 30 FPS. The reason it's slightly off is to do with competing standards introduced in the early days of television (NTSC and PAL, if you're interested). It's not any concern when we're editing in iMovie though, as it will read these files at 30 FPS, and export at 30 FPS. This means that when you're making the Berlin video in iMovie for macOS, you should set the project frame rate to 30 FPS. Because the video clips are 1080p, you should use the **1080p_30** project format file to determine your project settings.

> **Changing how iMovie treats frame rates**
>
> Although it is best practice to only use footage at the right frame rate for the project settings, iMovie does automatically slow down high frame rate clips so that they play smoothly in a project with a lower frame rate. If you want the clips to play at their original frame rate (remember, this can cause problems with clips stuttering):
>
> 1. Go to **iMovie Preferences** (⌘ + ,).
> 2. Untick **Apply slow motion automatically**.

With your frame rate and resolution now set, it's time to move on to the main editing process, starting with the assembly edit.

The assembly edit

The assembly edit in iMovie for macOS works just the same as you've come to expect: select your videos from the Project media folder and add them to the timeline using keyboard shortcuts such as *E* (append to the end of the project), and viewing shortcuts such as ⌘ + = and ⇧ + Z. Place the Berlin clips in whatever order you feel works best for telling the story of the trip. Maybe you want to split the video into scenes, by location. Or maybe, you want to put all day clips first and night clips second, so the video feels like watching a day unfold. So long as it's coherent, it's really up to you. Also, remember that you don't have to – and shouldn't – use every clip provided in the Berlin album.

When you're happy you have the spine of your story laid out, it's time to trim down your timeline. As you might expect, all you need to do to trim or extend a clip is click and drag on its edge – you'll be doing that a lot. Do also revisit the *Editing tools* subsection of *Chapter 4*, so that you can try out the time-saving keyboard shortcuts for trimming your assembly edit into a more concise **rough cut**. The more practice you get with assembly edits, the quicker they will go by. In this section, we're going to go over a couple of tools that may help make your assembly edit easier (and are good to learn anyway). Let's start with one you know – the Precision Editor.

Using the Precision Editor

The Precision Editor allows you to see how a transition works in great detail. It lets you move the out point of one clip and the in point of the next at the same time. You can move each one separately too, and change where the audio on the clip stretches to, to create J- and L-cuts. Perhaps more than any other edit, they make a video feel smooth and professional.

The tool works just the same as in the mobile app, but it is opened differently. This is because cuts in iMovie for macOS don't have a transition symbol. Instead, they are represented by a dark vertical line called an **edit point** (see *Figure 5.11*). Moreover, if two clips fit together perfectly with no time gap between them, no line is placed between them. This means that when you split a clip, the edit point will just be a tiny gap between clips:

Figure 5.11 – The two types of edit points for cuts in iMovie for macOS – where clips follow on exactly (left) and where there's a gap that's been cut out (right)

With that quirk noted, here's how to get to the Precision Editor on a Mac:

- To open the Precision Editor for a transition, click on the transition symbol and press ⌘ + /
- To open the Precision Editor around an edit point, do either of the following:
  - Select the clips on either side of it and press ⌘ + /
  - The easier option is to double-click the edit point

If you'd like more guidance, we covered how to use the Precision Editor in the *Making smooth audio transitions with J- and L-cuts* section in *Chapter 3*. We'll also use it in the *Using transitions* subsection of this chapter. Now, let's look at a similar tool that's macOS-exclusive.

Using the Clip Trimmer

The Clip Trimmer can be beneficial once you have your clips laid out and don't want to mess with their position on the timeline. This tool keeps clips the same length but allows you to use different parts of the source media, which is a type of edit known as a **slip edit**. It's useful for preserving timeline structure as we looked at doing when replacing clips in the *Understanding the magnetic timeline* section of *Chapter 4*. The Clip Trimmer works quite similarly to the Precision Editor in that it allows you to move in and out points at the same time. In this case, though, it's the in and out point of the same clip. Here's how to use the Clip Trimmer:

1. Select a video clip on the timeline (click or hover the playhead over it and press *C*).
2. Press ⌘ + \. The video strip for the clip in the timeline will jump up, showing the parts of the source media that go beyond the range of the timeline clip (*Figure 5.11*):

Figure 5.12 – The Clip Trimmer has long looked buggy but fulfills a useful purpose

3. Hover your cursor over the video strip – the cursor will change shape and the playhead will turn red (in this specific case, it's now called a skimmer: the name doesn't matter, but the change signals that you're hovering in the right place).
4. Click and drag on the video strip. The Viewer will split into two different frames (*Figure 5.12*): the left frame shows what the clip looks like at the start of the clip, and the right frame shows what it looks like at the end of the clip.
5. A tooltip will also appear below the clip in the timeline, telling you how many seconds forward or backward you have *slipped* the clip. In this case, I've gone to +1.15 seconds, so that the audience can see the plane taking off during the clip:

Figure 5.13 – The adjusted frames in the Viewer – before and after taking off

6. When you're happy with the slip edit, press *Escape* or click off the clip to exit the Clip Trimmer.

The Clip Trimmer allows you to work on refining the meaning of your video, as well as making it more coherent in some places. What you decide to show the audience is, naturally, a huge consideration in editing. Now, as we work toward the final version of our video, known as the **fine cut**, we're going to explore the different resources that iMovie makes available for adding meaning to videos.

Using iMovie media

iMovie for macOS has great creative scope, and that means that we can't cover all the tools you can use to add meaning in one chapter. Some of the creative tools available to you, such as using overlays, will be discussed in the next chapter. But for most of the rest of this chapter, we'll be going over the resources and tools that iMovie explicitly provides to you. First of all, we're going to check out the resources contained in the tabs above the Media Browser.

Using the Audio & Video tab

The Media Browser is split into five different tabs. The default view in the Media Browser is your Project Media or any Event you have selected. The shortcut to return to the **My Media** tab is ⌘ + *1*. But for the rest of the tabs, they provide resources to you, which you can add to the timeline and edit as you please. Pressing ⌘ + *2* takes you to the **Audio & Video** menu, which currently is still only really for iMovie's stock sound effects and jingles (we might see stock video appear there someday):

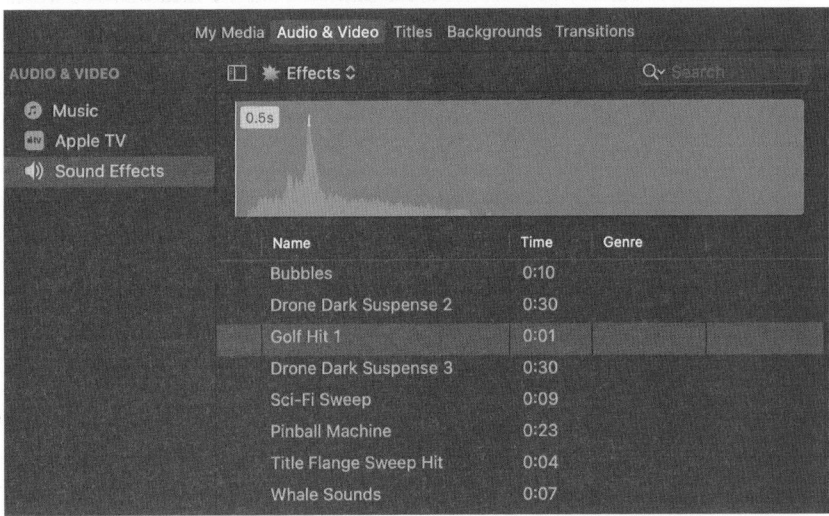

Figure 5.14 – The Audio & Video (but just audio, really) Media Browser tab

There are a couple of options on the sidebar beside **Sound Effects**, as you can see in *Figure 5.11*. If you have music in your Apple Music app, you can access it through this menu. The same is true of any home videos you might have opened in the Apple TV app (this will be the default opening location for `.m4v` files). However, the most useful section of the **Audio & Video** tab is the **Sound Effects** section.

In this section, there is a drop-down menu with the different categories of sounds available to you (*Figure 5.14*). All of them were recorded for iMovie and are part of the app. Whatever project you're working on, you can just drag and drop these sounds into your timeline:

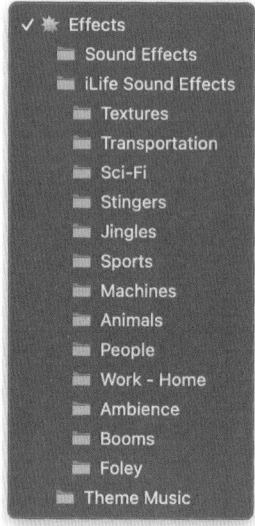

Figure 5.15 – You can also search for specific sounds using the search bar

In the *Layering sounds in Movie mode* section of *Chapter 3*, we saw that layering sounds can help to fill out a scene and make it feel more realistic, but the sound library in iMovie for iOS/iPadOS is sadly lacking. The macOS sound effects library is a little richer. The **People** and **Animals** folders help a lot, with crowd sounds, cheering, and clapping (and baa-ing, growling, and night-time ambient ribbeting) that all work as great **walla** – background sounds of people and animals that make a scene feel fuller.

Similarly, **Sci-Fi** sounds and **Textures** help to build scenes that require more mysterious and otherworldly sounds that we don't hear in real life. **Foley** helps to emphasize sounds that come from movement in the frame, especially for objects such as doors and clocks. That's just a sample of the sounds available too – use the search bar to search for more audio clips (make sure the main **Sound Effects** folder is selected if you do that).

Figure 5.15 is an example of creating a soundscape for a busy outside shot during the day. Here are a few things I noted:

- **Concrete jungle** and Traffic **work** well for making a space feel busy.

- There's not much in the way of birds under the sound effects, so I introduced some seagulls with very low volume just to get a hint of avian wildlife.

- I decided to arrange the audio clips in descending order according to how prominent they are in the scene. Later on, I might add a voiceover above all those clips and music below it.

- Because there are four layered audio clips, I used the ⇧ + ⌘ + - keyboard shortcut to reduce the size of the clips as they're shown on the timeline:

Figure 5.16 – A sound layering example for the Berlin project

- All of the audio has fade handles extended to introduce the sounds gradually, so the scene doesn't come in abruptly. The fade handles on audio clips are small circles at the start and end.

- I've reduced the volume of the audio clips. To do that, click and drag the white line in the audio clip downwards. Alternatively, drag it upwards to increase the volume. A tooltip will tell you the % volume of the clip, from 0% (silent) to 100% (original) to 400%.

So, sound effects. When used together and balanced with one another, they can transform a scene, and make your video a lot more engaging. However, you need to be a bit more careful when using iMovie's music options – they may not have quite the same effect.

Music choice

Apart from the sound effects available in the **Audio & Video** tab, there is also a **Theme Music** folder. It's not as well-stocked as the **Soundtracks** folder in iMovie for iOS/iPadOS, but it has a few nifty tunes. If you followed along with the exercise in *Chapter 1*, you will have already heard one of the theme music options as part of the "The Timeline" video: *Fifth Avenue Stroll*. I hoped you liked it, but perhaps it didn't suit the topic of the video, even though it sounded nice(?).

I ask this using guarded question marks because it's up to you to decide for yourself. You may want to ask yourself though about whether using iMovie's jingles is effective for your project. They're high quality in terms of production, and they're copyright free, but there are two main problems with using iMovie's jingles:

- They're very stylized, which means they're likely to sound a bit overenthusiastic and not very genuine or well-integrated into your project
- Everyone who uses iMovie has access to them, meaning a lot of people will be using the same jingle as you

When music is used in something narrative-driven such as a film or TV show, it's often expected to be unique, and to closely follow the emotion of every scene. When we've heard a tune before, we tend to associate the thing we're seeing now with what we saw before, and that doesn't help the film or show stand out as unique. That's why composers often work alongside production teams to create music just for a particular film, show, or episode.

The best we can do with no budget is to search for music that matches the story we're telling; something that's relatively subtle and hasn't been used much (or that you haven't heard before, anyway). This will help your music choice feel more unique and genuine, even if you can't find music that was designed to evoke the setting of the scene.

The exception to this rule is when you're putting music to something more style-driven, such as a montage. A well-known piece of music takes the audience out of what they're watching, just like editing for effect does. A montage (or similar) aims to be as un-immersive as possible – that's why stylized films such as *Baby Driver* and *Guardians of the Galaxy* are *soundtracked*, rather than *scored*. They rely on emotional connections people make to what they've heard before, be that road trip cassettes or childhood awesome mixes.

So, it's up to you to think when you're adding sound to your clips: do I want to immerse the audience in the scene, or draw attention to the video's style and encourage emotional connections to be made? Either is valid, it's just about choosing the right approach for the scene you're editing. And yes, once more for those at the back, "right" is subjective in editing. So, let's get our feet back on firm ground and look at something a little easier to quantify: titles.

Adding titles

Pressing ⌘ + 3 will take you to the **Titles** menu, which works a little differently from how it does in iMovie for iOS/iPadOS. To add a title follow these steps:

1. Drag and drop your title of choice from the menu onto the timeline (or position the playhead where you want the title to start and press Q).
2. Double-click on the blue title pane in the timeline.
3. In the toolbar above the Viewer (which we'll look at in more depth in the next section), a section dedicated to the title will open (*Figure 5.16*).
4. Double-click in the text box in the Viewer to edit the text.
5. The title pane on the timeline will change to reflect the text you've entered – this lets you see what your titles say at a glance while editing other clips:

Figure 5.17 – The title menu lets you change the font, size, text justification, color, and simple format options

The principal advantage of iMovie title panes is that although they behave like connected media, forming a clip connected to the video below, they don't count as a layer. That means they can be placed on top of an overlay without it being overwritten. This is not possible with videos or photos. Moreover, if you add an extra video where the title is, it will bounce above the clip you placed. This means you can set the title once and it will adapt flexibly to further edits you make.

However, the problem with these titles is that they lack flexibility. It may seem like there's a lot you can do to edit these titles, but the macOS titles are not nearly on par with the flexibility of the titles in the iOS/iPadOS version. The main reasons why are as follows:

- You can't move the title around the frame
- There are no options that change the shape of the frame, such as Mortise

Because iMovie titles are limited in their customizability, using them will make you run into the same problem as using iMovie's stock music: your titles will look the same as everybody else's. Perhaps more than anything else, a *Standard* title in *Avenir Light* font, expanding toward the viewer and – for no apparent reason – spilling into the next line, is what has always made people think poorly of iMovie. It's not especially fair, as you can make decent use of the stock titles. iMovie does also offer some themed titles (as well as transitions) if you choose a theme with the **Theme Chooser** menu (⌘ + 6). These can be useful because, like the titles we looked at in Magic Movie in *Chapter 2*, some of these titles can change the size of the frame:

Figure 5.18 – The Travel themed title placed at the start of a video

However, the problem with these titles remains the same as using other stock titles and musical tracks: your project will be just like everyone else's. This is especially true given that you can't even change the font in themed titles, let alone alter the graphics. In *Chapter 7*, we'll look at how to create titles where you can change every little detail to make titles uniquely yours; and even add custom animations.

Using maps

When you press ⌘ + 4, you'll be presented with the [maps and] **Backgrounds** tab, split into two sections that you can scroll down and see. Maps are very niche in their use case, but luckily for us, we're creating a travelog, so it makes sense to use them. Maps can help illustrate a journey you took. However, be careful what map you choose. Many of the maps available are just images: stills of a world map, and rather boring ones at that. However, hidden among these maps are much more interesting and customizable maps that animate based on places you enter. To customize a map, follow these steps:

1. Drag a map without the word "still" into the timeline or press *E*.
2. Check the toolbar above the Viewer. If the map is customizable, there'll be an extra symbol – a globe – highlighted on the left:

Figure 5.19 – The customizable maps let you plot destinations and styles

3. Click on the **Route** button to set a starting point.

4. A pop-up window (*Figure 5.19*) will let you enter a starting point, based on a large but not exhaustive list of towns, cities, and landmarks. You can also change the name of the selected location – for example, if you wanted to make a more specific note of the location:

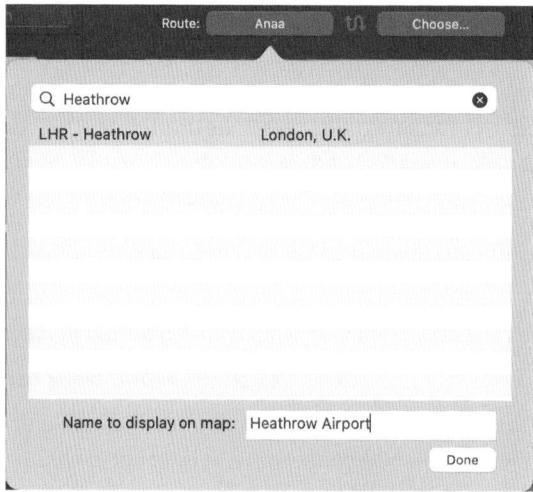

Figure 5.20 – Inputting the start point for the Berlin trip

5. Click **Done**.
6. Click **Choose…** on the other button and enter information to set a destination.
7. If you want to swap the start and end points of the journey, the squiggly arrow between the start point and end point switches the two.
8. If you click on the **Style** button (*Figure 5.21*), you'll be able to change the style of the map, as well as zoom in on your route if, like mine, it doesn't cross many countries:

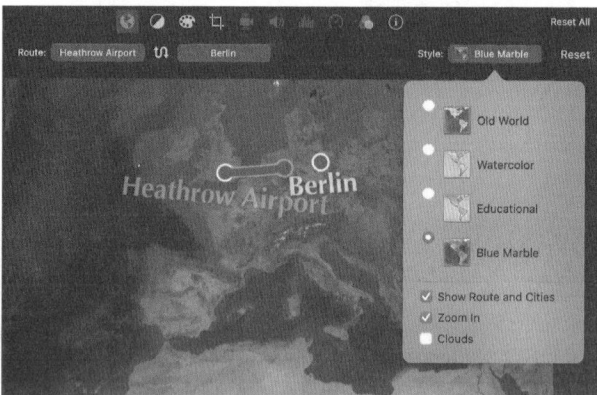

Figure 5.21 – When using the Blue Marble map, you can also add clouds to the frame

9. When you then play the clip, the map and journey line will animate, with a little pulse highlighting the destination.

Overall, maps have a lot more going for them than it seems at first, but they still lack customizability. You can see from *Figure 5.20* that the location text is bigger than it is for some European countries, and there's a lot of the map that isn't being used despite zooming in. We can't do anything about the text except use shorter words, but we'll use the toolbar in the **Crop** section to zoom the map in further. Overall, we have a fairly nice representation of our journey, and that's maps. Now, let's look at the backgrounds available in the same tab.

Using backgrounds

Backgrounds are an excellently versatile set of clips in iMovie. They're a set of block colors, gradients, and other designs that act like images in the timeline. They received a nice bit of extra customizability in iMovie update 10.2.4, which introduced customizable two-color backgrounds. To customize these backgrounds:

1. Drag a patterned or gradient background into the timeline (ironically, all gradient backgrounds besides the one called "gradient" let you change the colors).
2. Click the leftmost icon on the toolbar above the Viewer, which is a symbol of a landscape/painting (as shown in *Figure 5.19*).
3. Click on one of the colors shown above the Viewer to edit that color. The color you're editing will show a light gray border around it below the toolbar (**Color 2** is always on the right or bottom of the frame for gradients):

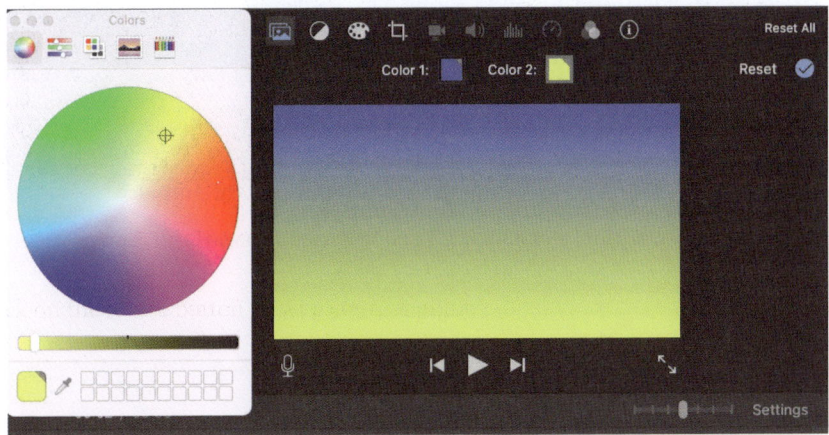

Figure 5.22 – Changing Color 2 to yellow on a Gradient Blue background

4. **Colors**, the macOS color selection wheel, will come up (*Figure 5.21*). Here's a quick guide on that:

   - Click anywhere on the wheel to select a color
   - The slider below the color wheel turns the whole wheel darker the further right you drag it
   - The eyedropper tool below the slider lets you move your cursor and click on the screen to pick an exact color

5. When you're happy, click the blue tick right of the toolbar to save your changes.

So, where would you use backgrounds? Block color backgrounds can make text *pop* out and are one of the few places where stock iMovie titles can be used to good effect. However, I'd still wager you can do a much better job making titles using Keynote, so stay tuned for that.

As clips within themselves, backgrounds can be very versatile: one example of their use is as placeholders. I like to use three colors of backgrounds to remind me where my clips will go, and what the status of those clips is: green is for clips I have imported into iMovie already, orange is for those I need to edit elsewhere first, and red is for those that still need to be recorded or otherwise sourced. You could use this at any point in the assembly edit to represent missing clips, and even edit title panes to describe what each placeholder represents, as shown in *Figure 5.22*:

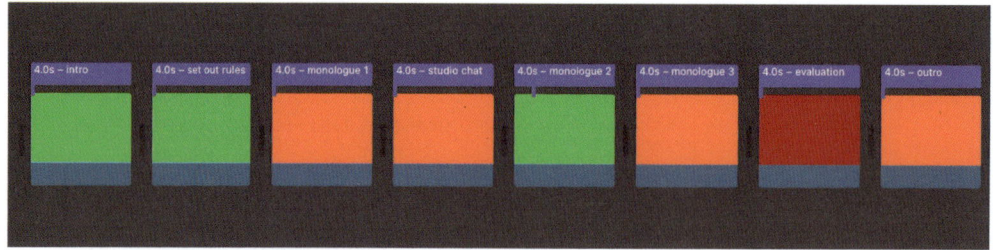

Figure 5.23 – Placeholder backgrounds with titles explaining what will replace them

You shouldn't need to do this for the Berlin video as all the clips are already available, but do try this out in a future project if you want to block out your narrative before you have all the clips you need. Speaking of clips, what do they always have between them? Transitions. Let's look at them now.

Using transitions

Transitions work similarly to projects in Movie mode on mobile devices, but instead of tapping on a transition to add or change it, you must do the following instead:

1. Go to the **Transitions** tab (⌘ + *5*).

2. Click and drag your transition of choice between two clips, or click on the transition symbol/edit point and double-click the transition you'd like to insert:

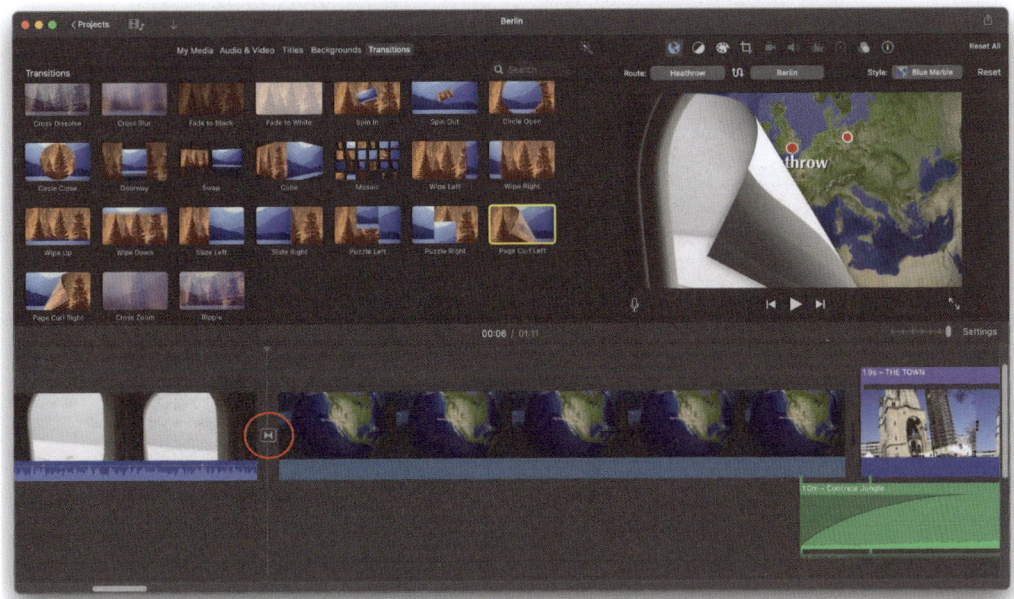

Figure 5.24 – Using a Page Curl Left transition to introduce the map we made earlier (transition symbol circled)

3. Once the transition has been placed, you can double-click on the transition symbol to change the length of the transition.
4. Press ⌘ + / to open the Precision Editor on a transition.

In this case, I've used the Precision Editor to continue the sound of the plane as an L-cut into the map clip (*Figure 5.24*). **Sound-bridging** in this way helps to make the clips feel even more connected by making the transition smoother:

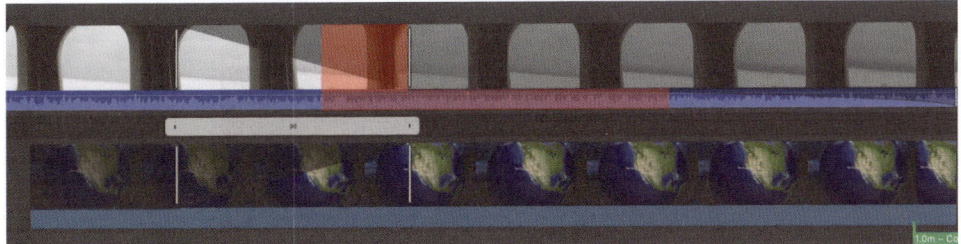

Figure 5.25 – The Precision Editor open on the Page Curl transition (L-cut is shaded red)

Another style note: beware of straying from cuts, cross-dissolves, and fades-to-black for most projects. Any other transition draws attention to itself, and if it's not directly serving the story you're trying to tell, it will make the video look like it's not taking itself seriously. That can be to your advantage if you're making a jovial video like our Berlin travelog, but if you're trying to be serious, the more *Powerpoint-y* transitions such as Spin, Doorway, Cube, and Puzzle will just look unprofessional. With transitions, the audience has to expect it to accept it – only a few films, such as the *Star Wars* franchise, get away with using wipes and star-shaped transitions!

And that's it for the media resources in iMovie! Now that your clips have been arranged and we've added sound, maps, and transitions to them, we're going to take a look at the editing tools in the toolbar. These tools allow you to change and refine what you see inside the frame itself.

Editing using the toolbar

It's time to move from the Media Browser sections of iMovie to the Toolbar, a set of useful functions that sit above the Viewer. You've already seen some guest entrants to the toolbar, which appear as the leftmost option when you have certain clips selected. Title customization shows a **T** symbol; map customization shows a globe, and if you choose a background with customizable colors, a picture icon appears for changing the colors. Finally, for extra toolbar options, **Overlay Settings** appears as an extra option when you click on connected videos and photos. We'll look at that in detail in *Chapter 6*; for now, we'll be exploring the standard tools in the toolbar, from left to right.

Color balance

The first menu on the toolbar holds the **Color balance** tools. Color is a stage of the editing process that usually takes place right before the final video is checked for approval and exported. It's a creative process as much as editing, but when you don't have much experience with it, it's easy to go mad with color changes and make clips look silly (I, for one, am guilty of that). iMovie's color tools are best used for correcting mistakes and ensuring your clips look broadly the same.

Within **Color balance**, there are four settings: **Auto**, **Match Colour**, **White Balance**, and **Skin Tone Balance**. I would suggest ignoring **Auto**: it's an option that automatically maximizes contrast because iMovie kind of presumes all the clips in the timeline will look grainy and dull and in need of sharpening up. However, you'll rarely have a clip that looks genuinely better for this treatment. Leaving clips and photos as-is often looks the best: remember, there's no point in making edits for the sake of it.

The next option, **White Balance**, can be useful for fixing clips that are very obviously discolored. When you film something, a good rule of thumb is to film with as much light as possible. This is because dark footage is **noisy**; visual noise is little specs, flecks, and fuzz that appear in dark areas of the frame. The more light you have, the less noisy the footage is. So, you're using all the light you can, but the problem for us is that the light's **temperature** is often too warm – with a light on, white objects in the frame will be cast in an orange shade:

Figure 5.26 – When you use standard house lights, white shades look like they've had a bad fake tan

This is where white balance controls come in: they make the white shades look white again. Here's how to use white balance control in iMovie:

1. Select a clip that looks too warm.
2. Look in the Viewer for a part of the clip that you know should be white (such as a piece of paper, or in this case, a sheep).
3. Click the **White Balance** button in the **Color balance** menu.
4. The cursor will turn into an eyedropper tool. Move the eyedropper tool to the area that should be white (the piece of paper/sheep's wool) and click on it.

5. iMovie will change the color temperature of the whole clip based on the chosen area being a crisp, clean white:

Figure 5.27 – Clicking the eyedropper on the sheep's wool balances the colors quite well

A word of warning, though: the changes this tool makes aren't subtle, and it only really works well if your footage is *very* orange. If you're looking for a small decrease in color temperature to get rid of a light orange shade (which might be left after the original correction), it's best to do this manually using the **Colour correction** menu, the next menu along on the toolbar. The changes that the color balance tools make are harsh, obvious, and just not very effective.

Matching the broad color scheme of clips is better done with your human eyes than by a computer, and the same is true for getting skin tones to look broadly similar. That's why I would suggest avoiding **Match Color** and **Skin Tone Balance** too. In most cases of clip color looking a little bit off, it's best to make small adjustments with the **Color correction** menu.

Color correction

In the **Color correction** menu, you'll see three different color sliders (*Figure 5.27*):

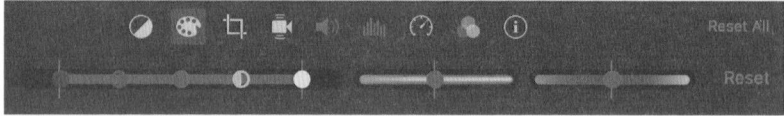

Figure 5.28 - If you ever forget what a slider does, hover over a circle for a tooltip

These sliders allow you to change different attributes of the color across the whole frame. From left to right, they are as follows:

- **Shadows**: Drag left to make them darker; right to *lift* them
- **Contrast**: Drag left to increase; right to decrease
- **Brightness**: Drag left to make the clip darker; right to make it brighter
- **Contrast** (reversed): Drag left to *decrease*; right to *increase* contrast
- **Highlights**: Like the brightness control, but only affecting the brightest areas of the frame
- **Saturation**: Drag right to make colors richer and fuller; dragging left desaturates colors to black and white
- **Color temperature**: Drag left to make colors bluer (cooler); drag right to make colors more orangey (warmer)

Directly on the right of the sliders is the **Reset** button, which will erase any changes to color and return the sliders to their original position (as shown in *Figure 5.26*). For color, as it is with all edits, it's best not to make big changes unless you want to draw attention to them. High saturation will make your clips look gaudy and samey; low contrast and extreme shadows will make it difficult to see anything in your clip. All such changes will take your audience out of the video, but if that's your goal, here are some creative ways you can use big color changes:

- Maximize **highlights** to create an ethereal look for a dream sequence
- Lower **saturation** to show that a scene is happening in the past
- Decrease **color temperature** to make a scene look sad

Finally, remember that the changes you make affect the whole frame. So, don't go pursuing the perfect color for one part of the frame at the expense of everything else. If in doubt, don't make any color correction changes at all. Natural beauty, and all that.

Crop

The **Crop** menu, to my mind, is the best part of iMovie for macOS. Having framing controls right above the Viewer that are easy to access explodes iMovie's creative scope. Creating refined movement and reframing is just a few clicks and drags away. In other NLEs, crop (or rather, *transform*) settings are buried below mountains of menus. In iMovie, all you need to do is this:

1. Select a clip.
2. Click on the **Crop** button on the toolbar.

What can you do with the magical crop menu? Well, that's dictated by which **Style** you choose. There are three different styles of cropping: **Fit**, **Crop to Fill**, and **Ken Burns**. When you add a clip to the timeline, one of these styles will be applied to it. The cropping style iMovie chooses depends on what kind of clip it is:

- Backgrounds, Maps, and videos will use the **Fit** style. The whole clip is shown, and none of it is cropped.
- By default, photos have the **Ken Burns** effect applied. This animates between two crop boxes: one for the start of the clip, and one for the end (as shown in *Figure 5.28*):

Figure 5.29 – The Ken Burns effect animates a zoom into the photo and avoids the area outside the image

If you're editing a project where you want photos to stay static, you can change how iMovie treats photos by default when they're added to the timeline. To do that:

1. Go to **iMovie Preferences** (⌘ + ,).
2. Change the option on the drop-down menu for **Photo Placement**.

You don't have to stick with the cropping style that iMovie gives a clip, though. Any clip can use any of the three **Style** options (**Fit**, **Crop to Fill**, and **Ken Burns**). However, I'd suggest avoiding **Fit** as it removes the transparency that can make pillarboxes and letterboxes versatile and useful in iMovie. It's well worth changing video clips from **Fit** to **Crop to Fill**. Here's how to do that:

1. Select the clip and go to the **Crop** menu in the toolbar.
2. Click on the **Crop to Fill** style, which will be shaded blue when it's selected.
3. Hover over any highlighted corner of the crop box – the cursor will change into two arrows, allowing you to change the size of the crop box.

4. Drag the box out until it fills the whole frame, including the black bars (**pillarboxes**) outside the image (as shown in *Figure 5.29*):

Figure 5.30 – Dragging the crop box to fill the frame for a portrait video of the Reichstag

Having a full-frame **Crop to Fill** makes the areas outside the photo or video transparent, which is extremely useful if you're using the clip as an overlay (we'll look at that more in *Chapter 6*). For now, let's think about why you might use the **Crop** tool creatively on the main video layer. Because only what's illuminated inside the crop box will be shown in the frame, you can use the crop box to reframe clips. *Framing in* like this can have several uses:

- Cut out a photobomber (or thumb!) at the edge of the screen
- Remove a part of the screen from the audience's view – especially if it contains something you don't want the audience to see
- Draw the audience's attention to a certain part of the frame that's relevant to the narrative
- Take the audience's attention away from the untidiness of a jump cut by reframing at the edit point

Chances are you've seen videos that have made use of that last suggestion. **Punching in** is a YouTube editing staple because it's an easy way to cut out dead air from the video while avoiding the jarring nature of a jump cut. One sentence ends with the full frame in view. Immediately, we cut to a closeup of the person in the frame, starting a sentence that was recorded several minutes later. The movement of the frame captures the audience's attention, distracting them from the lack of continuity in the video.

Overall, punching in allows jump cuts – made for the sake of coherence and conciseness – to be hidden quite effectively. The editing process is a process of disguising the truth to make a better video. In the words of editor Iain Anderson: "*video editors are liars, and the good ones get away with it.*" That concludes our look at static crop boxes. Impressive though they are, we're now going to top that by customizing the Ken Burns effect to our own needs.

Creating Ken Burns animations that settle

We first looked at the Ken Burns effect in *Chapter 3*; it's a very useful effect for making static images more interesting to the viewer. However, the mobile iMovie app doesn't have the customization capabilities that can enhance your visuals. But remember, in iMovie, there's always a workaround.

iMovie for macOS has one main advantage in its Ken Burns offer that allows you to make much smoother, more natural-looking animations: the ability to split photos. The mobile version only allows you to create an animation that starts right at the beginning of the clip and ends right at the end. This is limiting because you're never able to make the frame settle: constant movement can quickly become tiring or disorienting for the audience. *Figure 5.30* illustrates the Ken Burns animations used to make the "The Timeline" video from *Chapter 1*. Each animation settles before moving again, which (hopefully) stops the video from feeling messy and chaotic:

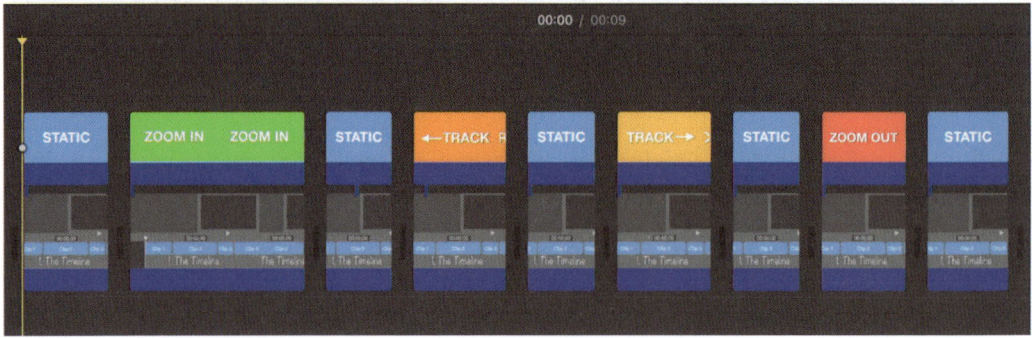

Figure 5.31 – The overlays here are purely for illustration, just showing the direction of each animation

Now, we're going to recreate the Ken Burns animations from the first part of that video. If you're following along, make sure to download the images from the `Chapter 5: 'The Timeline' stills` folder of the book resources. This process involves a lot of steps, but a lot of it is repetition, and with enough practice, this process will be part of your muscle memory:

1. Create a new project (⌘ + *N*) when you're on the **Projects** screen in iMovie.
2. Import the "The Timeline" stills you downloaded (⌘ + *I* or drag and drop them into the Project Media folder).
3. Select `Timeline-images.001` and add it to the timeline (*W*).

4. Extend the clip by dragging the edge to around 10 seconds so that the animations don't take place at breakneck speed.
5. Go to the **Crop** menu. **Ken Burns** is already selected as the cropping style, which is what we need here.
6. In the toolbar, click the *swap* button (circled in *Figure 5.31*). This swaps the crop boxes, starting the animation with a full frame and ending the animation after zooming into the frame:

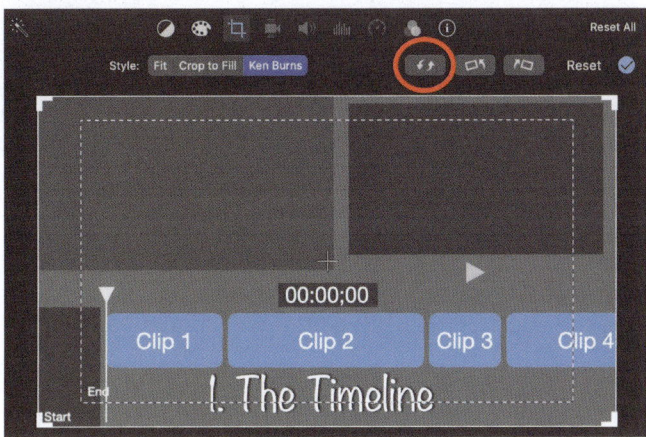

Figure 5.32 – The start and end crop boxes, swapped

7. Move and resize the **End** box to show the area you want to zoom to. Make sure the **End** box illuminates the text in the image and the timecode (as shown in *Figure 5.32*).

The animation will also be more pleasing to the eye if it's symmetrical, so try to make sure the **End** box snaps to the Viewer's yellow lines of symmetry. Also, check that the yellow arrow (showing the path of the animation) is pointing straight down:

Figure 5.33 – A good position for the end box

Now that we have a nice end position, we want the animation to settle there before it makes its next movement. Here's how to do that:

8. Split the clip at about the 00:02 timecode – this makes the animation go at a reasonable pace.
9. Select the second clip. If you scroll through it, you'll see that it repeats the animation of the first clip. We're going to use that to our advantage because it means that the **End** box is in just the right place to settle the animation.
10. Go to the **Crop** menu and click the *swap* button again.
11. Now, change the **Style** option to **Crop to Fill**. The Viewer should look like it does in *Figure 5.33*:

Figure 5.34 – The settled position for the animation

We had to swap back the animations on the second clip (*step 10*) because when the Ken Burns effect is changed back to **Crop to Fill**, the **Start** crop box is the framing that is used. Now, when you play the timeline, the frame should zoom into the illustrated timeline and settle in the zoomed position. We're now going to add one more animation to this, to showcase the power of the *swap* button. Here goes:

12. Split the second clip at about the 00:03 timecode – this means the animation will settle for a second before moving again.
13. Select the third clip and open the **Crop** menu. Change the **Style** option back to **Ken Burns**.
14. Click on the **End** box and drag it inwards from the top-right corner. Stop when it's the same height as the **Start** box (as shown in *Figure 5.34*). Be aware that it won't necessarily snap to this position:

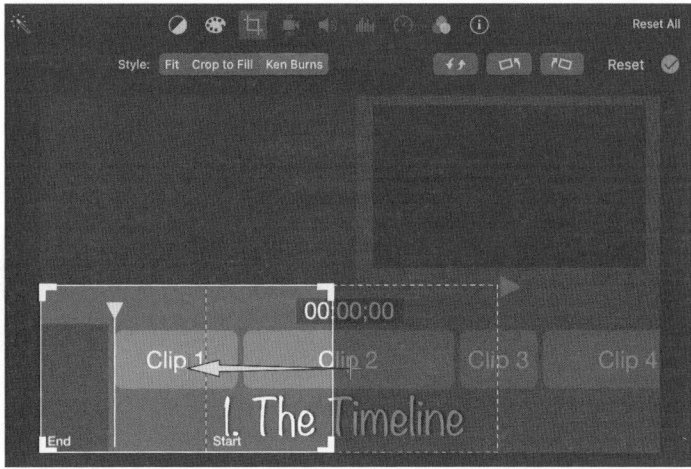

Figure 5.35 – Once again, make sure the animation arrow is straight

15. Move the **End** box to the right a bit so that the crop box goes just past the illustration of the playhead.

Now, when you watch the third clip, the frame will move smoothly across the illustrated timeline. Symmetry is important here because the straighter the animation path, the smoother the animation will feel. We moved the **End** box back to the right to reduce the pace of the movement in the frame – again, this makes the animation feel smoother. Now, we're going to – with incredible ease – animate back to where we were:

16. Split the third clip at about the 00:05 timecode, and split the now-fourth clip at the 00:06 timecode. This will create another 2-second animation that settles for 1 second.
17. Select the fourth clip, go to the **Crop** menu, **swap** the boxes, and then select the **Crop to Fill** style.

There may seem a lot to do in each of these steps, but it's because this is the same process we went through earlier (*steps 9* to *11*) to settle an animation. As I said, this is all about repetition. There's also a good reason we made two splits at once in *step 16* – it allows us to use the animation we made before.

18. Select the fifth clip, go to the **Crop** menu, and **swap** the clips. This will reverse the animation that moved across the illustrated timeline.
19. To settle the animation for the final time, split the clip at about the 00:08 timecode.
20. Select the sixth (and final) clip, go to the **Crop** menu, **swap** the boxes, and then select the **Crop to Fill** style.

Now, when you watch the whole timeline back, the frame should zoom in toward the timeline, settle, pan across the timeline, settle, pan back the other way across the timeline, and settle before the clip ends. *Et voila*, you've done it: the timeline should look similarly split to *Figure 5.35*, and you'll have an animation to write home about!

Figure 5.36 – The six clips of the animation we made

Having a 20-step process probably makes this task seem more complicated than it is. Creating settled animations is all about repetition and learning to do things in the right order. If your frame starts going haywire, undo (⌘ + Z) until you get back to a point where the animation was smooth, and keep on trying.

A few more notes on this. The preceding instructions are for working animations into images, but you might want to do the same for a video. You absolutely can, but remember that with a video, you can't necessarily just extend the clip like you would with an image. Start by deciding what length of video you want the *entire* animation to cover, then split that range off. From there, you can follow the same steps as you would with an image. And that's Ken Burns pretty much mastered. If you want to apply a similar effect to your Berlin video, go ahead – just remember to ask yourself whether your edit is helping to add meaning to the video as a whole.

Other Crop actions

Apart from the reframing and animation options that the **Crop** menu gives you, the tool can also be used to crop and rotate clips in a traditional sense:

1. Select a clip in the Media Browser.
2. Go to the **Crop** menu on the toolbar.
3. Click the button labeled **Crop** that appears within the **Crop** menu.
4. Drag the crop box to your desired shape.

5. Press the tick icon on the far right of the menu (see *Figure 5.36*) to perform the crop:

Figure 5.37 – Performing a crop on TV-Tower-Vid-2

The advantage of cropping in this way is that you don't have to crop to a standard 16:9 shape. The box is freeform, and you can make the image or video whatever size you like (so long as you like 90-degree edges). However, this won't change the shape of the iMovie frame: you'll just have pillarboxes beside the clip where before you might have had part of the image or video. For that reason, unless you need a custom shape, it's best to punch in or reframe photos and videos using the **Style** options.

Finally, let's look at rotation. You're likely to be familiar with this option from the Photos app and similar. In iMovie, rotation works the same way:

1. Select a clip in the timeline or Media Browser.
2. Click on the **Crop** button on the toolbar.
3. Click one of the rotation options (a rectangle and arrow symbol, as shown in *Figure 5.37*).
4. The clip will be rotated 90 degrees left or right. Keep clicking the button until you have the rotation you need:

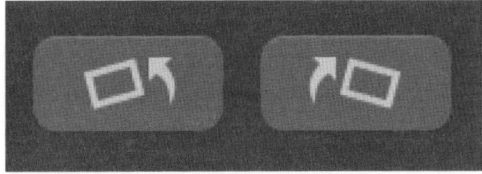

Figure 5.38 – The clip rotation buttons in the Crop menu

Because it's mostly for correcting images and videos that are the wrong way around, the rotation tool is a bit limited. You can't have the media at an angle that's not 90, 180, 270, or 360 degrees. Never fear, though: Keynote can rotate a photo or video in any way you like. More on that in *Chapter 7*! Next up, we have some features that can help fix issues in the way clips were recorded.

Stabilization

Next along in the toolbar is the **Stabilization** menu. This contains tools that smooth out subtle shakes and movements in footage, which is useful if you didn't have a tool such as a gimbal to keep your camera stable. To use it, follow these steps:

1. Select a clip that needs stabilizing (ideally, it will be framed wider than you need it, as stabilization zooms into clips).
2. Click the **Stabilization** button on the toolbar (a camera icon with lines at the top and bottom).
3. Click the **Stabilize Shaky Video** checkbox.
4. The checkbox will buffer and a circular progress bar will appear at the top right of the iMovie window while it analyzes the motion in the video (see *Figure 5.38*):

Figure 5.39 – Image stabilization calculations in progress

5. If you want to cancel the stabilization, click the circular progress bar, and then click the **X** button in the hover menu that appears (*Figure 5.39*):

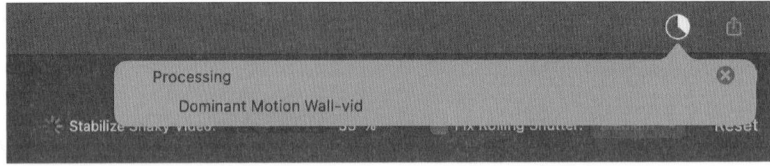

Figure 5.40 – The hover menu for canceling an iMovie process

6. The **Stabilize Shaky Video** checkbox becomes ticked when the task is finished. The strength of the stabilization will be shown in the slider; this defaults to 33%.

7. Give the clip a watch back – if it doesn't feel like the shakiness of the footage has been removed, you can increase the strength using the slider in the **Stabilization** menu.

Be careful increasing the strength slider too far, though – the higher the strength of the stabilization effect, the further iMovie zooms into the frame. *Figure 5.40* shows the same point in the same clip with stabilization at 10% strength (left) and 100% strength (right):

Figure 5.41 – You lose a lot of the frame when increasing the strength of stabilization

An additional word of warning: when I say *subtle* shakes and movements, I mean it. iMovie uses what is now quite an old form of video stabilization that isn't up to scratch compared to that of many other NLEs, or the in-camera stabilization available in many phones and cameras. If you attempt to stabilize a very shaky video with iMovie, instead of smoothing out the movement, the entire frame will warp and distort, almost like it's trying to come out of the screen at you, like the shark in *Jaws 3D*. The term *dominant motion* is key here – if there's enough movement from the camera's instability, iMovie will get confused as to what movement is the dominant one, and the whole video will be destroyed by the effect.

The other option in the **Stabilization** menu, **Rolling shutter**, seeks to fix a problem that occurs when you make a fast sideways movement with a camera, such as a **whip-pan**. During the motion, objects in the frame can wobble or slant in the direction of the movement, like they're being pulled by the camera. Just the same as image stabilization, iMovie analyzes the footage and performs a fix. This time, the strength options aren't decided from a slider, but from drop-down menu options of **Low**, **Medium**, **High**, and **Extra High** (*Figure 5.41*). Don't be tempted to use this effect if your footage isn't suffering from a rolling shutter, though: this will just add a counter-wobble to the clip:

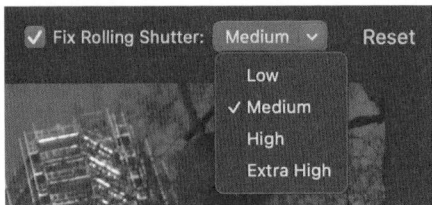

Figure 5.42 – The rolling shutter controls

That's the **Stabilization** menu covered – now onto two toolbar menus that you can use to make changes to all of the audio in your project.

Volume, noise reduction, and equalizer

To the right of the stabilization tools on the toolbar is the **Volume** menu. You'll be familiar with its loudness slider from iMovie for iOS/iPadOS. However, the **Volume** button on the toolbar allows you to make changes across all selected audio clips:

1. Select a clip containing audio.
2. Open the **Volume** menu in the toolbar.
3. The slider tells you the volume of the selected clip, or if multiple clips are the same volume, the volume for all of them.
4. If you have clips at different volumes, the slider will turn orange and read -- % (as shown in *Figure 5.42*). In iMovie, orange means that there's not one single setting.

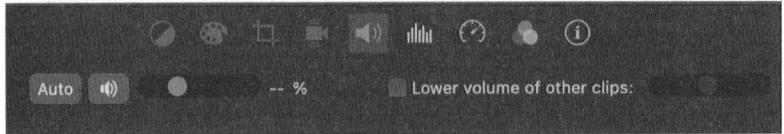

Figure 5.43 – The Volume menu when multiple clips at different volumes are selected

The main reason you should go to the **Volume** menu is to apply the **Auto** effect. This effect boosts the loudness of all of your audio without changing the volume percentage. This is useful if your audio is really quiet. The steps to remedy this are:

1. Type ⌘ + A to select all clips.
2. Click on the **Volume** button on the toolbar.
3. Click **Auto** below it.
4. The **Auto** button will be highlighted in blue (meaning all clips are using that setting), but the slider will likely still be highlighted in orange because although the clips have been boosted, they are at different volumes.

5. Regardless of the percentage volume your audio is now, 100% will be a lot louder than before.

This is why the **Auto** setting is useful for quiet clips – it gives further room for their audio to be boosted. Selecting all clips is important because if you don't apply the **Auto** boost to everything, it can be deeply confusing trying to deal with one clip at 112% volume blowing your ears off, and another at 112% being barely audible.

The speaker icon next to the **Auto** button is a toggle that allows you to mute all selected clips (although the ⇧ + ⌘ + *M* keyboard shortcut does this too). This is useful if you want to watch the timeline without hearing it or to **solo** particular audio clips by muting the others (as shown in *Figure 5.43*). Soloing is useful for diagnosing and solving problems in your audio when you have a lot of sound clips:

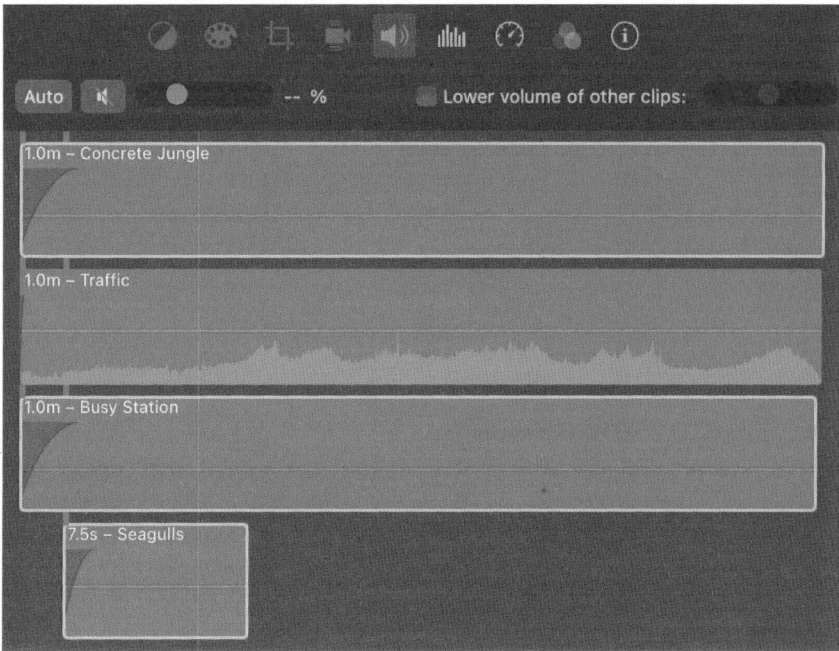

Figure 5.44 – Soloing one sound effect using the mute toggle

The other option within the **Volume** button is **Lower volume of other clips**. This is a control for audio ducking, an effect we discussed in the *Limitations of Magic Movie and Storyboard mode* section of *Chapter 2*. When the checkbox is ticked, the selected clip will lower the volume of the audio around it so that it can be heard. It can be useful for audio balancing (especially given that there is a slider you can use to change the strength of the effect), but it's no substitute for properly checking and balancing the audio levels yourself. Your judgment is better than your computer's.

Lower volume of other clips is automatically ticked whenever you record a voiceover in iMovie for macOS. The process of recording a voiceover is similar to in Movie mode on the mobile app, but it's worth going over:

1. Type *V* or press the microphone icon below the Viewer.
2. Place your playhead where you want your voiceover to start.
3. Press the red **record** button (which replaced the play button below the Viewer).
4. Wait for the prompt then record your voiceover, clicking the red button again to stop the recording.
5. There's no playback and re-record option on iMovie for macOS – the file you recorded is connected to V1 as a foreground audio clip.

The reason I mention voiceover clips is that as well as having audio ducking applied, voiceover clips are also given an equalizer effect, which can be found in the next menu along the toolbar: the **Noise reduction and equalizer** menu. Neither effect, as it turns out, is good to have on your audio. So, when your voiceover is recorded, do the following:

1. Click on the voiceover clip you just recorded; the **Volume** menu will open.
2. Untick **Lower volume of other clips**.
3. Click on the **Noise reduction and equalizer** menu on the toolbar.
4. Open the **Equalizer** drop-down menu and click **Flat** (which removes the **Voice Enhance** equalizer that was applied).

Voice Enhance, like any **equalizer** (**EQ**), plays around with the frequency ranges in your audio. EQs can emphasize a frequency range, such as **Bass Boost** (low frequencies) or **Treble Boost** (higher frequencies). However, because they're a computer's best guess and you don't have control of the effect, iMovie's EQs almost always make your audio sound *worse*.

Voice Enhance seeks to make your speech clear, but at all costs: it removes frequencies that make your voice sound smooth and balanced. It leaves your voice sounding tinny and abrasive. iMovie's Equalizer is another feature that makes it seem like Apple thinks every clip used in this NLE was recorded on a potato, in a blizzard. EQ-ing audio is very difficult to get right (just as creative color work is), and needs to be done manually at any rate. Often, it's best to just leave your audio alone or cover imperfections with some well-balanced sound effects and music:

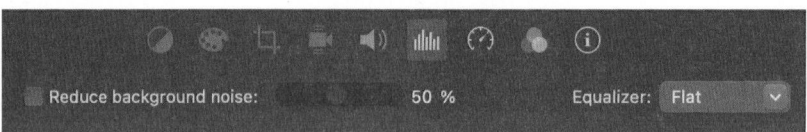

Figure 5.45 – The Noise reduction and equalizer menu

The other option in this menu, **Reduce background noise**, should be thought of as image stabilization for sound. It can be a useful tool to deploy when you use it at low strength, but it can just as easily ruin your audio at high strength. The process for adding this effect mirrors the image stabilization tool as well:

1. Select a clip containing audio.
2. Go to the **Noise reduction and equalizer** menu on the toolbar.
3. Click the **Reduce background noise** checkbox (see *Figure 5.43*).
4. When the processing is complete, the checkbox becomes ticked.
5. Change the strength of the effect with the slider.

You'll want to keep the percentage reduction low (almost always below 50%; I tend to find 10-20% works best). This is because high noise reduction starts eating into the audio you want to hear, cutting off the start and end of words to eliminate all background noise. It's much better to have some background noise and clear speech than unintelligible dialogue and no background noise. And once again, you can always obscure some of the background noise with some well-chosen, well-balanced sound effects and music.

Now, let's look at the final few toolbar tools – these offer similar features you'll be pretty familiar with from iMovie for iOS/iPadOS.

Speed

The **Speed** toolbar menu works almost the same as in iMovie for iOS and iPadOS, except you can tick a checkbox to reverse a clip. This is a feature that's mysteriously absent from the mobile app but can be very useful for creating stylized effects in your video. If you want to add a freeze frame, you'll need to use the ⌥ + F keyboard shortcut. There are a few automatic speed-related effects that iMovie offers, such as **Modify** | **Flash and Freeze Frame**. Remember though that, being stock effects, adding them won't help you make your video look unique. We'll look at a couple of custom speed effects in *Chapter 6*.

Filters and audio effects

As we discussed in *Chapter 2* and *Chapter 3*, filters aren't a great idea to add to your video if you're trying to make your narrative serious. Luckily, iMovie's filters on the Mac, such as in Movie mode, have a strength slider. This allows you to add an understated filter that gives your clips an interesting aesthetic edge. With a filter strength taken down below 50%, you can make your footage look stylized and unique without making details in the clip difficult to see:

Figure 5.46 – Cropping the top and bottom of the sheep clip and adding the Blockbuster filter at 45% strength gets you Sheep: The Movie(?)

Unique to iMovie for macOS are **Audio Filters**. Some of these filters can be useful, and it's a real shame that the strength slider doesn't affect these clips (it looks like it should, but click off and back onto an audio clip and you'll see the strength goes back to 100%). Still, some of the audio effects aren't so overstated at 100% that they'll ruin the coherence of a clip. Here are a few of my favorites:

- **Muffled** is good for suggesting that sound is coming from behind a window or wall.
- **Echo delay** makes sounds seem to bounce around and repeat; it's good for suggesting that a character is disoriented (especially if you match it with shaky camera footage, as if from their point of view!).
- **Telephone** may not sound very much like phone audio, but it's good for mimicking the sound coming out of a TV you can see in a clip.
- **Large room** makes audio sound distant and echoey. This helps create a sense of space with sound.

Information, Enhance, and Reset All

The final icon on the toolbar, **Information**, tells you some basic information about the clip:

- Its name
- When it was created
- How long the clip is relative to the whole timeline

You can also change the length of clips using the **Information** screen:

1. Select a clip in the timeline.
2. Type some seconds into the box (as shown in *Figure 5.46*):

Figure 5.47 – The Information menu

3. Hit *Enter*. The clip will be changed to that length, so long as there is enough source media to fill that length (iMovie won't speed up or slow down the clip).
4. If you select multiple clips, the duration you enter will be applied to each clip selected.

On the far left of the toolbar is the **Enhance** button, shown as a wand symbol (see *Figure 5.46*). Clicking this makes automatic changes to the selected clip, across all of the valid toolbar options (that is, not the video ones for an audio clip). Again, I would advise against clicking this: don't let iMovie decide what's best for your project. You're an editor now, and your judgment is king. **Enhance** is a shortcut that pushes you out of the edit, and often goes over the top with the strength of effects it uses, too.

Finally, on the far right of the toolbar is the **Reset All** option. You may have noticed that certain menus in the toolbar are shaded blue, and that means that one or more of their features has been used. Clicking **Reset All** removes all changes made with toolbar options, returning all the toolbar menus to an unselected white color.

Copy and paste toolbar edits

With the toolbar features covered, now is a good time to tell you about a set of shortcuts that allow you to copy across adjustments you made using the toolbar. All of these "paste adjustments" options are based on using ⌘ + C to copy the original clip. Here are some highlights that help you quickly gain uniformity in as many clips as you select:

- ⌥ + ⌘ + C pastes color correction settings
- ⌥ + ⌘ + R pastes reframing changes using the **Styles** options in the **Crop** menu
- ⌥ + ⌘ + A pastes the clip's volume level (for example, 71%, 126%, and so on)
- ⌥ + ⌘ + S pastes speed settings
- ⌥ + ⌘ + U pastes overlay settings (this is an important one for the next chapter!)
- ⌥ + ⌘ + V pastes all settings and changes on a clip

And that covers all of the main editing tools and menus in iMovie! Of course, no rough-to-fine edit is going to involve you going through every menu and using every tool you possibly can, but now that you know how to use these features (and which to avoid), you should be able to make the changes you want to add meaning to your videos while keeping them coherent and concise. When that process is done, make sure that you quality control your video first by proof-watching it. Then, it's time to export.

Exporting a project

The export menu is in a large Share icon in the top right of the iMovie window (*Figure 5.47*), and there is one option within it you should always select – **Export File**:

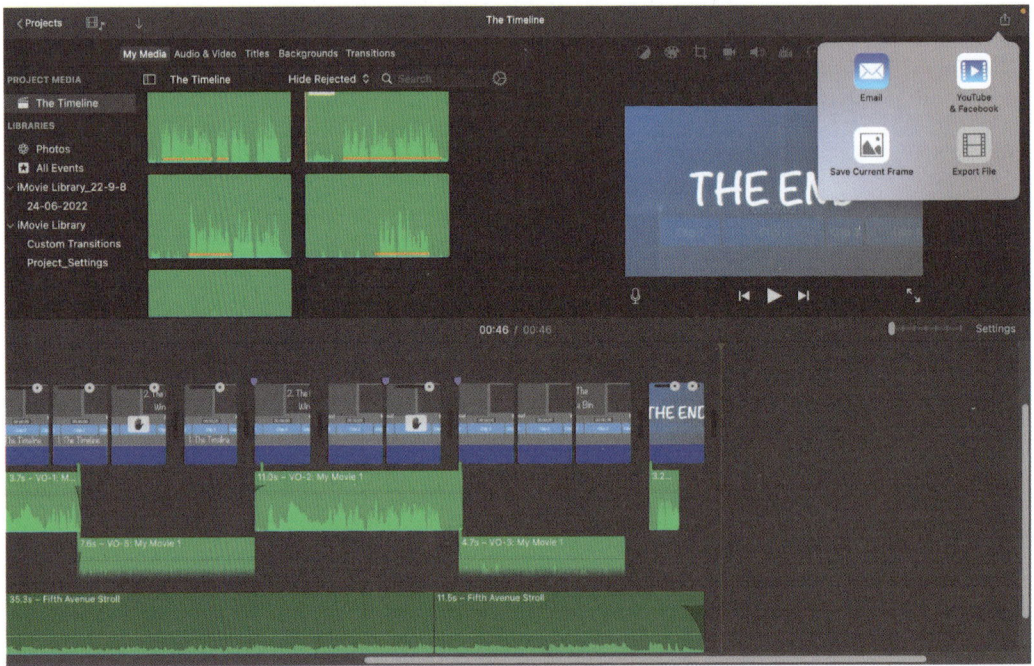

Figure 5.48 – Don't be vile, export to a file

Just like when we were creating safety copies when importing footage at the start of this chapter, it's important to have a version of your finished project in your filesystem. This means you'll always have a file that you can make changes to if the edit becomes corrupted, or footage is lost. Uploading straight to YouTube or Facebook might seem tempting, but please try not to – you'll thank yourself later.

The first file you export is known as the **master file**. We'll be diving into customizing your exports in *Chapter 8*, but the rules for exporting the master file in iMovie are simple:

- Export in the *highest resolution* you can (the maximum resolution is the resolution you set with your project format clip)
- Export in the *highest quality* you can fit on your computer
- Compress with *better quality* using the final drop-down menu:

Figure 5.49 – The best settings for exporting a master copy of your video

If you don't have the space for the **Best (ProRes)** quality (we'll see why it makes files so much larger in *Chapter 8*), do the following for your master file:

1. Click on the **Quality** drop-down menu and change the quality to **Custom**.
2. Drag the quality slider to the right.

With that, all you need to do is press **Next** or hit the *Enter* key and choose a location to export your file to. it's a good idea to export large videos to an external drive if you have one. This makes it less likely that iMovie will error during the export due to not having enough space on your computer. If you are having problems with iMovie exporting your video, check out *Chapter 9* for some solutions to try out.

Summary

Whew, that was a lot. The good news is, you're now totally clued in on how to bring an iMovie project from import to export. You know the principles of editing, some nifty tricks, what the menus and commands in iMovie for macOS do, and which to avoid. Let's recap.

First of all, we looked at how to import files safely and efficiently. Then, we looked at how to sort that media by marking your favorite regions. The final stage of preparation before the assembly edit is determining your project settings. In iMovie, the resolution and frame rate are decided by the first clip placed in a blank timeline.

The assembly edit involves the simple cuts and trims we covered in *Chapter 1*, *Chapter 2*, and *Chapter 3*. Make sure to use the keyboard shortcuts from *Chapter 4* too. After the assembly edit, we aim to make the video look and sound more polished. For sound, we looked at filling out our scenes with appropriate sound effects and music. We also looked at audio effects and iMovie's **Volume** menu on the toolbar.

For video, we looked at adding meaning by changing what the audience sees in the frame. Titles, maps, backgrounds, and transitions can make your video flow better and look more engaging, so long as you use them in moderation. Cropping tools let you frame out redundant parts of the frame, disguise jump cuts, and create smooth and professional-looking Ken Burns animations. We also covered correction tools such as image stabilization and color correction. Finally, color grading and clip filters can be used at low strengths to give your video a subtle but unique aesthetic *look*.

Concluding our editing work, we looked at exporting a master file in the highest resolution and quality you have space for. But maybe don't export quite yet! In the next chapter, we'll be continuing to refine our videos by looking at overlays, effects, and keyframing. It's editing on another level – literally.

6
Using iMovie Effects – Overlays and Keyframing

Welcome to the sixth chapter, which is all about using more than one layer of video – and sometimes more than one timeline – to achieve certain effects in iMovie. Now that you've been able to complete a fine cut of a video and export a master copy, it's time to build on those skills by learning some video effects. Some of the techniques in this chapter are intended to be part of iMovie, and some are workarounds. For me, workarounds are exactly what iMovie is about. Some may say that you should just start learning a more fully-featured NLE, but if you need to work your brain creatively to make great videos (and you do), finding workarounds is exercising exactly the right part of your mind for keeping your storytelling sharp and interesting too.

This chapter is going to revolve, mostly, around overlays. I've been teasing them for a while, and it's about time we covered them. Clips are always interacting with one another, but so far, we've only thought of this in terms of a linear progression: one clip after another. But we can also look upwards – clips above the main video layer can complement and affect the meaning of the clips below. Overlays aren't limited to iMovie for macOS. We saw their use very briefly in *Chapter 3*, but I've been refraining from mentioning them to make sure not to overcomplicate things. But as overlays are for everyone, this chapter will cover how to perform an edit in iMovie for macOS as well as iOS/iPadOS platforms, where applicable.

The topics we will focus on in this chapter include the following:

- The different types of overlays (cutaway, split-screen, green/blue screen)
- Animating picture-in-picture clips and audio ranges with keyframes
- Layering overlay effects through compound clips

Cutaways – introducing overlays in iMovie

An overlay is one clip sitting on top of another. As we know from looking at the magnetic timeline in *Chapter 4*, overlays in iMovie are treated as connected media, rather than being their own track. This means that overlays:

- Aren't attracted to the start of the project
- Don't move to the side when you hover a clip over them (in fact, they get overwritten entirely, because you can only have one connected video at a time)

Overlays are available in Movie mode for both iOS/iPadOS and macOS. However, in each version, overlays are added in different ways. Before you add an overlay, you will need a clip in the timeline. Now, here's how to add a clip as an overlay.

For iOS/iPadOS:

1. In the Media Browser, tap on the media you want to use as an overlay.
2. Tap the three dots next to the play icon.
3. Choose the type of overlay you want to add to the video.

To change the overlay type after you've added the clip, tap on the clip and select **Overlays** from the toolbar below the timeline (as in *Figure 6.1*):

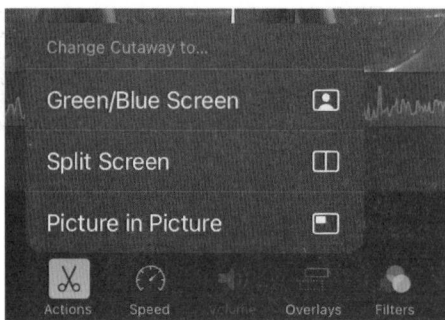

Figure 6.1 – The overlay settings menu for iOS/iPadOS

For macOS:

1. In the Media Browser, select a clip you want to use as an overlay.
2. Drag it on top of a clip in the timeline (or press Q).

3. The connected media will default to the Cutaway overlay type. To change the overlay type, click the **Video overlay settings** button on the left of the toolbar:

Figure 6.2 – The Video overlay settings menu in iMovie for macOS

Both versions of iMovie offer the same four types of overlay:

- Cutaway
- Split Screen
- Green/blue screen
- Picture in Picture

The cutaway is the type of overlay you're likely to use most regularly when editing. They come up so often because a cutaway can add meaning – or obscure problems – in several different ways.

Using cutaways to hide jump cuts

A cutaway sits on top of and obscures the clip below it. In editing, a cutaway is often used to hide cuts and splits and make a scene appear a lot smoother than it was. If you speak to the camera for a few sentences, hesitate, then say one more sentence before hesitating again, you can't punch in the frame the footage as we looked at doing with the Crop-to-fill tool in the previous chapter. If you do, you'll be left with jumpy footage where you're constantly bouncing around the frame as you jump between hesitations and sentences. It will be tiring to watch. The constant unnatural movement in visuals will also make it a lot more obvious that the words you're saying are isolated from each other – that will make what you say harder to follow as a whole.

However, if you use a cutaway that sits on top of all the jumps in the footage, the audience will see just one, smooth shot, and this will make the sentence – and the video – flow a lot better. Cutting to a shot that doesn't show the speaker's face allows you to condense and crossfade the audio freely, without fear of showing the jump cuts. There are different types of cutaways, and they include the following:

- **B-Roll**: Footage that is relevant to the story you're telling but *illustrates* and gives context to what's being said, rather than showing it directly. For example, a shot showing a computer while a reviewer talks about its tech specs.
- **Reaction shots**: This shows a different angle that complements the story. This could be someone staring, nodding, or shaking their head while someone else speaks. Switching between two shots of a conversation is a technique called **shot/reverse-shot**.

- **A better take**: If you filmed the same thing with multiple cameras, or shot multiple takes, you could use a cutaway to break from Shot A, take 1 before cutting back to Shot A, and then take 2 without the audience noticing.

You can see from these examples that cutaways aren't just about tidying up the edit – they're perfect for refining meaning. Cutaways can complement and add to the story you're telling, and intrigue the audience with new angles illustrating what's being talked about.

Cutaways are fairly simple in the way that they're used – you just place one clip on top of another, totally obscuring it. In fact, for iMovie for iOS and iPadOS, that's all you can do with cutaways – there is no deeper menu of settings once you choose **Cutaway**. However, in iMovie for macOS, there are extra settings within the **Video overlay settings** menu that make it far more capable.

Adding fade transitions to overlays

It's possible to fade in overlays in iMovie for macOS. This allows you to gradually introduce overlay clips instead of having a cutaway appear instantly. There are two ways to add them. Firstly, you can do the following:

1. Select the overlay and click the **Video overlay settings** button on the toolbar.
2. Click in the **duration editor** box and set a time for the fade in and fade out, accurate to 1/10 of a second:

Figure 6.3 – The duration editor

Alternatively, click and drag the fade handles at the top edge of the overlay in the timeline. It's quicker, it's easier, and it's more customizable. If you zoom in fully into the timeline, you can drag the fade handles to frame-by-frame accuracy:

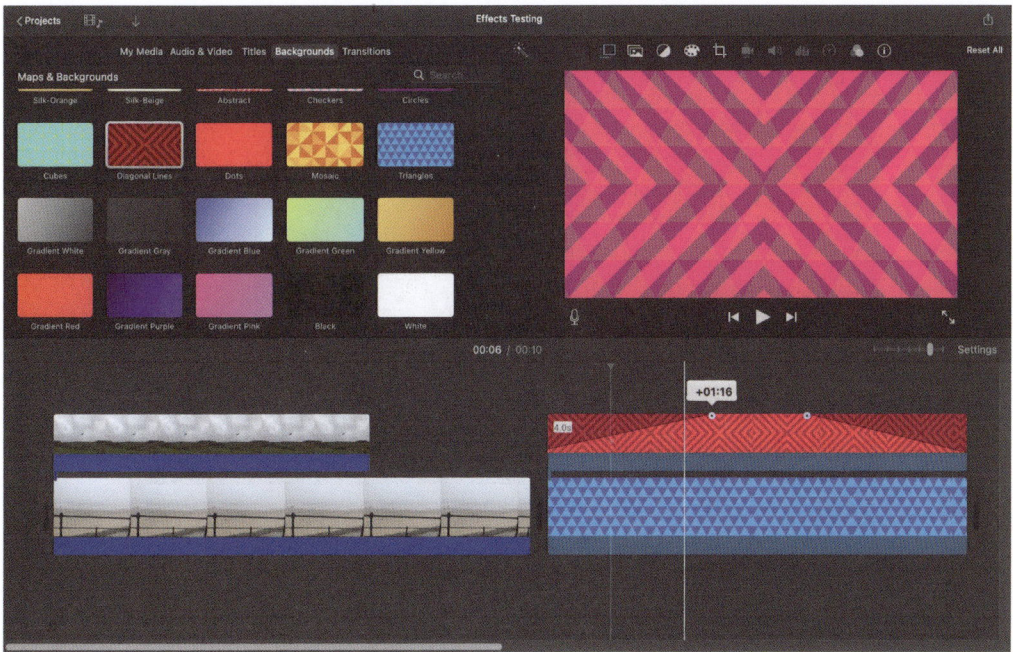

Figure 6.4 – A tooltip shows how far into the clip the fade goes

Using the fade handles also allows you to change the fade in and out length. Every fade-in on an overlay fades out of the same length. This will reduce the number of creative opportunities a fade transition is appropriate for because the fade out has to make sense in the video too. Luckily, however, it is possible to control the fade-in and fade-out lengths independently. To change the length of just one fade, follow these steps:

1. Press and hold the option (⌥) key.
2. Click and drag on the fade handle you want to move and drag it left or right.

> **The option key**
>
> The option key, ⌥, has a role in iMovie to increase your creative options, allowing you to make small and specific changes that make editing easier. You've already seen it at work moving clip connections in *Chapter 4*, and you're going to see it again when working with audio later in this chapter. In macOS, ⌥ is a modifier key that changes what some menus show, and what some actions do. As more actions are added to iMovie in the future, combining shortcuts and actions with ⌥ may help you to find more hidden customizability. So, have a go!

That's how to use fade transitions for cutaways. But apart from bringing clips smoothly, fading in overlays can create a brief **double-exposure** effect, where you can see two clips at the same time (like in a cross-dissolve transition). Next, we're going to look at the other option in the **Video overlay settings** menu, which provides a permanent way of doing that.

Creating Opacity effects

After it's faded in, a cutaway will sit on top of the main video layer and obscure it – that is, unless you change that layer's opacity. Here's how to do that in iMovie for macOS:

1. In the Media Browser, select the media you want to use as an overlay.
2. Drag it on top of a clip in the timeline (or press Q).
3. Click the **Video overlay settings** button on the toolbar. The style of the overlay will already be set to **Cutaway**.
4. Drag the **Opacity** slider to the left to reveal more of the clip underneath.

So, reducing opacity can create a sustained double exposure effect, but why would you want to? Won't it just create a mesh of clips that add up to nothing much? Not necessarily. In films and TV shows, double exposure suggests to the audience that the two clips are related in some way. It could be suggesting:

- Characters are dependent on one another
- The character or subject wants a particular object or is thinking about it
- Two different places or objects relate to each other or are both relevant to the story

These uses of double exposure lend themselves best to narrative fiction, but there are other ways you can use double exposure to add meaning. You could add images to give extra context to a factual clip such as a map. For *Figure 6.5*, I used an *old-world* customizable map and a photo of a ship out to sea to add context to a fictional cruise trip to the USA. The map clip is the overlay, allowing the dark blue sea to reveal the photo beneath when I drop the opacity. The photo of the ship is available in `Chapter 6: Double Exposure`, in this book's resources, so feel free to get in some practice by using **Overlay Settings** to recreate (or improve on!) the following image:

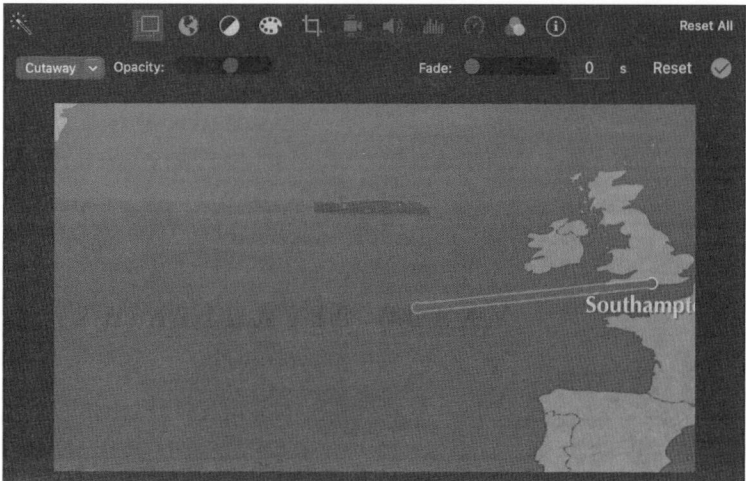

Figure 6.5 – Double exposure of the map and photo

Double exposure works best where the image is high in contrast – a large area of dark color and a large area of bright, light color. If the areas of color are pretty uniform, the dark area will disappear first and all at once when you drop the opacity. This allows you to superimpose other images while still keeping the bright areas, as well as text that's in a different color. Like everything else in editing, double-exposure effects are best used in moderation. Too many double exposures will take away from the novelty of the effect and will make it seem tacky.

That concludes our look through some artistic uses for opacity. But besides this, there are also practical uses for opacity. We're going to look at one that can make editing a lot easier for projects that use multiple camera angles.

Multi-camera editing with cutaways and opacity effects

The practical advantage of using overlays and opacity is that it makes **multi-camera** editing a lot easier. Multi-camera editing means cutting together two different shots of the same thing that were shot at the same time. Most TV shows (especially live ones) are filmed with five or more cameras at the same time; multi-camera setups are often used to record different angles of live events, so the editor can choose the best bits from each camera later. This second use of multi-camera setups is the kind of multi-camera editing we're going to look at here.

The `Chapter 6: Multi-Camera Editing` folder in this book's resources contains footage of a band performing a song. Two cameras were filming it: one getting a wide shot of all the performers, and the other getting creative and visually interesting close-ups of drum beats, guitar strings, and the lead vocalist singing. As an editor, your job is to choose the best bits from each angle to go into a video of the performance. But there's one problem – how do you keep everything in sync?

You can probably guess that if you place the *closeup-camera* file after the *wide-camera* file in the timeline and cut the best bits up, you'd be left with clips that are totally out of order, and out of sync with the background audio. So, instead of doing that, we need to edit each camera's footage at the same time, and that means using overlays. First of all, we need to get everything into the timeline:

1. Download the footage and audio of the band performing.
2. Import the footage and audio into a new iMovie project. You should have three clips: the wide camera footage, the close-up camera footage, and the audio of the performance.
3. Place the camera angle you think you're going to use most in the timeline, first.

    I would suggest adding the close-up angle first. This is because the wide angle is a safety shot – it's there as insurance in case the more exciting closeup angle is out of focus or changing shots.

4. Place the other shot on top, and the audio in the background audio track at the bottom of the timeline:

Figure 6.6 – Two camera perspectives and audio in the timeline

Our next job is to make sure that the two camera angles are synced with one another, as well as with the audio of the band performance.

Syncing multi-camera footage

When editing multi-camera footage, we need to make sure our shots are synced so that when we cut from one shot to another, movements on the screen still fit with the sound. If your audience can notice the discrepancy between them, the video will become difficult to watch, and harder to understand and enjoy.

The easiest way to achieve sync is to find a short, loud sound and a visual that accompanies it. If you remember to, it's always a good idea to clap in front of the camera just after you press record. That way, you have the visual cue of two hands meeting and the sound of the clap to match up. In this edit, the wide camera catches a band member clapping to the drum beat; exactly the kind of cues it's good to sync with. Ignoring the main video layer for now, let's sync the wide angle:

1. Play the timeline (*L*) and find where the guitar player starts clapping above their head.
2. Now, we need to find the exact point that the guitar player's hands meet. Look in the Viewer for where the hands first connect (using the ← and → arrow keys to move frame by frame).
3. Press *C* while hovering over the top clip to select it; then, press *M* to add a marker where the hands meet.
4. Mark the second and third claps using *steps 2* to *3* again. This will help make the sync more exact.
5. Now, select the audio track and listen, looking at the waveform too. After the singer encourages people to clap their hands, there are a series of claps, each of which makes a small peak in the waveform. Mark the first, second, and third peaks with *M*, as in *Figure 6.7*:

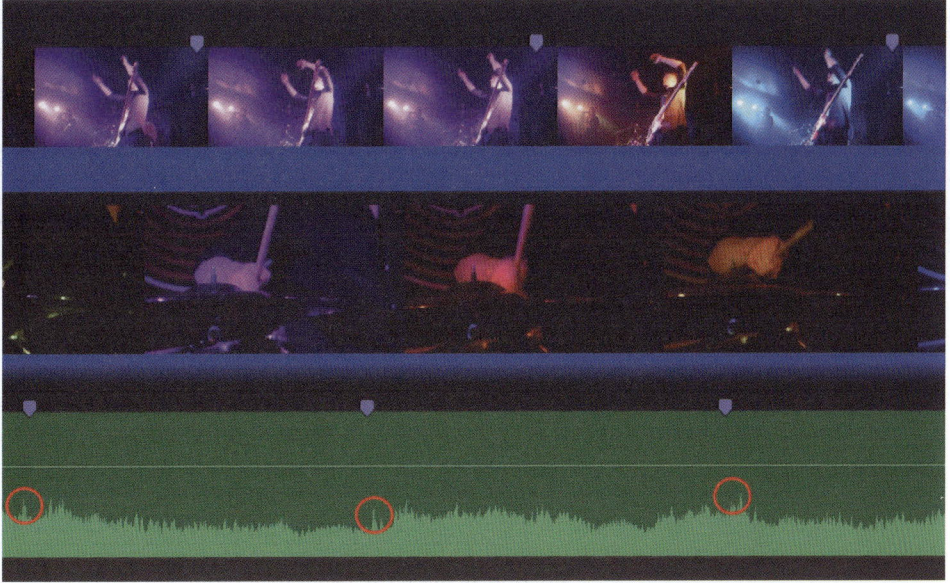

Figure 6.7 – The claps in the top clip and audio clip (peaks circled)

6. Now, we need to sync the two clips. Move the audio clip to the right so that the pairs of markers snap together (if they don't snap, toggle snapping on with *N*). They may not all match exactly, but you should be able to roughly draw a straight line through each pair of markers. If you can't, make small adjustments and play the clip back until the drum beats and claps feel synced when you watch the clip.

With that, we have the wide angle and the audio synced, but we still have to sync the closeup angle. For this, we're going to need to find a different visual cue because, unfortunately, the clapping isn't visible in the closeup angle. Sometimes, it can be challenging to sync footage up, which is why prior planning (such as remembering to clap at the start of a recording) is so important. To sync the closeup angle, we'll be focusing on the guitar in the closeup shot:

1. Click on the top clip and in the **Video overlay settings** menu, drag the **Opacity** slider to the left so that the clip is invisible. Now, when you move the playhead along the timeline, you'll see the close-up angle.

2. After the first few drum beats of the song, the guitar will begin to be played. In the simplest sense, for a guitar to be played, fingers and thumbs need to be moving the strings. Knowing that allows us to sync this clip.

3. Just as the close-up camera pulls away from the guitar, the thumb in the shot bends to hold the leftmost string. At that point, add a marker (*M*). Remember, for finer control moving the playhead, use the arrow keys (← and →):

Figure 6.8 – Mark at this point – the thumb bends, and the footage blurs

4. Now that we've marked the point in the video just before the guitar is played, let's do the same for the audio. Playing the timeline before the marker, listen out for the first guitar chord. To help, it comes in after six drum beats. Mark the peak where the guitar playing starts with *M*:

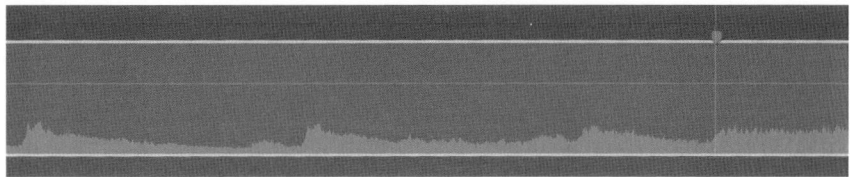

Figure 6.9 – The sync point for the guitar – the waveform becomes flatter once the guitar comes in (the peaks beforehand are drum beats)

5. Finally, it's time to sync everything up properly. Move the background audio to the right so that the first audio marker snaps to the marker we placed on the closeup shot.

6. This will take the wide angle back out of sync again, so move that top clip to the right so that its clapping markers snap to the three clapping markers later on in the audio, as in *Figure 6.10*:

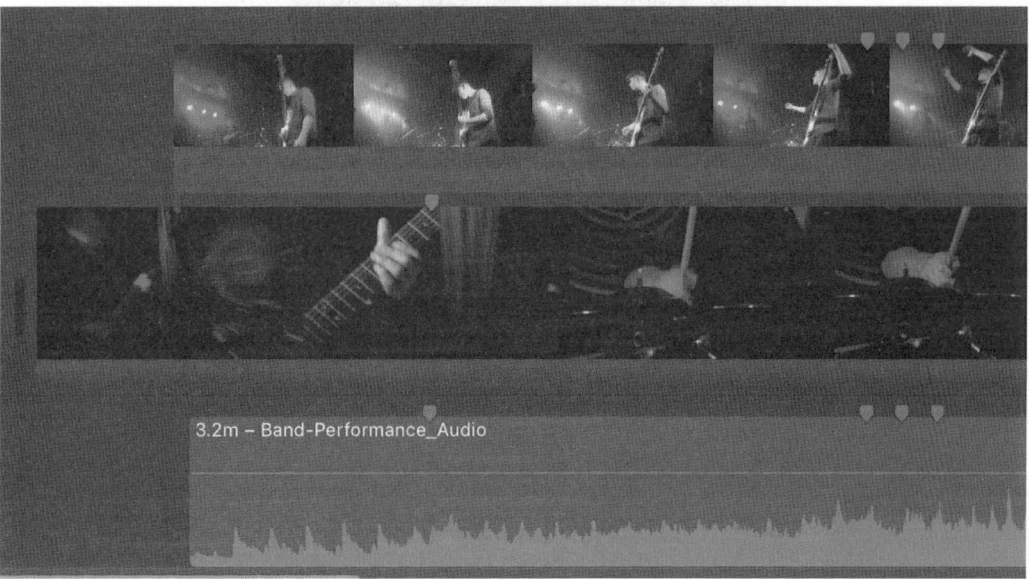

Figure 6.10 – The wide angle, closeup angle, and audio correctly synced

What you've just done there is about as difficult as syncing clips can get, so don't worry if it feels complex. If this didn't work out for you, here's a quick fix to get the footage synced for this particular exercise:

1. Trim 2.8 seconds off the start of the closeup angle.
2. Trim 0.3 seconds off the start of the wide angle.
3. Make sure the audio is dragged as far left as possible.

If you synced the clips using markers, you'll want to trim off the same sections so that there's no dead air in the video before the audio starts. Now, we can move on to the creative side of multi-camera editing.

Editing multi-camera footage

While syncing footage in the previous section, we reduced the opacity of the top layer (the wide angle) so that we could look at the closeup angle without moving clips out of the way. Moreover, we didn't make any splits or changes to the clip on the main video layer, and no footage was removed. This means that all the footage, still correctly synced, is kept on the timeline in case we want to make changes later.

When adding the clips to the timeline, we chose a preferred camera angle because, with the opacity of the other angle reduced to 0%, the shot on the main video layer is the shot you are going to see the most of. Using opacity for multi-camera editing in iMovie works best by prioritizing one shot, and turning the opacity back up on the other whenever the preferred shot cannot be used. Here's how to do that:

1. When the preferred angle doesn't look good (for me, this was when it was out of focus or the footage was too shaky), select the overlay with *C* and make two splits around that area with ⌘ + *B*.

2. In **Video overlay settings**, drag its opacity to the right:

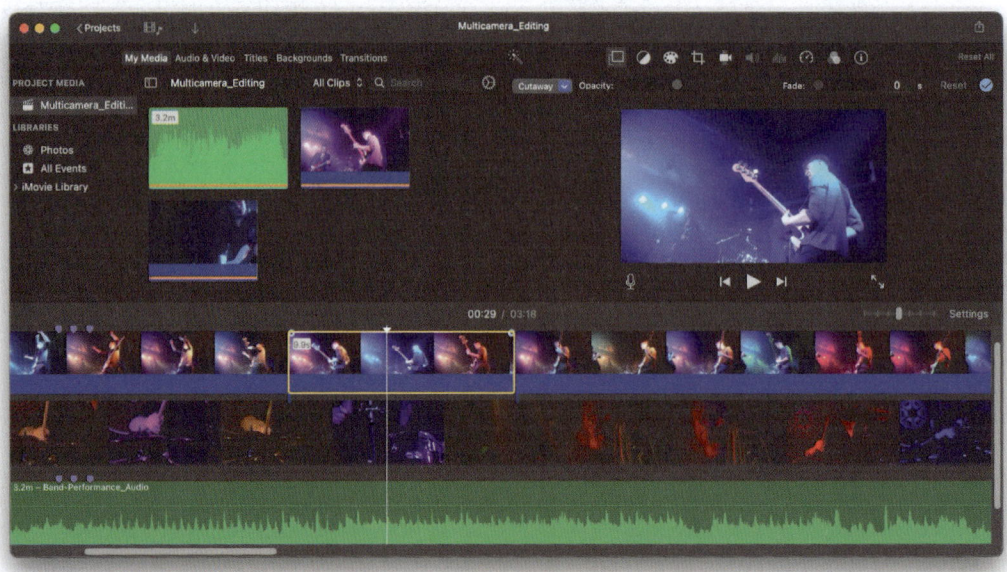

Figure 6.11 – Bringing up the opacity where we want to cut to the wide angle

3. When you watch the video, the footage will cut away to the overlay for just the time it needs to.
4. Find the next place where the preferred angle doesn't work and repeat *steps 1* to *2*.

Editing multi-camera footage is much more straightforward than syncing it in the first place. The most important thing now is exercising your judgment as an editor, deciding where it's best to stay on the preferred angle, and where you want to cut away to the other angle. Apart from avoiding bad-looking parts of the preferred angle, you might want to cut away:

- To reorient the audience (occasionally showing the audience the whole space makes the video feel more coherent)
- To show interactions between all the people in the space (the lead singer may gesture to the guitar player, for example, and for that, you'll want to see both)

As we know, iMovie only allows one main video and one layer of connected video, so editing footage that involves three or more simultaneous shots requires a workaround. If you do have three or more shots, start editing with the two you think you'll use the most; we'll cover adding the extra angle later. That's our foray into multi-camera editing for now. It's time to take a look at the other styles of overlay available in both versions of iMovie.

Split screen and blue/green screen effects

We're now going to take a look at the other ways iMovie lets you represent overlays. In the **Video overlay settings** drop-down menu, Split Screen is a fairly simple but still useful overlay style. In Split Screen mode, the overlay clip is placed next to the clip in the main video layer. Split-screening clips is useful when you want to imply that two things are happening at the same time, or are in a direct comparison. It's a great way to bring together shots filmed at different times and in different places: it makes the audience feel like they're happening right next to each other. You could even use Split Screen to show two different shots of one person; game shows sometimes do this with a shot of a contestant's face, and their fingers on a buzzer.

To create and customize a split screen effect on iOS and iPadOS:

1. Add a clip you want to have in a split screen on top of another clip in the timeline (tap the three dots and select **Add as...** | **Split Screen**).

2. Tap **zoom controls**, which are in a magnifying glass icon at the top right of the Viewer (circled, *Figure 6.12*). Pinch to zoom into or out of the overlay image, which will be on the right by default:

Figure 6.12 – A split-screen shot (zoom controls circled)

3. To move the perspective of the other clip, tap the main video clip on the timeline, then tap **zoom controls** again. The clip will fill the Viewer until you have finished adjusting and tapped **zoom controls** again.

4. Below the zoom controls on the Viewer is the **rotate** button. Tap to rotate the entire split screen arrangement by 90 degrees. One or three taps switches to a horizontal rather than vertical split between the clips (as in *Figure 6.13*).

5. The bottom icon toggles a white border between the clips in Split Screen mode:

Figure 6.13 – A rotated split screen effect with no border. The zoom on the overlay has been adjusted

The border is unique to the mobile version of iMovie, so if you'd like to make the visual split between the clips a bit more obvious within the program, do make use of it. Now, here's how to add split-screen effects to iMovie for macOS:

1. In the Media Browser, select a clip you want to have on a split screen.
2. Drag it on top of a clip in the timeline (or press Q).
3. Click the **Video overlay settings** button.
4. Choose **Split Screen** from the drop-down menu of overlay styles.
5. You can control where the overlay sits on the screen with the **Position** drop-down menu (see *Figure 6.14*). Whatever that menu says (top/bottom/right/left) is the location of the overlay clip:

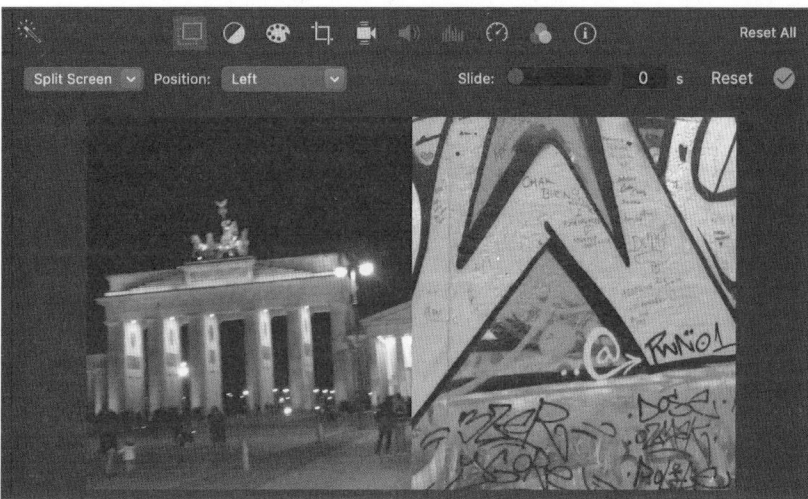

Figure 6.14 – Split screen effects in iMovie for macOS

When using **Split Screen** on Mac, you also can transition into the split screen effect by having one clip move over the other. This animation, called **Slide** (see *Figure 6.14*), slides the overlay clip in from the side of the frame given in the **Position** menu until it occupies half the screen. It's similar to the slide/wipe transition we looked at in *Chapter 3*, but this one stops halfway across the frame. Unlike fade transitions, there is no fade handle on the timeline for you to manipulate the **Slide** transition with. To customize the transition length:

1. Go to **Overlay settings**.
2. Click in the duration editor box and write the length of time you want the transition to take.
3. Hit *Enter* to save the change.

The time you enter will be how long the slide-over animation takes to complete, from the start of the overlay clip. The reverse of the transition will take place at the end of the clip, with the overlay sliding back out of the frame again. With the split screen effect, there is unfortunately no way to independently control the in and out animations.

That's split screen overlays. There's not too much to shout about – it's a straightforward effect that can visually enhance your projects when showing an additional clip simultaneously would add context to the video. Now, let's look at something a little fancier.

Using Green/Blue Screen effects

The **Green/Blue Screen** overlay style allows you to cut out specific areas of the frame based on color, a technique called **chroma keying**. This technique is useful for superimposing yourself onto a different background (what you might think of when you hear *green screening*), or cutting a shape out of the frame so you can see the clip beneath. In a strange reversal of the usual feature sets, the chroma keying feature on iMovie for iOS and iPadOS is a lot more advanced; allowing you to key out any color you like based on where you tap. Here's how you do that:

1. Add a clip containing a block of green or blue color on top of another clip (tap the three dots and select **Add as… | Green/Blue Screen**).
2. The effect will usually be applied automatically. Tap **Reset** (the top left of the Viewer) to remove the effect.
3. Tap on the color inside the frame that you want to remove. The **Tap to remove color** effect works best on green and blue areas of the frame, but it is possible to tap on a different color to make it transparent, so long as it's bright and consistent:

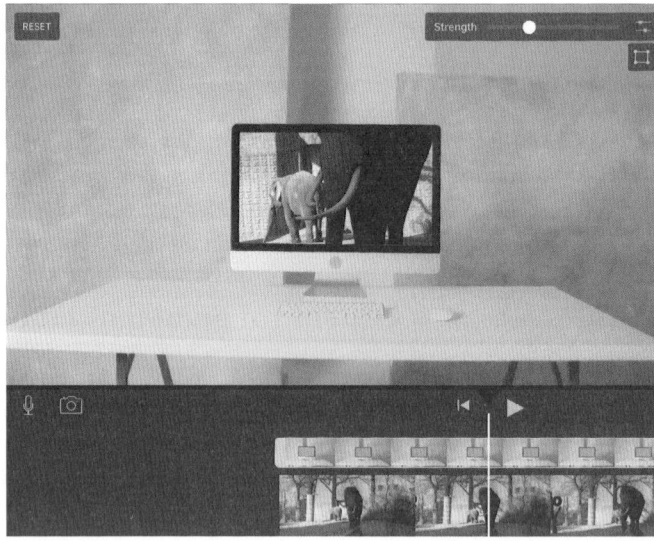

Figure 6.15 – Green screen footage from Pexels overlaid on Berlin zoo footage

4. You can change the strength of the keying with the **Strength** slider (top right, *Figure 6.15*).
5. Just the same as with the split-screen effect, you can tap on the main video layer and adjust the zoom with **zoom controls**, changing what we see in the green screen area.

Now, let's learn how to use this effect on macOS. There are a few differences in the blue/green screen options between the iMovie versions. iMovie for macOS only allows two colors to be keyed out (green and blue), and you can't click to make a color transparent. The effect is applied automatically based on which color (green or blue) is filling up most of the frame. To create a green/blue screen effect on Mac:

1. Select the clip you want to key green or blue out of and drag it on top of another (or press *Q*).
2. Click the **Video overlay settings** button.
3. Choose **Green / Blue Screen** from the drop-down menu.

For *Figure 6.16*, I added the **Green/Blue Screen** effect to a clip where a blue circle expands on a green background. Keying out the background shows `Aquarium-vid-2`. Do be aware that where you place your playhead is important on macOS: the position I used the effect at was the furthest point into the clip where iMovie keyed out the green color (as the majority of the frame was still green). Any further and it tried to key out the blue, which didn't work well because the circle uses multiple shades of blue:

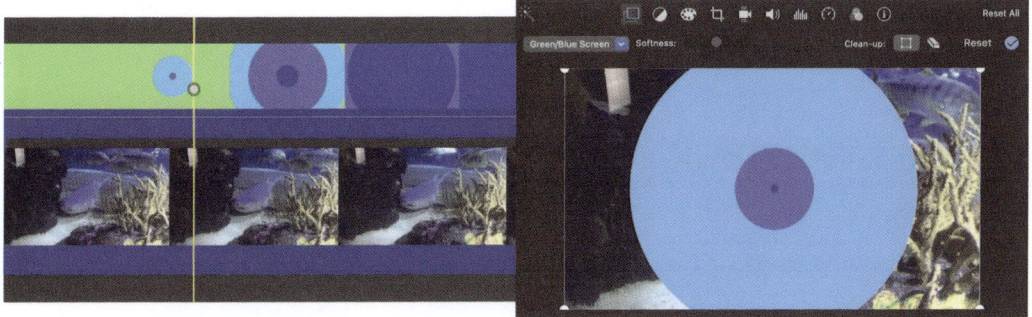

Figure 6.16 – Keying out a green background on iMovie for macOS

4. You can change the strength of keying with the **Softness** slider beside the drop-down menu (*Figure 6.16*).
5. You can adjust the framing of the clip in the main video layer by going to the **Crop** menu in the toolbar and adjusting the **Crop to Fill** crop box.

Both versions of iMovie have a **Crop** option (selected under **Clean-up**, *Figure 6.16*). This allows you to remove whole parts of the overlay that you don't want to keep, thus **masking out** areas of the clip. Unfortunately, this tool is quite limited because you can only drag four points. This only allows you to mask out blocky areas of the frame, which would be useless if you wanted to mask out the shape of someone's head, for example.

Also in the **Clean-up** menu is the **Eraser** tool, which allows you to key out any green or blue areas that are still showing by clicking on them. This acts a little like the **Tap to remove color** option in the mobile version, but unfortunately, you can't use it in the same way, because the green/blue screen effect is always automatically applied. Even if there is no green or blue in the frame, iMovie looks for the closest thing to it, often with bad results. Instead, the eraser tool is useful for clearing up little specks of green or blue that haven't been fully keyed out. And that's about it for the **Green/Blue Screen** tool. Now, we're going to look at the final style of overlay, which takes the whole overlay clip and places it within the main video.

Using Picture in Picture effects in iMovie

Picture in Picture (**PiP**) is perhaps the iMovie effect that gives you the most creative scope. It allows you to resize the overlay clip so that it fits within the frame of the main video, and, as we'll see later, animate that clip around the frame as the video plays. PiP is a great way to display extra information with more flexibility than a cutaway. PiP is not the most subtle of effects, but it can be used to add a significant amount of extra meaning and context to your video. Here's how to add a PiP.

For iOS and iPadOS:

1. Add the clip you want to feature within the frame of another clip (tap the three dots and select **Add as...** | **Picture in Picture**).
2. The clip will appear as a smaller version of itself inside the main video:

Figure 6.17 – A PiP clip of jellyfish in a photo of the aquarium

Now, you can customize the PiP using the options at the top right of the Viewer (see *Figure 6.17*). From top to bottom, they are:

1. Tap **zoom controls** (magnifying glass icon) then pinch the image to zoom into and out of the PiP.
2. Tap **compass points** then drag the PiP to move it; pinch in and out to resize the PiP.
3. Toggle the bottom option to remove the border automatically placed around the PiP. You should remove the border if you want the PiP to blend into the image, or if it has a transparent background (otherwise, the border will look like a weird picture frame).

Those steps cover about all you can do with PiP in iMovie's mobile version, but iMovie for macOS has more options for customizability. Here's how to add a PiP there:

1. Select the clip you want as a PiP and drag it on top of another (or press Q).
2. Click the **Video overlay settings** button on the toolbar and choose **Picture in Picture** from the drop-down menu.

From the **Video overlay settings** menu, you can customize the border with more detail than in the mobile app (see *Figure 6.18*):

1. The **Border** selector allows you to change the border to one of three settings:
   - No border
   - Thin border
   - Thick border
2. Next to the **Border** selector is an option to bring up the macOS **Colors** wheel to choose a color for the border.

3. Ticking the **Shadow** checkbox to the right of the menu will give the image a drop shadow that helps it stand out further. The shadow is quite straight and blocky though, so it's probably only worth using if the audience would struggle to see the PiP on the screen:

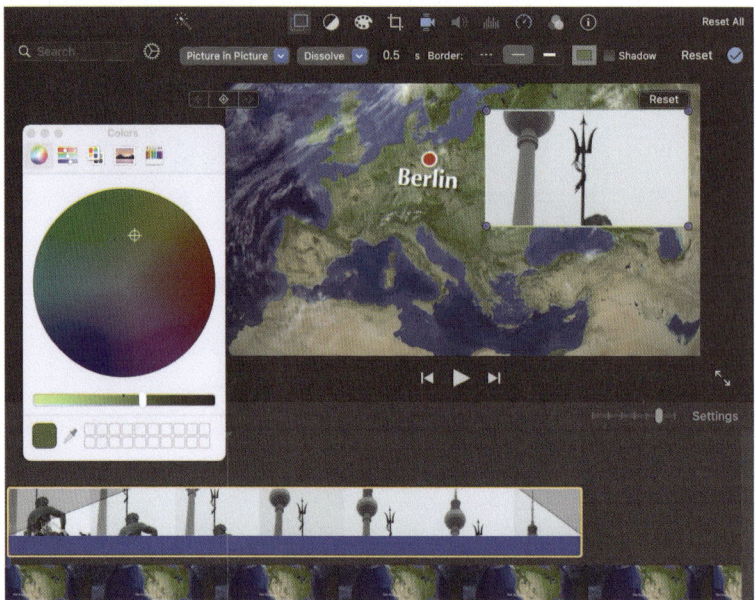

Figure 6.18 – I've used the eyedropper tool on the color wheel to choose a border that matches the green on the map

The example PiP in *Figure 6.18* uses the timeline's fade handles to transition in, but PiP overlays in macOS can make use of different transition styles. Let's take a look at those.

Using Zoom and Swap transitions with PiP

Dissolve is the transition you'll most likely use with overlays as it allows you to gradually introduce an overlay with the fade handles on the timeline. But when adding transitions to PiP, we have the option to be a little bit gaudier – if the tone of the video calls for it – by using the **Zoom** or **Swap** animation style . First, let's look at **Zoom**. Instead of fading in as a whole image, this animation makes the PiP (and its border) scale up from whatever corner is nearest the edge of the screen. To change the transition:

1. Click on the second drop-down menu in the **Video overlay settings** menu and choose **Zoom** (as in *Figure 6.19*).
2. Change the length of the zoom animation with the **duration editor** box.

3. Hit *Enter* to save your changes:

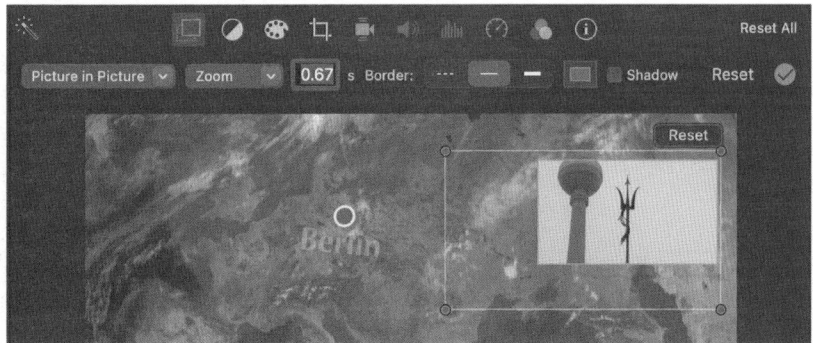

Figure 6.19 – The PiP and border scale to full size over 0.67 seconds

Do be aware that you can't change the transition length of a zoom on the timeline – fade handles only appear, and work, for **Dissolve** transitions. Because of this, there will always be an equal-length zoom-out animation that you cannot change (the same as with **Slide** for split-screen effects). Unfortunately, having this in the video limits your creative options with **Zoom**, so for that reason, it's usually best to stick with dissolves.

The final transition style is a little different. **Swap** changes which clip is shown in the PiP, without you having to move anything in the timeline. This scales the main image down from filling the whole frame and into the PiP box, over the amount of time set in the **duration editor** menu. To set this up:

1. Click on the second drop-down menu in the **Video overlay settings** menu and choose **Swap**.
2. Change the length of the zoom animation with the **duration editor** box.
3. Hit *Enter* to save your changes:

Figure 6.20 – Over 0.67 seconds, the full-screen map shrinks into the PiP box

You might be able to see the reason this transition is called **Swap**: the overlay clip becomes the one that fills up the whole frame, with the clip in the main video layer acting as a PiP. Swapping has great creative potential, but it can also be confusing when the clips swap roles. Maybe marking the clips (*M*) to show when they're swapped might help.

Although the **Zoom** and **Swap** transitions can work well for stylized videos such as our Berlin travelog, **Dissolve** transitions using fade handles remain the most versatile setup for overlays. They can cut instantly like a cutaway or introduce clips gradually just like a normal cross-dissolve transition, and we can control fade-in and fade-out transitions independently. **Dissolve** is also the only transition type that allows you to use the keyframe editor, and that's very important.

Using keyframe animations on macOS

The keyframe editor (see *Figure 6.21*) is a macOS-only tool that opens up a world of animation possibilities, but let's define a keyframe first so that we know what we're dealing with. A keyframe is like a save point for animations. If you set a keyframe for an object at the 00:03 timecode and you move the object again at 00:08, you can always go back to its position at 00:03 because you set a keyframe there. A keyframe holds a state of animation that won't be lost:

Figure 6.21 – The keyframe editor in iMovie for macOS

When you set two keyframes, the thing that's being animated (in iMovie, this can be a PiP clip or an audio level) moves from its position in the first keyframe to its position in the second, as smoothly as possible. Therefore, by setting multiple keyframes, you can create an *animation path*. We're not talking hand-drawn animations here, though – think more of a character avatar bouncing across the frame, imitating a speaker who isn't on camera. In that spirit, let's look at animating a PiP with keyframes:

1. Add a clip as an overlay (*Q*) and change the overlay style to **Picture in Picture**.
2. Move the playhead to near the start of the overlay clip, or where you want the PiP to start moving.
3. In the Viewer, click and drag the PiP to select the starting position you want.
4. Click the middle button in the **keyframe editor** area: **add a new keyframe at playhead**.

5. The diamond in the center of the **keyframe editor** area will show a cross (as in *Figure 6.22*). This means that a keyframe has been set at the playhead's position:

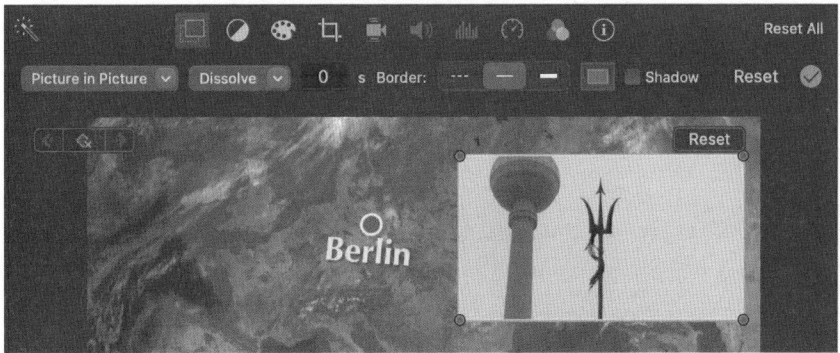

Figure 6.22 – The first keyframe has been set

> **Creative choices for PiP animations**
>
> If you want your PiP to move in one smooth motion, you'll want to set just two keyframes: one at the start and one at the end of the clip. That way, the PiP will animate in a smooth line, similar to a Ken Burns effect.
>
> If you want more natural, shaky movement, you'll want to set more keyframes across the clip. However, be aware that setting multiple keyframes close together with lots of movement between them will make the animation look chaotic.
>
> Always try to keep keyframes a similar distance from one another so that the PiP doesn't speed up and slow down hugely. Similarly, try not to resize the PiP, as the overlay scaling in size while moving will look strange. Of course, if you have a creative reason for doing either of these – or a *motivation* within your narrative for them happening – that's fine. It's about making sure the audience understands and accepts what you're doing.

6. Move the playhead along the timeline to where you want to set the next position.
7. Click the middle button of the **Keyframe editor** area again to set the second keyframe at the playhead position.
8. Click on the arrow keys on the left and right of the **Keyframe editor** area to navigate between the keyframes you've set.
9. When you're on a keyframe, the icon in the middle will show an **x** symbol, along with the square. Click the middle button again to remove that keyframe.

It's worth remembering that even though you're animating the overlay across the frame, you can still change the cropping style and add Ken Burns effects to the image itself. Do the following:

1. Click on the overlay clip in the timeline.
2. Click the **Crop** button on the toolbar.
3. Change between **Crop to fill** and Ken Burns styles as you please. To show the whole image, choose **Crop to fill** and drag the crop box to show the whole image.

This is where using **Crop to fill** comes into its own: when you drag the crop box to fit the whole frame (but don't use the Fit style), the black bars aside the clip go transparent, and won't show up in the PiP. Although you can use the keyframe editor to animate any PiP, the effect is best used on smaller images with no background. Animating a rectangular 16:9 frame around a larger 16:9 frame won't look as unique and interesting as a more organic shape. And that concludes our look at PiP animations – but that's not the only thing you can animate with keyframes in iMovie.

Using audio keyframes

Animation doesn't necessarily mean the movement of a visual object. An animation is a change in something over time, and this can apply to audio levels too. You'll remember from editing audio that iMovie shows volume as a line. If you change the volume of a clip, that whole clip's **volume level** line will go up or down, and it will stay straight. But with keyframes, you can animate a path for that audio line, making audio decrease and increase in volume as you decide. Smooth shapes on the timeline translate to pleasingly smooth audio transitions for your audience. To create audio keyframes on Mac:

1. Click on the audio level line and ⌥ + *click*.
2. This will create an audio keyframe, which is represented as a dot on the timeline (as in *Figure 6.23*). This first keyframe is the starting volume for your audio animation.
3. ⌥ + *click* to create another audio keyframe further along the clip, where you want the volume animation to change.
4. Click and drag to move the second keyframe up or down.
5. Listen to the audio. You should hear the audio gradually become louder or quieter:

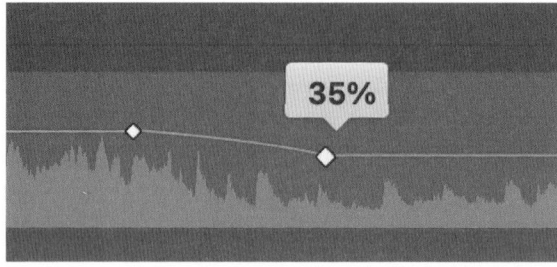

Figure 6.23 – Animating the audio volume down from the original volume to 35%

6. You can move an audio keyframe along the timeline by clicking and dragging it. The longer between keyframes, the more gradual the volume change.
7. If you can't seem to place a keyframe, you're probably too close to the previous one. Move the playhead a little and try ⌥ + *clicking* again.
8. If you want to delete a keyframe, right-click on the keyframe and click **delete keyframe**.

Creating and using audio keyframes is great for gradually fading sound when you're not at the end of a clip, so you can't use the fade handles. Moreover, because you can create as many keyframes as you like, you can make custom fades that fit whatever shape you like. This is especially useful if you want to cut audio in an interview, for example, where the person you're filming says something interesting but then immediately starts a new sentence you don't need. Creating a fade curve similar to what's shown in *Figure 6.24* is a good way to silence the next sentence but still avoid it sounding like you cut the speaker off unnaturally:

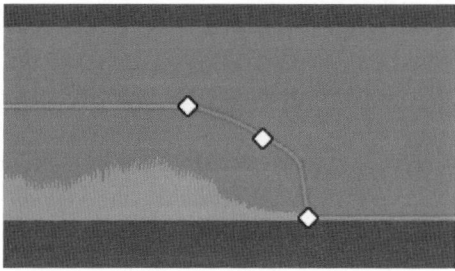

Figure 6.24 – Using keyframes to quickly but smoothly fade out audio

There are so many ways in which audio keyframes can be useful, but I'll give just one more – using a range (*R*) to isolate and remove unwanted sounds:

1. Find the waveform of the sound you don't want – knocks and other unwanted sounds are usually short, sharp peaks.
2. Draw a range around the waveform (as small as possible to encompass the sound) by holding *R* and clicking and dragging over the audio clip.
3. Inside the region, drag the volume level line to 0% (as in *Figure 6.25*). Two keyframes on either side of the region will keep the rest of the clip at its original volume:

Figure 6.25 – An audio range keyframe edit

4. Copy some background noise (known as **room tone**) from somewhere else to fill the gap you created. Otherwise, there'll be a jarring stutter in the audio when it goes to 0%:

    If you can, make sure the room tone you copy contains no voices or recognizable sounds. If it does, it will be obvious when you listen back that you copied audio from somewhere else, because the sound will repeat itself.

5. Play the audio back: if you can't tell there's an edit there, you've done it right!

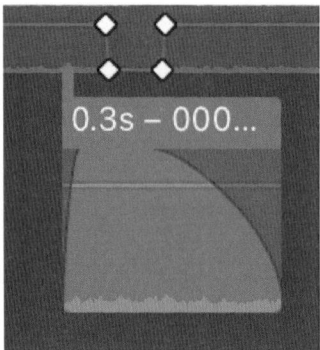

Figure 6.26 – The unwanted sound has been removed, with room tone covering the gap

The edit in *Figure 6.26* is applied to audio that was part of a video clip, but the technique is just the same for audio in its own clips. This was one way to gradually introduce a change. Now, we're going to look at introducing visual changes gradually by using transitions.

Using transition effects – speed and color ramping

In *Chapter 5*, we looked at speed and color effects that you can apply to clips in the timeline. The problem is that if you change color information, there'll be a sudden change in how the clip looks, and that's not good for audience immersion. Changes that happen gradually keep the audience enveloped in the narrative, and allow you to subtly tweak how you're telling that story.

In iMovie, you can use individual clips as keyframes, with **cross-dissolve** transitions between them making gradual speed and color changes – an effect called **ramping**. iMovie has some stock color effects that do this: **Modify | Fade to**. But if we edit the effect manually, we can do more: ramping works for changes in color, clip filters, and speed – all toolbar options. Here's how to ramp up any of those effects on macOS:

1. Split the clip (⌘ + B) you want the effect on with the playhead as close to the middle as possible:

    For their animations, transitions use an equal amount of the first and second clip (for example, for a 3-second transition, 1.5 seconds of each)

2. Make the speed or color changes you want to transition to on the second clip.
3. Add a cross-dissolve transition between the two clips (⌘ + *T*).
4. Watch the transition. If you want the change to happen more slowly (maybe even imperceptibly), increase the length of the transition by double-clicking on it, writing a new value in the box (*Figure 6.27*), and hitting *Enter*:

Figure 6.27 - The transition duration box

So, why might you want to gradually introduce effects? Well, it all helps to avoid taking the audience out of what they're watching. Effects introduced imperceptibly are useful in a couple of ways, both of which involve not wanting the effect to be seen:

- Introducing a color change to subtly change the emotion of a scene (for example, make it sadder by lowering the color temperature)
- Ramping up to a higher speed to make a clip fit to a shorter time – the more gradual the speed change, the less likely the audience is to notice it

However, be aware that because we're using a transition that doesn't happen instantly, this technique doesn't work with clips with shaky movement or Ken Burns animations. When there is lots of movement, you'll see the two clips in separate places at the same time while the transition takes place – a kind of unwanted double-exposure effect. That, unfortunately, destroys the immersion. You also might not want to use these effects if, for example, you are introducing a heavily sped-up section, such as a **timelapse**. Equally, if you're creating a montage, where you want to draw attention to the differences between clips, cutting to a color or filter change can be just the right kind of jarring to make your audience sit up and take notice. Nothing in editing is wrong, *per se*: you just need to be doing things for a reason.

Now, it's time for the final part of this chapter, where we're going to return to the limitations of one layer of connected media and find a good old-fashioned workaround for it.

Combining effects – creating compound clips

Whether you're trying to edit footage from three cameras or want multiple PiPs, iMovie's limit of one connected video layer comes up very regularly as a roadblock. Luckily, there's a simple – although not ideal – way around this: turning two clips into one *compound clip*. This is quite a simple process, but there are a few things that can help:

- A new project dedicated to your compound clip
- Plenty of space on your hard drive, or external storage space
- Some time and patience for exporting and reimporting clips

Creating compound clips in iMovie revolves around a few simple steps:

1. Complete a fine cut with two video layers, making sure everything is to your liking.
2. Export that fine cut to a master copy.
3. Reimport the master copy, now one layer, and add a new layer as connected media on top of that.

Here's the rub: because we're exporting and reimporting clips, we can't edit the originals. That's why it's a good idea to keep the individual parts of your compound clip in a separate project. That way, if you re-import your combined effect and only then realize that something isn't quite right, you can make edits and export the compound clip again. Nothing about creating compound clips in iMovie should be difficult; it's just very repetitive and takes a long time to complete. That's why you really should ask yourself whether you need to layer more visual layers on top of your project. Apart from risking cluttering your frame, it's going to be a big time sink – especially if you don't have a plan for where to stop.

Because you can export and reimport over and over again forever, the only limit on how many PiPs you can add to your effects, or shots to your multi-camera edit, should be your creative restraint (remember, never make an edit just for the sake of it!). So, let's have a look at creating compound clips with a couple of the examples we looked at earlier in this chapter in the *Using opacity for multi-camera editing* section.

In the example of the band performance, we had two camera angles that we edited together – the two most important for showing the musicians on stage. But suppose we had a third angle, of the crowd's reaction. This might be a nice angle to use when the crowd gets excited in reaction to the music. It'll help us reinforce the video's core message: that the band is entertaining and worth watching and listening to. We'll go through the whole technique, starting with the first edit with two cameras.

There is no footage of the crowd from the actual performance, so like all good editors, we're going to pretend. I searched "Gig crowd" on Pexels and found a plausible shot of a crowd called *Video Of People Having Fun At Concert*. If you're following along, see if you can find something similar – exercise those creative muscles! Let us go through the following steps:

1. If you haven't already, check you're happy with your multi-camera edit of the band performance, and export a master copy.

   You must export in the highest quality settings possible here to avoid quality loss from exporting and re-importing more than once.

2. Download some footage of a crowd that you'd like to use.
3. Go to the iMovie **Projects** screen (*2*) and create a new project (⌘ + N).
4. Import both the crowd footage and the compound clip you've made of the performance.
5. Add the compound clip to the timeline first (*W*) then add the crowd shot as an overlay (*Q*).
6. Go to the **Video overlay settings** menu and drag the **Opacity** slider to the left (as in *Figure 6.28*). This is the technique we used previously to see through to the main angle of the performance:

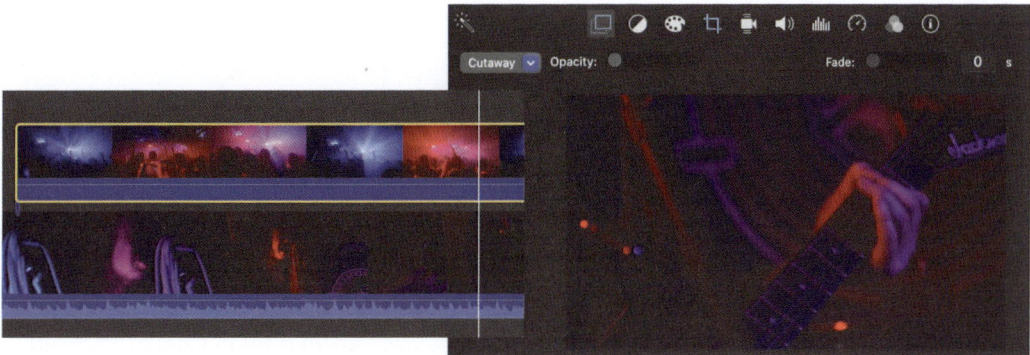

Figure 6.28 – Multi-camera opacity editing with the compound clip and the reaction shot

The shot of the crowd isn't synced with the performance (and is much shorter), so we're just going to choose the best places to cut to the crowd: wherever nothing in particular is happening in the performance, or if you find any areas you missed before where the camera is moving between shots or out of focus:

1. Split the crowd clip into several clips of about 3 seconds each. We'll place these throughout the performance.
2. Where you want to cut to a clip of the crowd, move the short section of the crowd clip to the desired location and drag the **Opacity** slider back to the right. With that, you've created a standard cutaway to the crowd.

   Try and make sure to cut to – and away from – the crowd in the middle of words if you can. This makes the cut itself less obvious, which is what we want when creating a seamless video of the band's performance.

3. When you're happy you've added all the cutaways to the crowd that you want to, export a master copy of the band's performance (*Figure 6.29*):

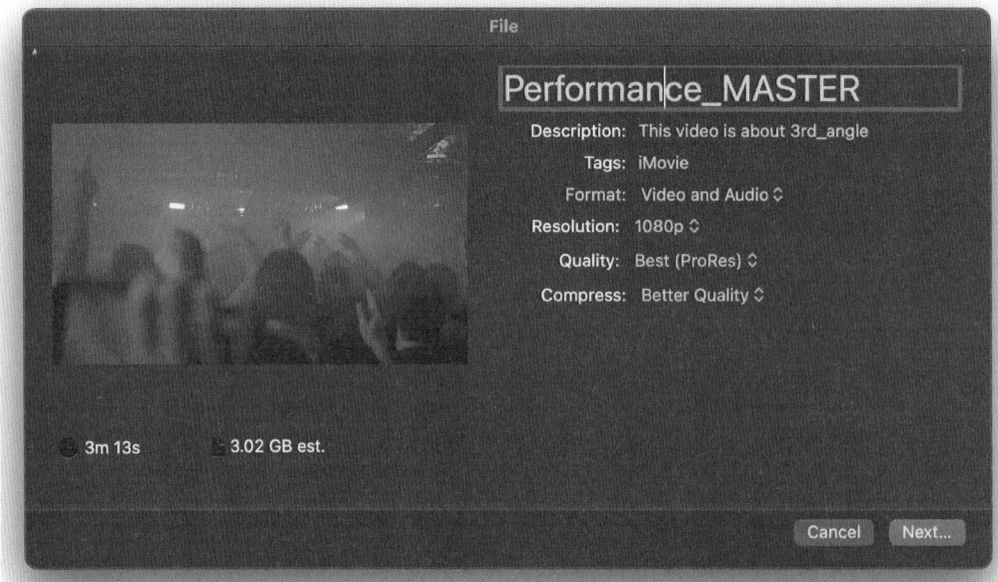

Figure 6.29 – Exporting the final three-camera edit

With this technique, we're editing in almost the same way we did before. That's the nature of using compound clips in iMovie: rinsing and repeating standard editing until we've added all the extra angles or clips that we need to. Sure, this method is inelegant, but without an official compound clip feature (or more video layers to work with), it's about making what you have work for you. Creative problem-solving is only going to make you a better editor, after all.

One thing – what about doing this in iMovie for iOS and iPadOS? There's no reason why this technique for making compound clips shouldn't work in iMovie's mobile app, but beware that what is a labor of love on Mac can quickly become arduous on an iPhone or iPad. As we discussed in earlier chapters, editing with a keyboard makes editing a lot faster and more efficient. Having to work with touch actions is going to make this process take longer – but maybe that doesn't have to be a bad thing. Let the outlay of time be a point to consider: do I need this edit for my video to tell its story effectively? Often, the simplest editing is the best.

Summary

Well done – this summary marks the end of our creative process of just using iMovie. First, we looked at the simplest and most versatile form of an overlay: the cutaway. Cutaways allow you to show different clips such as reaction shots and B-rolls. They can also hide jump cuts you made to make the video more concise. Changing opacity on cutaways allows you to create a double-exposure effect, and can speed up the process of multi-camera editing. Other overlay effects we looked at include split-screen effects and chroma keying, which allows us to remove parts of the frame based on color.

PiP effects allow you to show different clips simultaneously with a lot more freedom than split-screen edits. PiP effects are also the only type of overlay you can animate with keyframes in iMovie. Creating multiple keyframes along the timeline will make an overlay follow an animation path. You can also animate audio levels with keyframes, allowing you to fade volumes up and down smoothly and organically. For video, adding a cross-dissolve transition between clips can *ramp* up the effect so that the change – such as a speed or color change – comes in gradually.

Finally, we looked at combining effects and clips to get around iMovie's limit of one layer of connected video. Getting your effect just right and then exporting a high-quality clip will turn two clips into one when you reimport, allowing you to repeat the process to add as many video layers as you like.

What we saw in this chapter isn't an exhaustive list of the effects it's possible to create, but it should provide a jumping-off point for you to explore effects and combine them. In the next chapter, we're going to carry on increasing production values by bringing in Keynote – another macOS app – to create our custom titles and animations. See you on the other side.

Part 3 – Customizing Your Videos

iMovie most likely gets a bad rep because lots of the videos made using it look the same. The way to get around this isn't to buy or subscribe to a paid NLE – that won't make you a better editor. It's all about looking around at what's available to you and using that to make your videos unique.

In this part of the book, we're going to use other apps to change what's possible within iMovie. To start off, we're going to learn how to create custom titles and animations in Keynote that improve on both the titles iMovie provides and the keyframing available for PiP overlays.

We're then going to look at customizing our exports from iMovie using Keynote, Handbrake, and even iMovie itself. Gaining an understanding of video compression – especially how ProRes works – should help you to choose the best settings for encoding your video, and the video you're editing. Knowing your way around Handbrake will also allow you to tailor your videos to the requirements of websites and clients.

Finally, we're going to look at how to solve and avoid some of the most common problems that crop up while using iMovie. Any NLE, regardless of how much you love it or how much you paid for it, is going to do things you didn't want it to or expect. Hopefully, by the end of this book, however, you'll be better prepared for any questionable shenanigans from iMovie.

This part of the book comprises the following chapters:

- *Chapter 7, Integrating Keynote – Titles and Animations*
- *Chapter 8, Custom Export Formats, ft. Handbrake*
- *Chapter 9, Common iMovie Problems and Their Solutions*

7
Integrating Keynote – Titles and Animations

Well done – you've basically mastered iMovie. No, really. Throughout *Chapter 4*, *Chapter 5*, and *Chapter 6*, you learned how the magnetic timeline works, how to navigate through the iMovie for macOS interface, how to edit and refine clips in the timeline, and how to add and compound effects together. With that, you can comfortably create effective videos that get their intended meaning across coherently and concisely and contain added meaning and context. But because you've done all of this within iMovie – which doesn't leave a massive space for customization – your videos still may not seem totally unique. This final part of the book is all about bringing more individuality to your videos: customizing them to you and your needs. Although we've looked at ways to avoid making our videos sound like everyone else's, it is more difficult to give your videos a unique visual identity. This is what we aim to do in this chapter by using Keynote. But why Keynote?

The best tool for a job is one that is focused exactly and only on doing that job. That's why we're going to be using a word-processing application to create worded titles. Besides this, we're also using Keynote because it's video-minded. It allows both images and videos to be exported with an **alpha channel** – a transparent background. This makes using custom titles and animations in iMovie super-easy because we can add our titles as both cutaways and **Picture-in-Picture** (**PiP**).

This chapter will start with an introduction to Keynote, explaining how it can be used as an artistic extension to iMovie. We'll then look at how to create custom titles for your video project, before introducing animations to your titles that really make them pop. Finally, we'll look at creating custom animations that go beyond what keyframing allows in iMovie. The main topics we'll cover in this chapter are as follows:

- Creating custom titles in Keynote with transparent backgrounds
- Creating custom animations using shapes and moves
- Creating custom transitions using build orders and Magic Move

Technical requirements

Because iMovie for iOS and iPadOS has more customizability in its titles than the macOS version, we'll be focusing on Macintosh in this chapter. However, the method shown here should be transferable if you want to create static custom titles using Keynote (the first technique we cover) on mobile devices.

As we're creating titles and animations from scratch, you can follow along with all the steps as long as you have Keynote open. One animation exercise has a Keynote file you can work with, and that can be found in `Chapter 7: Keynote Car Animation` in the book resources. To access features such as dynamic backgrounds, you will need Keynote version 12.1, which requires macOS 11.0 (Big Sur) or later. Keynote is a default Macintosh app: if it's not on your Macintosh computer, you'll just need to go to the Mac App Store to download it.

Creating custom titles with Keynote

The first step towards creating custom titles is to make a dedicated Keynote file you can keep coming back to. This means you won't need to repeat the same first steps every time you want to create titles for your projects:

1. Open Keynote (double-click on the app icon or search for it using Spotlight, ⌘ + *spacebar*).
2. Click **New Document** or use the shortcut ⌘ + *N*.
3. You will be met with the theme chooser (*Figure 7.1*).

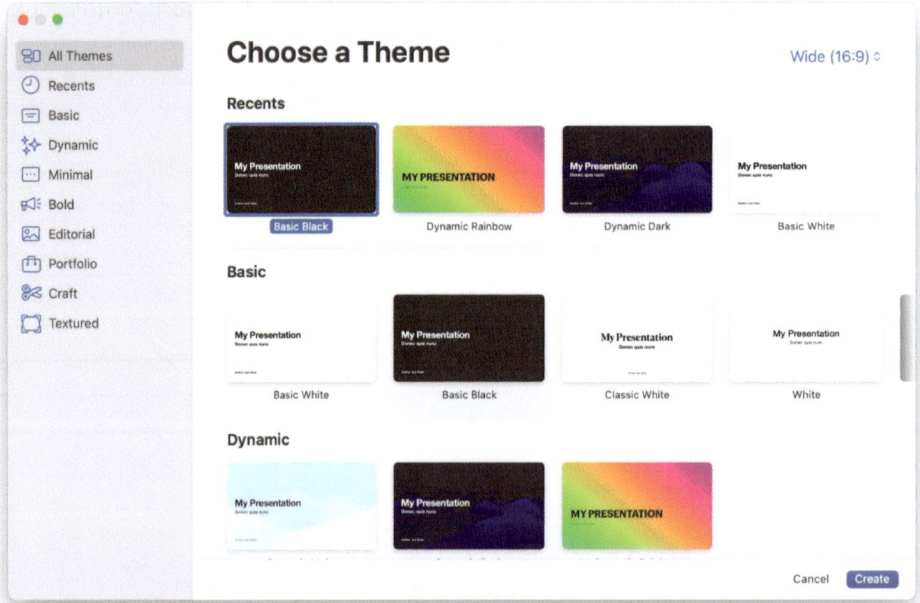

Figure 7.1 – The Keynote theme chooser

For creating titles with alpha channels, we want the simplest presentation possible. Select the **Basic Black** format, then click **Create**.

4. You'll now be in the main slide editing menu. Click on the background of the slide: you'll know if you've done this because the **Format** sidebar on the right-hand side will have the **Slide** heading, as in *Figure 7.2*.

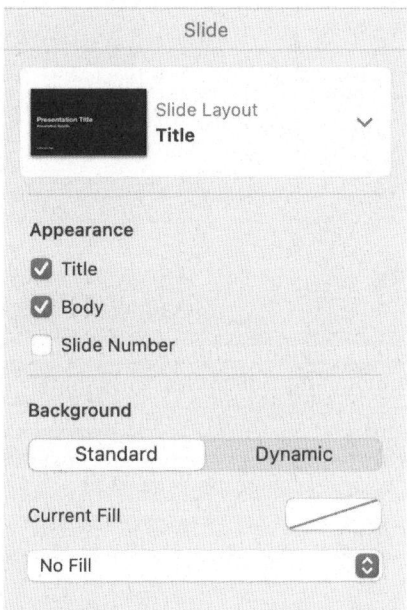

Figure 7.2 – The correct settings for making an alpha channel slide

5. Look for the **Current Fill** option at the bottom of the sidebar. This is the option that decides the color of the back of the slide. To get an alpha channel, we need no color there at all, so click the drop-down menu and select **No Fill**.

6. Depending on what kind of title you want to create, remove the unnecessary text boxes by clicking on them and hitting **backspace**.

   I like to remove the **Presentation Subtitle** and **Author and Date** boxes to leave just the main title to customize.

7. Double-click on **Presentation Title** and type the text you want in your title. Now **triple-click** or press ⌘ + *A* to select all the text, as in *Figure 7.3*.

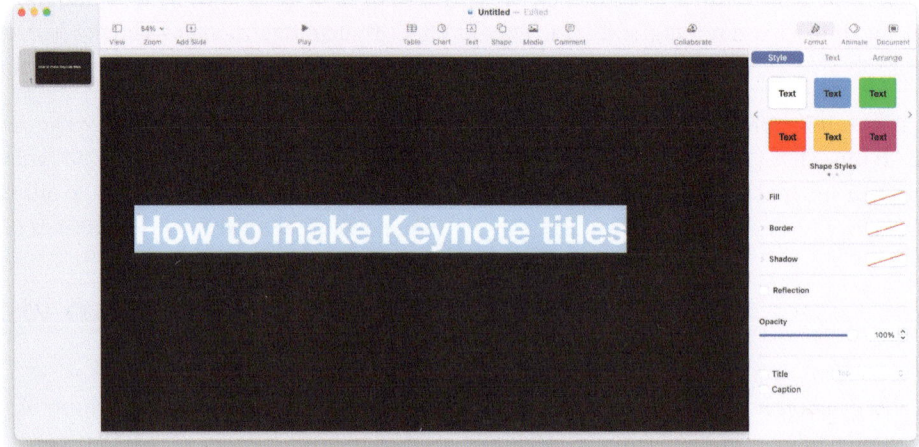

Figure 7.3 – Selecting text in the Keynote slide

8. When you look at the **Format** sidebar now, there should be three tabs: **Style**, **Text**, and **Arrange**. To change the font and text color, click on **Text**.

9. You can make whatever changes to the font you like, but I would definitely advise giving the font a drop shadow, which makes it stand out from your video background. To create a drop shadow, click on the cog icon below the point size indicator (circled in *Figure 7.4*), and then check the **Shadow** box in the hover menu that appears.

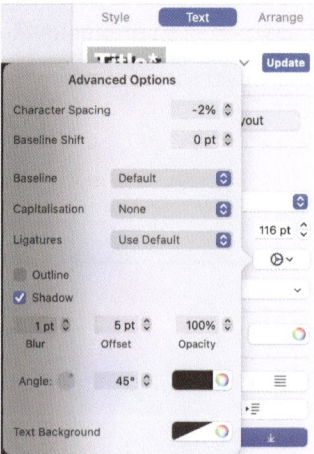

Figure 7.4 – You can customize the shadow to your heart's content, but having one is the most important thing

10. You now have a Keynote file that works as a great foundation for creating custom titles. Before you customize this title further, save the document with ⌘ + S and choose a location and name that are easy to remember.

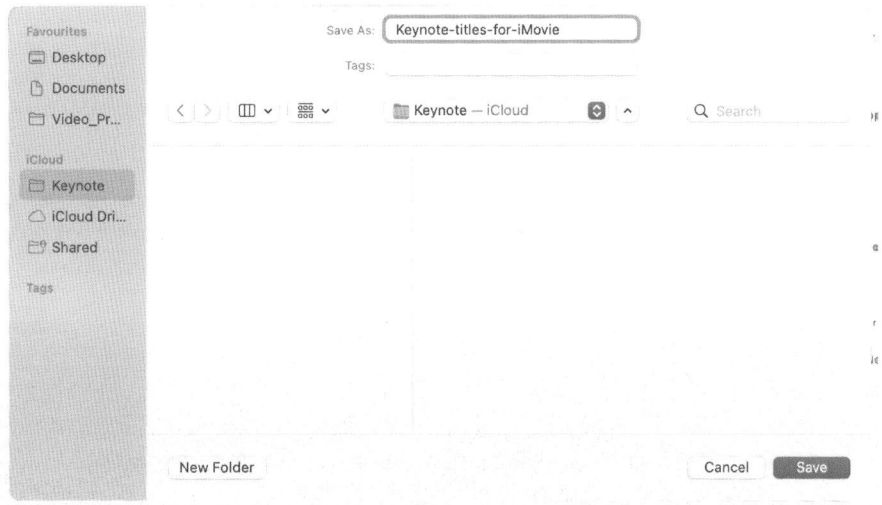

Figure 7.5 – An ideal save location for your title files

The default save location is Keynote's iCloud folder, and I'd definitely suggest keeping your title documents there. Keynote files (.Key) are small files and won't take up much iCloud storage, and having them to hand in your iCloud Drive means that you can always access your title documents on any Apple device you own, as long as you're connected to the internet.

Exporting Keynote titles

Now that you have a good stock title that you can rename and reformat for different needs, it's time to have a go exporting the title and bringing it into iMovie. It's the options you choose in the export menu that decide whether your title works in iMovie, so make sure to follow along to get some practice with your title:

1. When you're happy with your title slide, click on the slide to check once more that **Background** is set to **No Fill**.
2. In the menu bar, click **File** | **Export to** | **Images…** (there is no keyboard shortcut for this).

3. You'll be shown the **Export Your Presentation** menu. Make sure you're on the **Images** tab; you should see the menu in *Figure 7.6*.

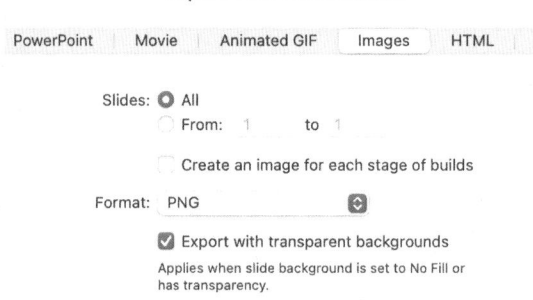

Figure 7.6 – The Keynote export menu for images

4. If you have more than one slide (usually for different titles), click the **From** circle and change the number in both boxes to be the slide number you want to export (e.g., `1` to `1`).

5. Make sure the format is set to **PNG** or **TIFF** in the drop-down menu, and tick the **Export with transparent backgrounds** box if it isn't ticked already.

6. Click **Next…** at the bottom right of the menu and choose an appropriate place to save the title. If you set up a dedicated video folder in Finder, as we talked about in *Chapter 5*, it would be a good idea to save the title image there.

> **Images and transparency**
>
> When looking up images with no background, some people put `PNG` in the search to make sure they get something with transparency rather than a white background (in search engines, transparency looks white).
>
> Unfortunately, they often don't find what they're looking for. That's because the `.PNG` format *allows* images to have an alpha channel but doesn't *give* them one. It's useful to remember the following:
>
> > `.JPEG` files cannot carry transparency
>
> > `.PNG`, `.HEIC`, and `.TIFF` files can carry transparency
>
> `.PNG` is often the best choice because it has great compatibility but cleverly compresses images to give you small files compared to `.TIFF`, which is a lossless image format.

Importing Keynote files into iMovie

When you've exported your `.PNG` image from Keynote, you can import it into iMovie. Because they have a transparent background, these title images can be used as cutaways or PiP. For the most flexibility, it's best to use title images in a PiP format. That allows you to resize the title to make the text fill the screen or move the title around with keyframe animations. Here's how to get your title in the timeline:

1. Open iMovie and double-click on the project you want to use the title in.
2. Click on the **Project Media** tab and press the import shortcut ⌘ + *I*.
3. Locate and import the title image. It will be in a folder with the name you gave when you exported from Keynote, and the first title image will have `.001` added to the filename, even if you didn't export multiple images.

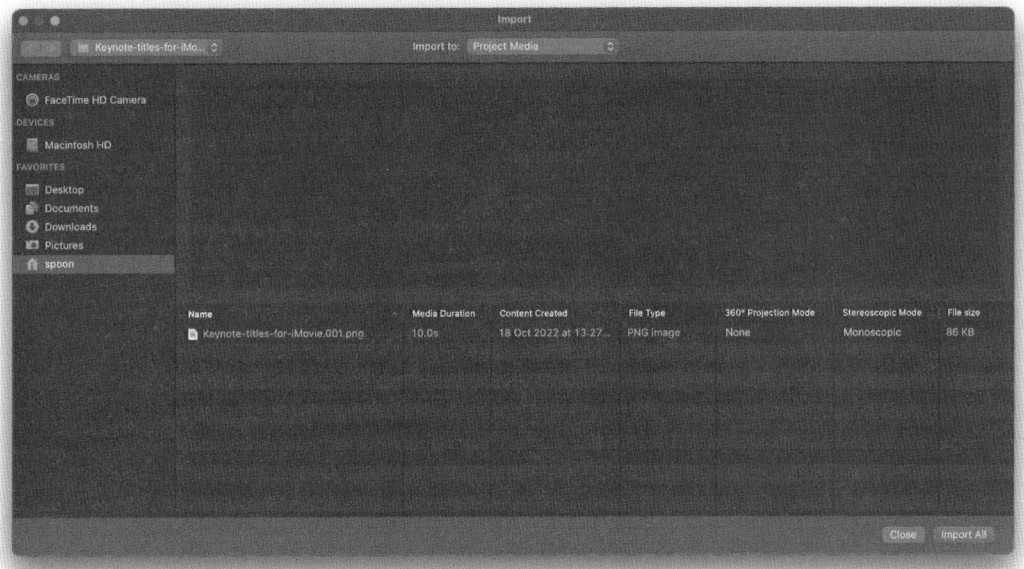

Figure 7.7 – The exported Keynote title in the iMovie import menu

4. Go to the **Backgrounds** Media Browser tab (⌘ + *4*) or find a clip of your choice to act as the background to the title. Add that clip to the timeline.

    As a rule, you'll want the title background to be as uncomplicated as possible. The more different colors and patterns on the background, the stronger a drop shadow or text outline you'll need to make the title readable, as in *Figure 7.8*.

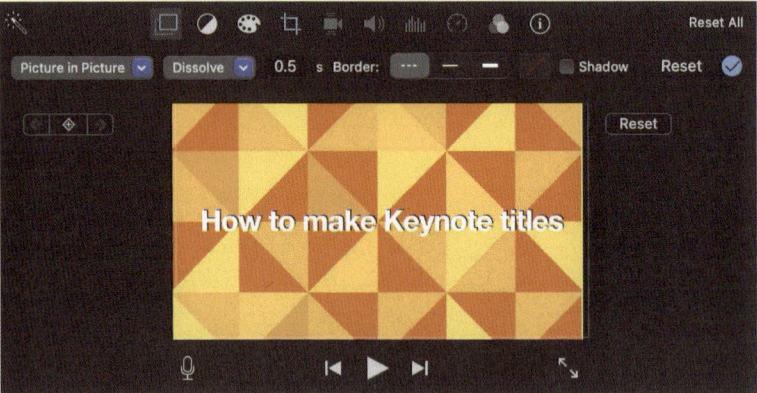

Figure 7.8 – Keynote's drop shadows help titles stand out against even complex patterns

5. Go back to the **Project Media** tab and add the title image as an overlay (*Q*).
6. Select the title image, click the **Video overlay settings** button on the toolbar and use the drop-down menu to change the overlay style to **PiP**.
7. If you want the title to come up instantly, drag the fade handles to the edge of the clip on the timeline. Alternatively, change the transition duration to 0 in the **duration editor** box (*Figure 7.8*).
8. Click and drag the blue handles at the corner of the PiP outwards to make the title larger until it fits most of the screen.

   For a title that's pleasing to the eye, ensure the PiP snaps against the yellow vertical and horizontal symmetry lines in the Viewer.

You don't need to have a title that fills the screen or is symmetrical, but remember, if you're being unconventional, do it for a reason: the audience will notice.

That covers things for custom static titles in Keynote. Change the color and font of your text, and mess around with **Advanced Options** (the cog icon) in Keynote for shadow weight, blur and opacity, character and line spacing, and more, to get just the title you want. The process for exporting and importing into iMovie will be the same however you design your static title. Now, we're going to take a look at animating titles, which requires a slightly different export process to allow the animation to be captured.

Creating animated titles in Keynote

In iMovie, you'll be familiar with titles that ripple, fade, and expand into place. You can also do this with Keynote using its **Build In** / **Action** / **Build Out** animations. You may be familiar with these kinds of animations from *PowerPoint* presentations: text falling, speeding, and swirling onto the screen. With Keynote, we can apply these animations and still export just the title with an alpha channel behind it. So, here's how to create a title that introduces itself:

1. Open the Keynote file you created for iMovie titles.
2. Click on the text box around your text and click **Animate** at the top right of Keynote's toolbar (*Figure 7.9*).

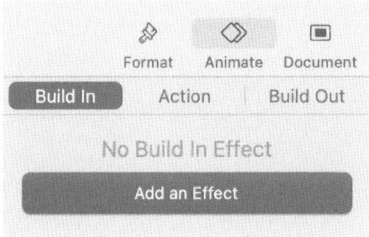

Figure 7.9 – The Animate sidebar

3. The **Build In** section should be highlighted, but select that tab if not. Click on the **Add an Effect** button.
4. There are a huge number of effects you can place on your title text: they're shown in different sections for different types of movement. Hover over an effect and click **Preview** on the right of it to see what the animation looks like.
5. When you've decided on an effect, click it, and a customization menu will appear in the **Animate** sidebar. The options will vary based on the animation you choose, but most allow you to change the following:

   - **Duration** of the animation
   - **Direction** of the animation (from the left or the right)
   - **Delivery** (allowing you to break up animations for larger bits of text, slow the start and end of animations, or add extra icons to the animation)
   - **Order** (ignore this for now unless it's not **1**, we'll cover this in the *Creating multi-stage animations with Build Order* section of this chapter).

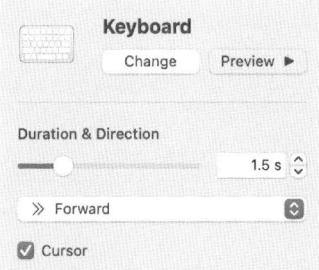

Figure 7.10 - The Keyboard animation makes it look like your title is being typed in real time and has an animated cursor you can add

6. Once you've fine-tuned the animation settings, click **Preview** to check that the text appears in the way you'd like. If not, keep making small changes and previewing them until you're happy with the title animation.

Exporting animated titles from Keynote

When you're happy, it's time to export. Because we have an animation that takes time to complete, we can't export the title as an image. Instead, we need to export a Movie and change its settings to preserve the transparency of the slide.

1. Go to **File | Export To | Movie…** in the menu bar.
2. Make sure the slide range is as you intend (e.g., 3 to 3 if you're exporting one animated title of many).
3. At the bottom of the menu is the **Resolution** drop-down menu. Click on that and select **Custom…**.
4. A few extra options appear. Check that **Frame Rate** is the same as your project, and change it if need be using the drop-down menu.
5. The option we need to change in order to export with an alpha channel is **Compression Type**. Click on that drop-down menu and select **HEVC**.
6. The final option below this menu will now become selectable. Check the **Export with transparent backgrounds** box if it isn't already ticked. The menu should look like *Figure 7.11*:

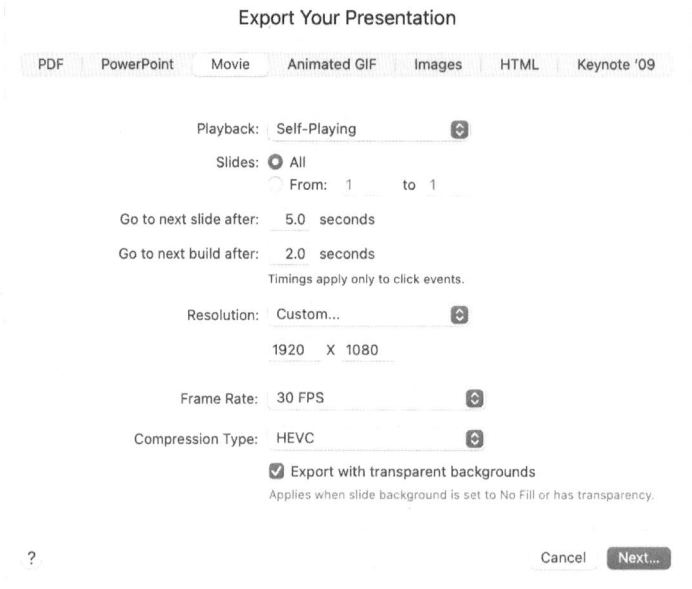

Figure 7.11 – Use these settings as a basis for exporting your animated title

7. Click **Next...** and save the video file to your project folder.

> **Exporting transparency in video**
>
> We saw earlier that `.PNG` and `.TIFF` files carry transparency, but `.JPEG` files don't. With videos, many formats actually remove transparency. In the Keynote export menu, the two **Compression Type** options that keep transparency are:
>
> > **HEVC**
>
> > **Apple ProRes 4444**
>
> Like `.PNG`, **High-Efficiency Video Coding (HEVC)** creates smaller files that keep transparency and most of their quality. ProRes 4444 delivers a file that's almost totally uncompressed and like `.TIFF`, means the file is going to be massive. It's very unlikely you'll need the extra detail ProRes 4444 allows.

After you've exported your animated title from Keynote, the process for importing it into your timeline is very similar to the process for images. One thing to note, though, is that when you add your title clip to the timeline, you may see that the title only starts its animation midway through the clip. It's nothing to worry about – it's just because we haven't edited the **build order** settings for the animation. That's something we're going to look at next.

Creating multi-stage animations with Build Order

At the moment, we have a title that builds in (appears with an animation). We're going to add to this by creating a second part of our title that animates using a different effect. So, let's add another text box to our title slide and give that a **Build In** animation:

1. Open the Keynote title slide you were working on.
2. Click once on the title text box; copy and paste it (⌘ + C and ⌘ + V) to ensure your second text box has the same style settings for the text.
3. Triple-click the new text box to select all the text, and type your new title.

4. Check the **Animate** sidebar for your second text box and make sure **Order** shows **2**, as shown in *Figure 7.12*.

Figure 7.12 – The Animate sidebar for the second text box

5. At the top of the **Animate** sidebar, click **Change** and choose a new animation. I've chosen **Sparkle** to compliment the text.

6. It's now time to make these animations work together. At the very bottom of the **Animate** sidebar, click on the **Build Order** button.

7. In the **Build Order** menu that comes up (*Figure 7.13*), click on the second animation and change the **Start** drop-down menu to **With Build 1**.

Using these build events instead of click events means that animations will now automatically follow each other rather than following delays that Keynote puts in automatically.

Figure 7.13 – The Build Order menu should look something like this

8. Click **Preview** at the bottom of the menu: both text boxes should animate at the same time.
9. To change how the animation looks, you can change the following options:

    - The duration of each transition
    - The delay on the second animation

This is now the time to take charge and change the settings according to your creative vision. Make little changes and evaluate them. Then, repeat. To illustrate the controls, I'm going to give examples of what I'd change to refine these animations.

At 1.5 seconds, the **Keyboard** animation looks too quick when I preview it – certainly for my typing speed! To make it look more like natural typing, I'm going to slow it down. To do that:

10. Click on the first animation in the **Build Order** menu. In the **Animate** sidebar, drag the **Duration** slider. Preview and evaluate: `2.5` seconds seems natural but not too slow.

    Now I'd like the second title to build in when the first animation is nearly complete. To do that, we need a delay similar to the duration for the first transition.

11. Click on the second transition in the **Build Order** menu and edit the value in the **Delay** box. Preview and evaluate: a delay of `1.8` seconds works well.

Figure 7.14 – It's unlikely a hundredth of a second makes a difference, but you can set delays to two decimal places if you want

When you're happy with your title, it's time to export this title as a video with exactly the same export settings as before. However, now that we are using build order (**With Build 1**) instead of click events,

Keynote is going to use the delay we've set between transitions instead of choosing its own delay. If you want the animation to start as soon as the video begins, you'll need to click on the first animation in the **Build Order** menu and change **On Click** to **After Transition**. With that covered, we're now going to add to our animation build order even further by animating the titles off the screen too.

Building out animations

We've got animations that introduce our titles, but at the moment, they just sit there until the clip ends. We could just fade them out by pressing ⌥ and clicking and dragging the fade handle at the end of the clip on the timeline, but say we want to animate the titles out of view too – how do we do that?

1. Click on the first text box again.
2. In the **Animate** sidebar, click on **Build Out** and then **Add an Effect**.

You're now creating a separate animation on the same text box, but don't worry – the **Build In** animation isn't being overwritten. Any object in Keynote can have one **Build In** animation, one **Action** (see the next section), and one **Build Out** animation. All of them will be shown in the **Build Order** menu.

3. Choose a **Build Out** effect by clicking on it, then repeat these steps *1-3* for the second text box.

For my first text box (with the Keyboard animation), I've selected **Keyboard** again as its **Build Out** animation. On the **Animation** sidebar, I set **Build Out Direction** for the **Keyboard** animation to << **Backward**. This makes it look like the text is being deleted with the backspace key. For the second text box (with the **Sparkle** animation), I've chosen **Vanish** as its **Build Out** animation.

4. Click on the **Build Order** button – if you're following along, the menu should look something like *Figure 7.15*, depending on the animations you've chosen.

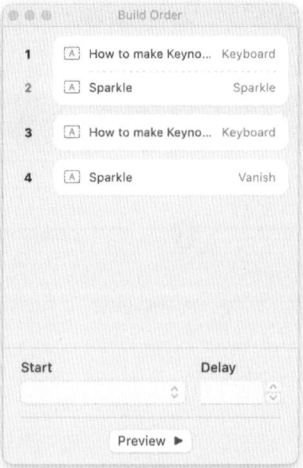

Figure 7.15 – All the Build In and Build Out actions we'll be using

Now we have all the actions in place; it's time to organize them in the **Build Order** menu. Firstly, we need to make sure that all the animations take place automatically:

5. At the moment, Builds **3** and **4** are set to start **On Click** – we can see that from the way their banners are visually separated from the other builds in the menu.
6. Click on Build **3** and choose **After Build 2** from the **Start** drop-down menu.
7. Click on Build **4** and, in that same drop-down menu, choose **With Build 3**. The **Build Order** menu should now look like it does in *Figure 7.16*.

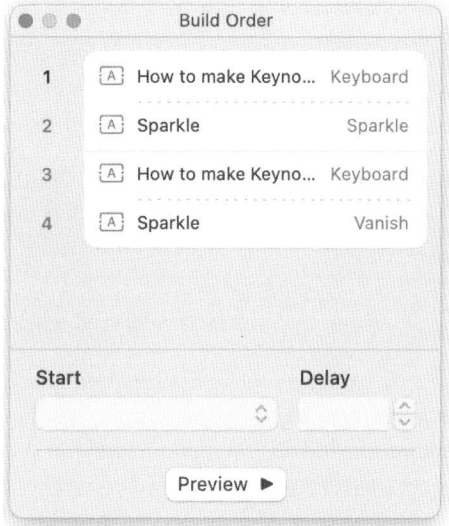

Figure 7.16 – Together, these four builds complete the Build In and Build Out animations

Keynote also has a helpful visual shorthand that tells you what the builds are doing at a glance. You may notice that in *Figure 7.16*, there are incomplete dotted lines between some builds and complete solid lines between others:

- A dotted line between two builds means they happen *with* one another
- A solid line between two builds means they happen *after* one another

Looking at these lines helps you more easily see the relationship between your animations, thus making it easier to target and change the correct delays and actions when building more complex animations.

Our next job is to set the delay for the **Build Out** animations. This will decide how long the title as a whole stays on screen before building out, and change whether both text boxes build out at the same time.

8. Click on Build **3** and type a time in the **Delay** box. Hit *Enter* to save the changes.

    I've gone for a 2-second delay, but your choice depends on how long you want your title to stay on screen.

Preview the animation, and you'll be able to see if anything's gone wrong, and you can evaluate it to decide what you want to change. I'd like my **Vanish** animation to complete at the same time as the **Keyboard** animation but without the animations starting at the same time. To do this, we need to delay the start of one animation but make sure that its animation takes less time to complete. That way, the total time of *delay + duration* is the same for both.

9. Click on Build **4** in the **Build Order** menu and add a delay of 0.5 seconds. Hit *Enter* to save your changes.

10. Click on Build **3**. In the **Animate** sidebar, edit **Duration** so that it's 0.5 seconds longer than Build **4** (e.g., 2.5 seconds versus 2 seconds).

Previewing the animation, we can see that although the timings are correct, **Vanish** causes the word to disappear into dust before the animation completes. To fix this, I'm going to do the following:

11. Add an extra 1 second of delay to Build **4** (**Vanish**) so that the word **Sparkle** disappears when the **Keyboard** animation ends (as seen in *Figure 7.17*).

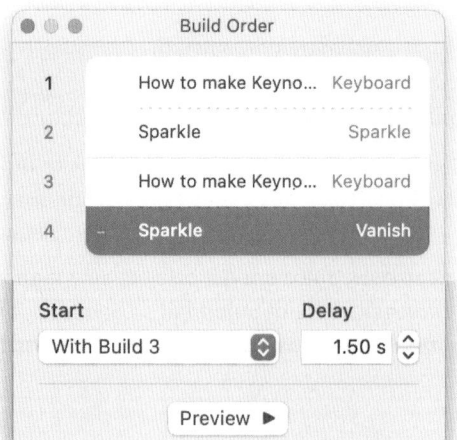

Figure 7.17 – Build 4 with added delay

And that's the animation – with two text boxes building in and building out – completed. Time to export.

Exporting, importing, and adjusting multi-stage animations

Because we've already exported an animated title clip, we're going to make use of some of the tricks of the timeline to make the process of bringing in an updated title clip a little bit easier:

1. Go to **File | Export To | Movie…**.
2. Make sure the compression type is still **HEVC** and **Export with transparent backgrounds** is ticked.
3. Click **Next…** and save the video file in your project folder.
4. Go to the relevant project in iMovie and import the file with ⌘ + I.
5. Before you bring the new title video into the timeline, copy the old title clip (⌘ + C).
6. Select the new clip in the Media Browser; click and drag it over the old one (overwriting it).
7. Select the new clip and paste the overlay settings from the old clip (⌥ + ⌘ + U). This saves making the same PiP adjustments again.

Also, now that we've built the animation for the title, we can make changes to the formatting of the title without having to reorganize the **Build Order** menu. If you've imported the title video into iMovie and decide the shadows need moving again, or you want to entirely change the color of the titles, you can do so without needing to change or re-edit the animations. For *Figure 7.17*, I went back into Keynote and made the following changes using the **Format** sidebar:

- In the **Text Color** drop-down menu, I added **color fill** to all words except **Keynote**, which got a **gradient fill** of yellow to blue
- I created an **image fill** with polka dots for **Sparkle**
- Using the cog menu, I oriented the shadows to the bottom of the words and increased their blur

It's not necessarily a title I'd submit for any beauty contests, but it does show how creative you can get with formatting. If you are planning to make a bit of an out-there title like *Figure 7.17*, first of all, make sure there's a good creative reason for it. Then make sure it has stronger drop shadows or outlines around the letters to make sure it stands out well against the background. Wherever the situation, there's no use in having a title the audience can't read.

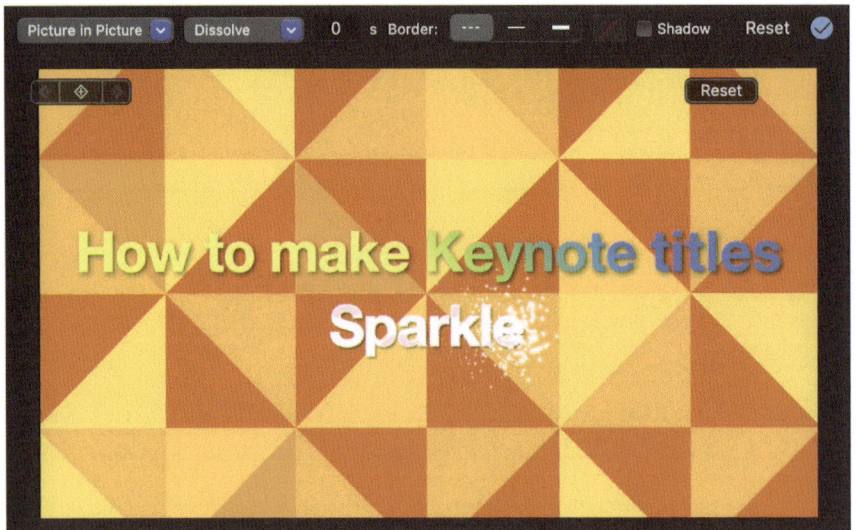

Figure 7.18 – The full animated title with formatting changed. I've also removed the fade handles in iMovie

And that's the expansive world of titles in Keynote. But that's not all the app is good for. In the **Animate** tab, between the **Build In** and **Build Out** actions is the **Actions** tab. This allows you to **Move** any object on screen with an animation path of your own choice, and that opens up a world of possibilities for creating professional-looking animations.

Creating path animations with Keynote

You can already animate images and video in iMovie with keyframes, so why would you want to do this in Keynote? Well, animation in Keynote has three key advantages over iMovie, and if any of them are crucial to your project, you'll want to use Keynote instead:

- You can export animations with transparent backgrounds
- You can animate multiple objects at once
- You can rotate objects to a 1-degree accuracy and rotate relative to a path

We've already seen the advantages that exporting with transparency can give us when it comes to titles. Let's explore the other advantages by animating a little scene of a countryside road. The following image has been created entirely in Keynote, and the file is available in `Chapter 7: Keynote Car Animation` in the book resources. There you can open the file see the color and gradient tweaks, stock shapes, and use of the Keynote Pen tool that helped create it. But at the moment, it's a still image. Your mission – should you choose to accept it – is to get some movement in the frame.

Figure 7.19 – The Keynote scene we'll be working with

Our goal is to guide the car on the far left of the image across the road in a natural-looking way. With a curved road, this would be impossible in iMovie. The best you could do with keyframing is to create a shape that looks curved by setting tens and tens of keyframes. This would make the car follow the course of the road, but crucially, the car won't turn to follow the road: it'll look like it's sliding the whole way. Here's how to create the path in Keynote:

1. Click on the car, which has multiple shapes grouped into one so that you can animate the whole thing at once.
2. Go to the **Animate** sidebar, click **Action** and then **Add an Effect**.
3. The **Move** action is the one we want for path animations; click that. You'll see a faded version of the car joined by a line to the original car.

    - The red line is the animation path
    - The faded car is where the animation path ends
    - The red diamond lets you add an animation when you click on it. If you click off the **Move** animation, clicking the diamond again will open the path editor back up.

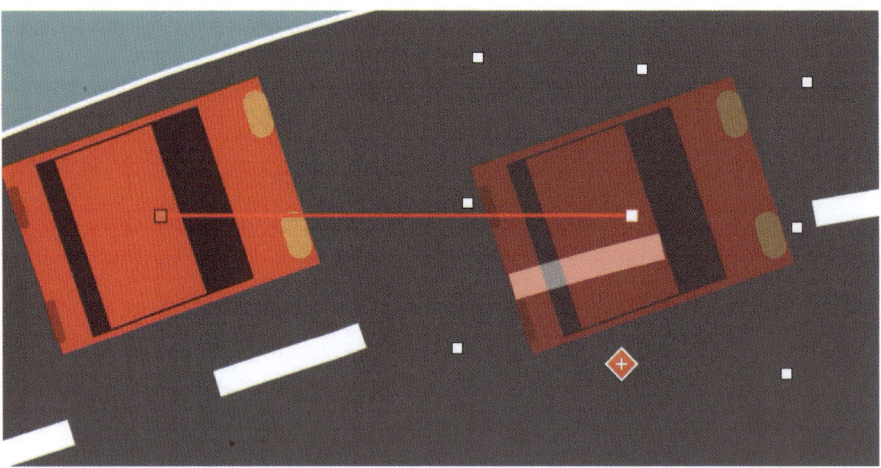

Figure 7.20 – The car and the animation path

4. Click on the faded car and drag it to the end of the road. Like the original car, it should be facing in a natural-looking direction for the road.

At the moment, the animation path of the car is straight, but adding curves to follow the road is pretty easy:

5. When we hover over the animation path, we see a white circle (a keyframe) in the middle. Click and drag the circle to where the road curves the furthest upward (circled in *Figure 7.20*).

Figure 7.21 – The keyframe (circled) turns red when you select it

6. Now you've moved the first white circle, a new white circle will appear around the clump of three trees when you hover over the animation path.
7. Click and drag the new white circle to where the road curves the furthest down. The area to aim for is shown in a square in *Figure 7.20*.
8. Now, the car will follow the road in a smooth path from the start to the end point of the animation. To make the car rotate correctly to follow the road like a car really would, go back to the **Animate** sidebar and tick the **Align to Path** box.

For such a simple option, **Align to Path** is a lifesaver. And with that, the animation path is sorted. But we still need to make the speed of movement look natural and to make the car look like it's coming from somewhere and is going somewhere. Take the following steps to do so:

9. Still in the **Animate** sidebar, change **Duration** to something above 5 seconds, so the car doesn't move too quickly. Hit *Enter* to save the duration change.

The car will now drive at a reasonable speed along our road, but at the moment, it's starting and stopping on the road. To make it look like our piece of road is just part of a larger road the car has been driving on, do the following:

10. Click on the square in the middle of the car at the start of the animation path and drag it outside of the slide. Zooming out of the slide with ⇧ + ⌘ + , (comma) will help with this.
11. Do the same with the faded car at the end of the animation path.
12. In the **Acceleration** drop-down menu, select **None**; otherwise, it won't look like the car has been driving before entering the frame.

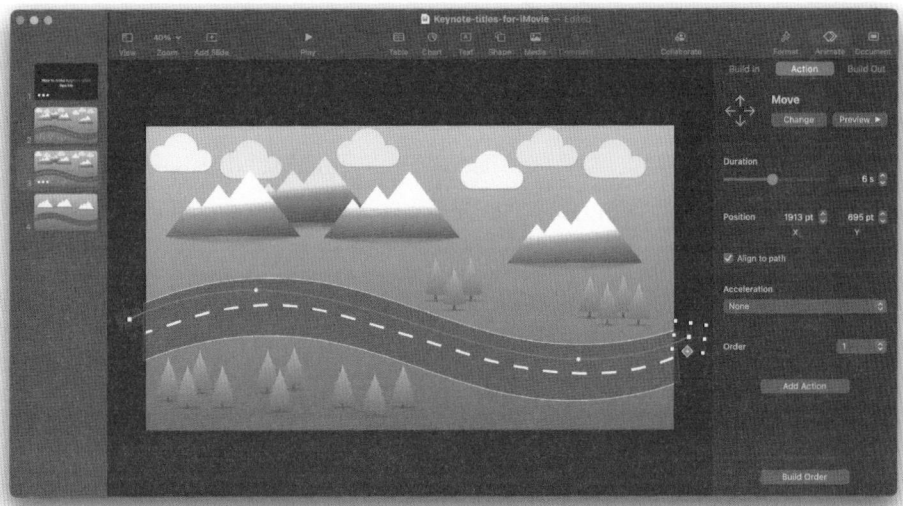

Figure 7.22 – The completed animation

If you click off the animation path and can't see the red diamond outside the frame slide, click the **Build Order** button at the bottom of the **Animate** menu. Then click on the Build for the car (**Group**), and the path will reappear. Now it's time to review and evaluate: when you watch the animation, check for the car exiting the road at any time or perhaps going too straight. To make the curve smoother, do the following:

13. Hover over the animation path and click and drag another white circle. You may want to do the same further down the road to balance out the curve again.

As a guide for the white circle keyframes, they always appear exactly in the middle of the two nearest keyframes. You can drag them wherever you'd like, as long as you don't cross over the next keyframe.

But what about the other advantage of animating with Keynote? Well, now we've done the hard bit of getting to grips with animations, it's easier to add more of them. Let's have another car going the opposite way and get those clouds moving:

14. Copy the car (⌘ + C) and paste it (⌘ + V) on the other side of the road.
15. Click the **Format** sidebar. Click and drag the circle on the **Rotate** tool (*Figure 7.22*) to turn the car to face the opposite direction.

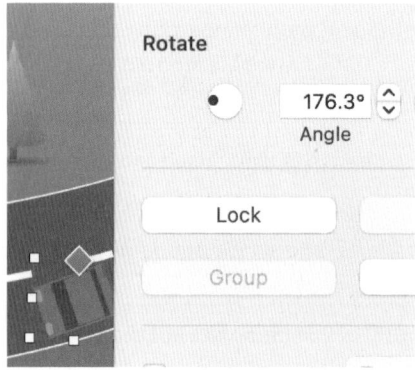

Figure 7.23 – Objects in Keynote can be rotated to an accuracy of one-tenth of a degree

16. Go to the **Build Order** menu and hit *backspace* to delete the animation path for the second car (as it currently goes in the wrong direction).
17. Click on **Animate | Action | Add an Effect | Move**, then follow steps *4–13* again to create a smooth animation for the second car (you can do it!).
18. Go to the **Build Order** menu, change the second car to animate **With Build 1**, and add a delay so that the cars drive across the road at different times (*Figure 7.23*).

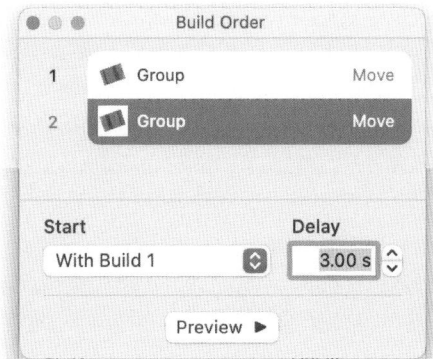

Figure 7.24 – Delaying the second car's journey

Finally, let's sort out the clouds. As there are so many, we're going to animate them all at once:

19. Use ⇧ + *click* to select every cloud, then click **Animate** | **Action** | **Add an Effect** | **Move**.
20. Change **Duration** to `10` seconds or more and select **None** under **Acceleration**.
21. With the clouds still selected, open the **Build Order** menu and select **With Previous Build** under the **Start** drop-down menu.

Preview and evaluate: both cars should go on normal-looking journeys while the clouds slowly, imperceptibly move above them. How lovely. Perhaps even more lovely that you've made this all in Keynote – very impressive. If something's clearly wrong, check back over the steps, especially steps *4–13*, for repeating the animation path for the second car. You'll have to adjust the keyframes to sit within the other lane, but the principle is the same: one keyframe at the peak of the top bend, one at the trough of the bottom bend.

When you're ready to export this animation, the process is much simpler than before because we don't have any alpha channels in this scene:

22. Go to **File** | **Export To** | **Movie….**
23. Click **Next…** and save to a place you'll remember. That's it!

Toward the end of this process, we looked at animating multiple objects at once. The next animation feature we're going to look at helps you to do this, but with entire slides instead of objects.

Using Magic Move animations

Not to be confused with Magic Movie, Magic Move is a Keynote feature that creates a smooth animation between slides, with the individual slides acting as the keyframes. Whatever the state of slide one, it will transition to look like slide two when you place a Magic Move transition on it. It's a tool principally used for jazzing up slide transitions with ease, but it also has uses in animating objects for videos.

Apart from taking care of all the animations on a screen at once, Magic Move can help you get around certain limits. For example, when we use the **Scale** action on a tiny shape, the maximum increase in size of 1,000% only increases the circle to a modest size. This means that if you were trying to create a custom transition such as the one I was keying green out of in the *Using Green/Blue Screen effects* section of *Chapter 5*, the circle wouldn't be able to scale large enough to fill the screen and hide the cut to the next clip.

If, however, you had a tiny circle on one slide and the same circle resized to fill the whole slide on the next, Magic Move would allow us to transition between them. Moving shapes in this way is the foundation of creating custom transitions, and so as our final task in this chapter, we're going to create one. First, though, let's look at how to use Magic Move:

1. In the Keynote toolbar, click **Add Slide** or use the shortcut ⇧ + ⌘ + N.

    To follow on exactly with the slide numbers quoted, you might want to create a new basic presentation (⌘ + N), so you can start on slide one.

2. Remove any text boxes on the slide.

3. Click **Shape** in the toolbar, and under **Basic**, click the circle.

4. Change its color in the **Format** sidebar if you wish.

5. Click on one of the square points around the circle and drag inwards while holding ⇧ + ⌥ (as in *Figure 7.24*).

    ⇧ + ⌥ makes sure the shape retains its lines of symmetry so doesn't become skewed or irregular. When resizing, make sure to release your click before you release the shortcut keys.

6. Zoom into the slide with ⇧ + ⌘ + . (full stop) as far as you can, so that you can still see the circle when it gets really small. A hovering tooltip tells you the size of the shape: keep shrinking the circle until it's about **5pt**.

Using Magic Move animations   203

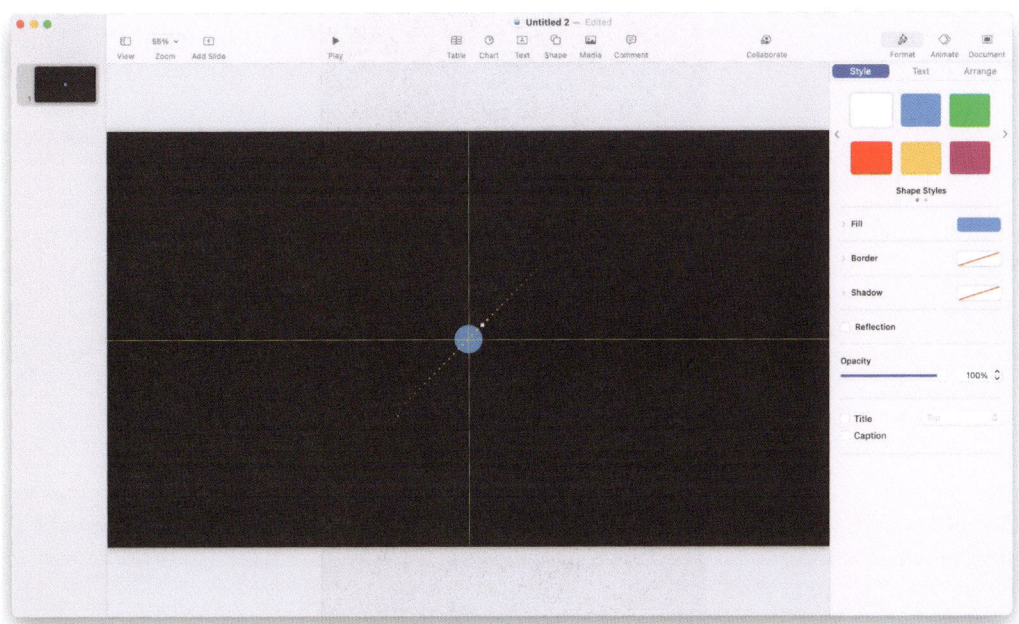

Figure 7.25 – Making the circle super small so that our transition looks like it starts from nothing

7. Click on the slide in the left-hand panel (**Slide Navigator**) and duplicate it with ⌘ + D.
8. On the duplicated slide, click the circle and drag outward while holding ⌥ + ⇧ until the circle fills out the entire frame. You'll need to stop mid-way and zoom out of the slide (⇧ + ⌘ + ,) in order to do this.

Figure 7.26 – The two slides that will make up the Magic Move

9. Click back on the first slide and click on the **Animate** sidebar.
10. Click **Add an Effect** | **Magic Move**

When you preview the Magic Move, the tiny circle in the first slide should smoothly increase in size until it fills the entire slide. That is your first Magic Move complete. But what does this have to do with custom transitions?

Custom transitions using overlays

As we discussed in previous chapters, at its most basic level, a transition takes us from clip one to clip two. Most transitions manipulate the frame itself to make a transition, whether that's a drop in opacity until the next clip takes over (dissolve) or the new clip wiping or sliding over the old one.

However, the transition we are creating here is an object that will fill the frame. With the audience distracted by the object filling the screen, the footage can change in the background without the audience seeing the cut. Going to such lengths to obscure the cut may seem peculiar, but it's useful if you want to transition to footage that your audience is unlikely to expect. Live sports, for example, often use these overlay transitions to introduce a live replay, which is both going back in time and showing the audience something they've already seen. Having a transition that announces itself in this way helps the audience to understand that their TV sets haven't suddenly got stuck on repeat. That way, they can enjoy the live replay.

Creating simple transitions with Magic Move

Now we know what animated transitions are used for, and what they usually involve, let's create one using the circle we animated with Magic Move. We're going to use the circle to obscure the screen and then use another Magic Move to return that circle to its original position. Then, we'll export the transition for use in iMovie.

1. If you haven't already, go to the **Background** drop-down menu on the **Format** sidebar and change the background of your slides from **Color Fill** to **No Fill**.
2. Duplicate the first slide and drag it to the bottom of **Slide Navigator**.
3. Select the second slide (the one with the circle filling the side), and click **Animate | Add an Effect | Magic Move**.

Magic Moves don't appear in the **Build Order** menu, so we need to string the builds together using **Slide Navigator** and the **Animate** sidebar (*Figure 7.24*).

1. Click on **Slide Navigator** and press ⌘ + A to select all the slides.
2. In the **Animate** sidebar, set the **Start Transition** drop-down menu to **Automatically**. The other default settings work just fine for this transition.

Figure 7.27 – The Magic Move controls in the Animate panel

Setting multiple Magic Moves has allowed us to chain the animation across multiple slides. This makes the animation easier to edit and understand at a glance because you don't have to add two different animation paths for the same object on the same slide. However, because Magic Moves have no build order settings, it isn't possible to animate different objects at different times. This means that if you want two animations to interact with one another, falling in and out of sync for visual interest, as we did previously in the chapter, you will need to use the standard animation actions.

Exporting and importing multi-stage Magic Move animations

Because we're using multiple slides, the export process changes to include a range of slides. To export your Magic Move transition, do the following:

1. Go to **File | Export To | Movie…**
2. Choose the correct slide range. If you created a new **Keynote** document, **All** or Slides 1 to 3 both work.
3. Select the **Custom…** resolution from the drop-down menu.
4. Choose the **HEVC** compression type and tick **Export with transparent backgrounds**.

5. Click **Next…**, choose an appropriate name, and save the location.

Figure 7.28 – The Magic Move animation represented in the QuickTime Player video strip

With your three slide range exported as a video with transparency, it's time to import to iMovie to see if the transition works. In iMovie, take the following steps:

1. Import your exported transition with the ⌘ + *I* import menu.

   If you created an Event for custom animations as I mentioned in *Chapter 4*, click the drop-down menu at the top middle of the **Import** menu and choose that Event to import to.

2. Add two visually different clips to the timeline to test the transition, such as a red and green background.

3. Drag the middle of the transition clip over the edit point between the two clips, adding the clip as an overlay.

4. Hover over the transition overlay and press *C*, followed by / (forward slash). This selects the clip and plays just the transition.

5. If the transition has worked, you'll see the circle expanding over the clip in the main video layer, but you shouldn't notice one color cutting to the other because the circle fills the frame at that point. You may need to move the overlay clip to make sure that it does this.

The transition created won't be incredible – it is just one circle after all. But it certainly does the job of grabbing the audience's attention. Like everything we've looked at in this chapter, this is a jumping-off point for further exploration. Now you know the tools, you have great creative scope to create titles and animations that really reflect your video, you as a creator, or the people you're making a video for. The final kind of animation we're going to look at is much easier – almost automatic.

Dead easy animation with Dynamic Backgrounds

Introduced in Keynote version 12.1, Dynamic Backgrounds animate the background of your slide based on a series of colors you choose. If you're in a tight spot with a video where you need to fill a space and don't have B-roll to do so, dynamic backgrounds will look a little more interesting than a static image held for a long time. Using a dynamic background is no substitute for making a video full of engaging and relevant footage, but it's helpful to have a dynamic background to hand, just in case. Here's how to make and export one:

1. Create a new Keynote presentation (⌘ + *N*).

2. Choose **Dynamic Rainbow** (or **Dynamic Dark** for a darker background – both allow full customization of the colors in the animation).
3. On the **Format** panel, there is a color bar showing the gradient of different colors on the screen. You can change the colors by clicking on the markers.
4. You can also add more colors by hovering over the color bar and clicking on a space with no markers.

Figure 7.29 – The color bar for Dynamic Rainbow

5. Also, in the Format panel, you can change the following:

   - **Scale**: How close the colors appear together on the slide (a higher value means the colors are closer)
   - **Speed**: How fast the colors move across the screen

6. When you're happy, export the dynamic background as a standard 1080p video. Whatever time you set for **Go to next slide after** in the export menu will be the length of the video, so make that as long as you need.
7. Creating an iMovie Event (⌥ + N) for these backgrounds could be a good storage option for them, so they're in iMovie when you need them.

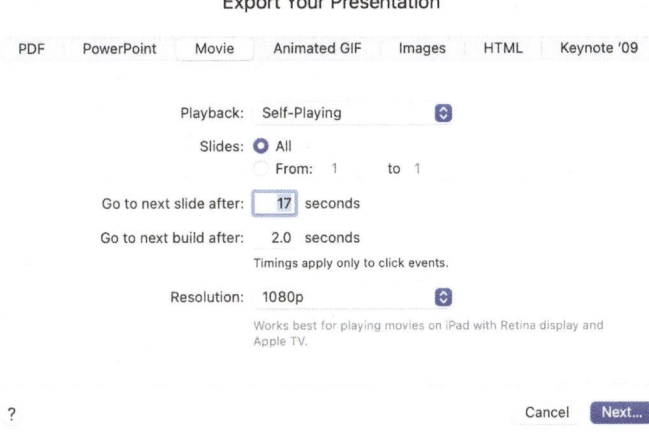

Figure 7.30 – We've ignored the "next slide" and "next build" timings so far: they are the automatic delays applied to click events

And those are dynamic backgrounds, ready for use in the direst video editing emergency. Hopefully, you won't end up in that kind of situation, though – with all you've learned in these seven chapters, you're definitely capable of making exactly the kind of video you're hoping for.

Summary

This chapter was all about using Keynote to expand your creative scope in iMovie by creating unique titles and animations. Firstly, we created and exported a static title, using the **No Fill** option for slide backgrounds so that only the text appears in iMovie.

Keynote also allows you to create and export animations as video files. Dynamic backgrounds are an easy way to fill parts of the timeline where you don't have B-roll, and they're a bit more engaging than block color backgrounds or still images. You can also animate individual elements and text on-screen in Keynote. Using **Build In** and **Build Out** animations, as well as custom export settings, we created an animated title that plays as a video in iMovie.

Moving onto more complex animations, Move animations allow us to make objects follow a path of our choosing. We used these to convincingly animate a car driving along a road. We used the **Build Order** menu to sync up multiple animations and add delays where appropriate, fine-tuning the overall animation to play exactly how we'd like.

Finally, we used Magic Move to create a custom transition that can put a unique creative stamp on your video and introduce a sudden step-change of style in your video. Keynote's high level of customization, which includes changing slide sizes, means that this isn't the last you'll see of Keynote in this book. In the next chapter, we will be using Keynote (and other programs) to customize our exports.

8
Custom Export Formats, ft. Handbrake

The creative process is over. Okay, that's a bit of a grand statement, but it's time to turn our attention to making changes to our video master copy, to make it suitable for different export locations. We've looked at making your video coherent, concise, and bursting with extra context, meaning, and your own unique style. We've made it sound good, and we've added extra effects to engage our audience. But as good as our video is, it won't be one-size-fits-all.

In earlier chapters, we briefly touched on the idea of aspect ratio, which is the relationship between the height and length of a frame. Screens are changing all the time, and content is increasingly being made specifically for portrait phone screens. Unfortunately, iMovie only allows the default 16:9 widescreen, which won't be the right shape for some destinations for your video. We need a way to put our videos in a different shape, and luckily, there's always a workaround.

There is also the matter of formats. Websites are generally very clever, accepting any kind of video file you upload and making it viewable. But it's worth understanding the different formats and technical aspects of video because if you're ever making a video for a client, they're going to have specifications that you'll need to stick to. And if you're making a video to intrigue on Instagram, or for dropping into Discord, there are going to be file size limits. The world of the web is filling up, and space is at a premium. For that reason, we're also going to look at changing our master file to fit different sizes – not just in terms of the frame, but how much space the file takes up. Armed with this knowledge, you can maximize quality without sacrificing space. The main topics we'll cover in this chapter are as follows:

- Changing the video aspect ratio
- Handbrake, and when you'd use a transcoder
- Compressing videos for file size limits

Technical requirements

In this chapter, we'll be using an app that isn't compatible with mobile devices, so you will need a Mac to follow the steps. ProRes exports, which we'll be looking at further in the *What is ProRes?* section of this chapter, are is only available on the macOS version of iMovie.

This is also the first chapter in which we'll be downloading something outside of the App Store: Handbrake. Handbrake is a free, open source app that allows you to customize video outputs, and we'll be using it to convert our videos into different formats ready for exporting. It can be found on Handbrake's website at `https://handbrake.fr/`, or on GitHub at `https://github.com/HandBrake/HandBrake`.

The version of Handbrake used in this chapter is 1.6.0. Older versions are available on Handbrake's website, and you need at least version 1.4 to take advantage of speed improvements for Macs with Apple Silicon chips (M1, M2, and so on). If a newer version is available, though, there's no reason not to use the latest version available to you!

Why all this video jargon?

This book, for the most part, has tried to introduce you to just the editing terminology that you need, so you may be wondering why we're jumping into the complex world of video technology. It's because iMovie hasn't given us export flexibility in the first place. We don't need to look at complicated ways of doing other stuff in editing (chroma keying, keyframing, and so on) because iMovie makes them simpler. For exports, though, it misses out on many of the features you need to increase your creative scope and conform to the needs of different platforms. Therefore, we need to use different applications for this job, and that means that you need to know what you're looking for when you download an outside application.

Open source applications such as **Open Broadcast Software** (**OBS**) (an **encoder** – something that turns a recording into a video file) and Handbrake (a **transcoder** – something that changes information about the video file) are put together by a wonderfully generous and very clever set of volunteers. Do be aware though that these apps are very functional and feature-dense: they're aimed at being able to do as much as possible, and this can make them quite daunting for a new user. The mission of this chapter is to help you make use of the most important parts of Handbrake so that you can create a version of your video for any requirement. But before we get to all of that, we're going to revisit something we know, and which we can edit using Keynote: aspect ratio.

Working with aspect ratio

When we looked at the Ken Burns effect in *Chapter 3*, we briefly touched on aspect ratio. To recap, aspect ratio is the ratio of a video's length to its height. So, for a 16:9 screen, for every 16 pixels (it could be any unit) that we go along the screen, the screen goes 9 up. Different aspect ratios will give a video frame a different overall shape – a 4:3 frame will be taller than a 16:9 frame, so if you overlayed

4:3 footage over 16:9 footage, pillarboxes – which are the sides of the 16:9 video underneath – would show through. You would need to crop the 4:3 video to reduce its height or crop the 16:9 video to reduce its length for the two to fit the same shape of frame.

> **Aspect ratio examples**
>
> To give you an idea of what aspect ratio means in practice, here are some examples:
>
> > The modern HD TV standard is 16:9.
>
> > Old TV shows were shot in 4:3, which is taller than 16:9. This leaves pillarboxes at the side of a 16:9 screen.
>
> > Cinema widescreen goes as wide as 2.39:1, making the picture shorter and wider than most screens. This creates **letterboxes** above and below the picture when viewed on a 16:9 screen.
>
> > MacBook screens are 16:10, slightly taller than 16:9, which leaves small letterboxes when watching videos in full screen.

It's also useful to know that the resolution of any screen will tell you its aspect ratio. If you have a full HD (1920x1080) frame, it will be:

- 1,920 pixels long and 1,080 pixels tall
- If we simplify 1,920 and 1,080, we get:
  - **192:108** (1,920 and 1,080 both divided by 10)
  - **16:9** (192 and 108 both divided by 12)

Similarly, if you had a recording of your phone screen that was 720 pixels long and 1,280 high, dividing both 720 and 1,280 by 10 gives 72:128; and dividing both 72 and 128 by 8 gives us the aspect ratio **9:16**. My apologies for the heavy dose of numbers, but it's handy for seeing that resolution and aspect ratio are interlinked. Any resolution, when simplified as far as possible, tells us the aspect ratio of the frame.

On macOS, you can check the aspect ratio of a video (as well as lots of other information) by opening the inspector:

1. Right-click on a video file and select **Open With | QuickTime Player**.
2. Bring up the Video Inspector with ⌘ + *I*.

3. Open the **Video Details** drop-down menu:

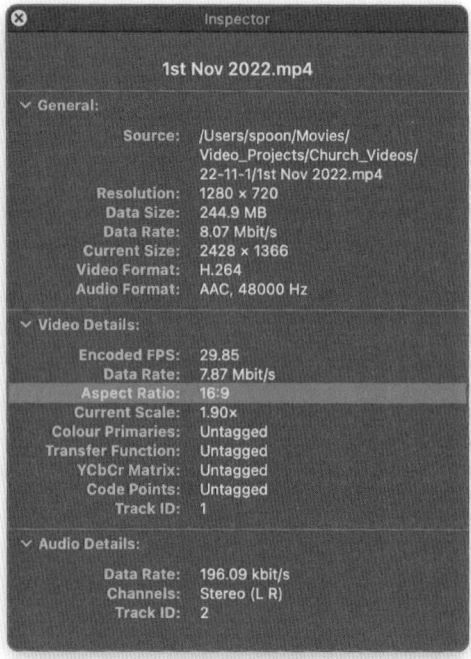

Figure 8.1 – Aspect Ratio (highlighted) in the inspector

4. Ignore the **Current Scale** information – anything with the word **Current** is referring to the size of the video window you have open on your Mac, not the video itself.

We've seen that iMovie will only export your video in 16:9, regardless of the shape of the footage that you use. If you need to change the aspect ratio, it needs to be done outside of the app. You can change the aspect ratio of your video in a transcoder (and we'll look at that next), but you can also use Keynote because it allows slides – which we know from *Chapter 7* can act as the frame of our video – to be exported in whatever aspect ratio you like.

Changing aspect ratio with Keynote

The first thing we need to note here is that Keynote, however capable, is not an NLE. We should always use software dedicated to our specific cause, so before we change the aspect ratio of our video, we need to make sure we're happy with it, and then export a master copy from iMovie. To recap, the master copy should have the following:

- The highest resolution possible (what you set the project resolution as)
- The highest quality possible (ProRes if you have the space, or slide the Custom quality slider fully to the right if not):

When we see **Quality** in iMovie, this refers to the video's **bit rate**. More on that later.

Once that video has been exported, we can bring it into Keynote and change its aspect ratio. Here's how to do that:

1. Open a new basic Keynote project (⌘ + N).
2. On the far right of the toolbar, click **Document** to open the Document sidebar.
3. Click the **Slide Size** drop-down menu and then click **Custom Slide Size…**
4. Change the **Width** and **Height** values so that they match the aspect ratio you'd like:

Figure 8.2 – This slide is set to a 4:3 aspect ratio, but with a higher resolution than Keynote's default 4:3 option

5. Click **OK** or hit *Enter* to go back to the slide, which will have changed shape.
6. Drag and drop a video file from Finder onto the Keynote slide; the video will come up as a resizable thumbnail with a play button in the middle.
7. Resize the video so that it fills the slide and snaps to the yellow lines of symmetry:

    - If your video is wider than your chosen aspect ratio (you're creating a *pillarboxed* version of the video), you want to fit the height of the slide exactly

- If your video is taller than your chosen aspect ratio (you're creating a *letterboxed* version of the video), make sure to fill in the length of the slide exactly:

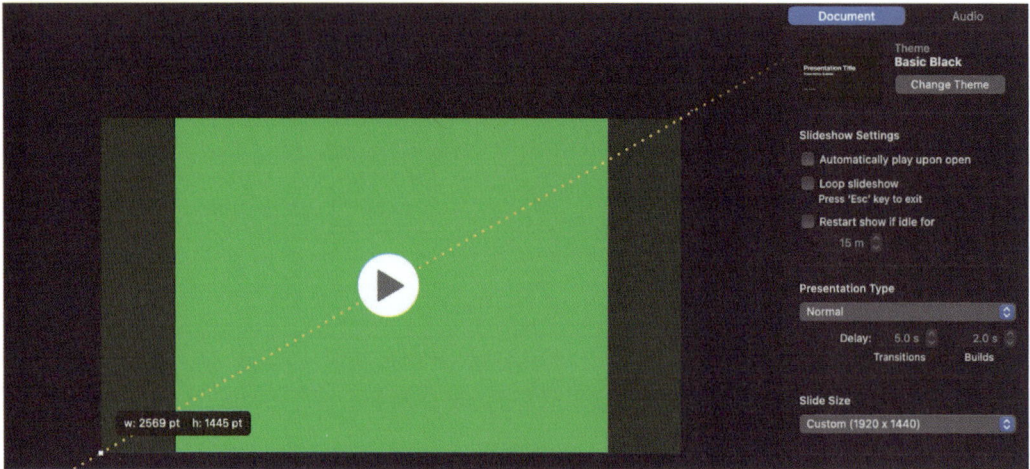

Figure 8.3 – My 16:9 video, which I'm making 4:3. The diagonal line of symmetry crosses through the play button in the middle

8. Go to **File** | **Export To** | **Movie…**
9. If you need to change the frame rate of the video, you can change this using the Keynote export menu too.

In the export menu, the slide size (which we set earlier) decides the aspect ratio you export, but we still need to set the resolution to make sure that Keynote isn't reducing the resolution of our video.

1. If your resolution is above 1,080 pixels for width (which it's likely to be), you'll need to change the resolution to **Custom…** and edit the values to be the same as the slide size you set (as in *Figure 8.4*):

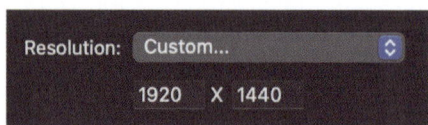

Figure 8.4 – Setting a resolution that matches my slide size

2. Click **Next…** and save the file in a place you'll remember with a name you'll remember.

Hey presto: the video has been resized! Using Keynote is a really simple way to change the aspect ratio of your video. Whatever parts of your video sit outside the slide are essentially cut off when you export, like using a guillotine to cut paper to size. So, if you had a video you made entirely in portrait, you could drag the video into Keynote, change the slide size to a 9:16 aspect ratio such as 1080x1920, and export just the portrait footage. However, the problem with that is that however you set the export resolution, you're deleting most of the frame. For portrait videos, there's a way to preserve all their resolution.

Exporting sideways from iMovie

We know from looking at aspect ratios that a portrait screen, 9:16, is the opposite way around to an HD widescreen, which is 16:9 – it's like the height and length have been swapped. This means that any footage that's in landscape 16:9 format just needs to be rotated 90 degrees to become portrait. And you can do just that within iMovie.

This technique involves rotating all your portrait footage by 90 degrees so that it sits on its side. Then, after exporting, you can use QuickTime Player to rotate the video back to be the right way up. The advantage of this is that you're exporting from iMovie with the whole frame filled. This means that a 1920x1080 portrait video made this way will be of better visual quality than one made by chopping off the majority of a 1920x1080 frame in Keynote.

Where possible, you should try to edit as normal and then rotate your clips just before exporting. It makes the editing process easier because you won't have to stare at your computer screen with your head tilted. However, there are a few things you need to bear in mind before you start:

- All clips you're editing with must be portrait: if you have a portrait section of the video and rotate only that, QuickTime Player will turn most of the video on its side when you correct the video
- For the same reason, when you rotate the clips, they must all be rotated in the same direction
- Crop to Fill boxes and Ken Burns effects will reset when you rotate clips

If you still want to use this technique but need to make use of crop boxes and Ken Burns animations, you'll need to rotate those clips before you start editing them. Even then, reframing won't work in quite the same way. Here's the process for exporting and correcting a portrait video:

1. Edit as many of your portrait clips as you can in their normal orientation.
2. For the clips where you need to use crop effects, first mark them all on the timeline (*M*).
3. On a marked clip, click on the **Crop** menu in the toolbar and click the left-hand **rotate** button (circled, *Figure 8.5*):

    - You can rotate the clip in whichever direction you like, so long as you do the same to the other clips. In this example, we're sticking to a counterclockwise (to the left) rotation in iMovie:

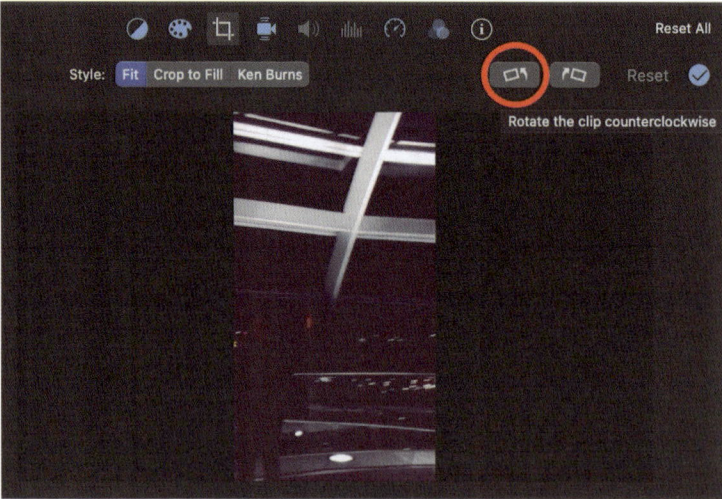

Figure 8.5 – The crop menu and the portrait video

4. Now, change the crop style to **Crop to Fill** or **Ken Burns**, depending on what kind of reframing you want to do.

Here's where you might run into an issue, though. When you use crop boxes on the rotated video, the crop boxes, which are fixed to a 16:9 aspect ratio, won't rotate. In practice, this means that you can't have a crop box that stretches along the whole top edge of the frame (unless you show the whole video). *Figure 8.6* illustrates this – remember you're looking sideways at the frame while editing this:

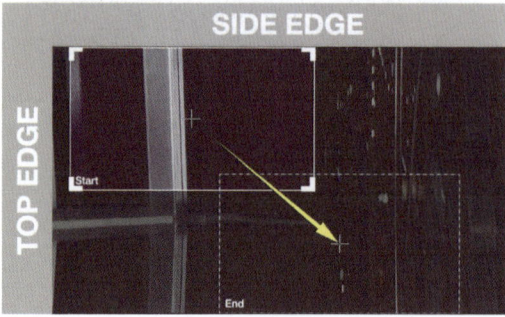

Figure 8.6 – The normal 16:9 crop boxes are in place on what will be 9:16 footage

This is a bit of a creative limitation, but hopefully, it won't stop you from doing what you wanted to do with reframing and zooming. If it does, you'll need to edit and export your portrait video as normal and then chop off the sides of the video with Keynote. But do remember the effect on resolution if you do. Now, back to the main steps:

1. Repeat *steps 3* to *4* for all the marked clips.
2. Select all the unmarked clips by ⌘ + *clicking*.
3. Go to the **Crop** menu and click the **Rotate the clip counterclockwise** option.

Now that all of your clips have been correctly rotated and have the edits you made preserved, it's time to export:

1. Go to **File | Share | File…** in the menu bar:

   This is the same path as clicking the Share icon and **Export File**, but a different way of getting there

2. Set all the settings to the maximum, as you would with any other master export (*Figure 8.7*):

Figure 8.7 – The rotated export

3. Click **Next…** and save the file somewhere temporary, such as your desktop.
4. When the file has finished exporting, double-click the file to open it in QuickTime Player.
5. Use the ⇧ + ⌘ + R shortcut to rotate the video 90 degrees back round to the right, making it portrait again:

   If you rotated all your videos clockwise in iMovie, do the opposite in QuickTime Player by using ⇧ + ⌘ + L to rotate the video to the left

6. Save the edited video by clicking the red circle at the top left of the window and following the prompt to save (*Figure 8.8*):

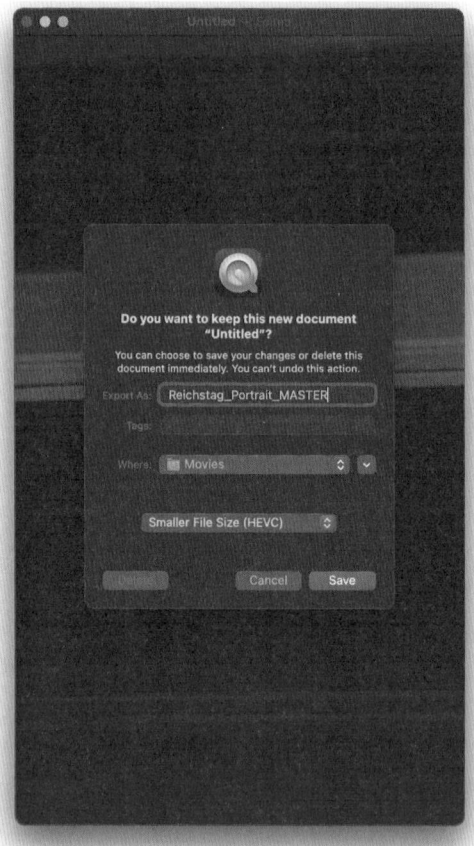

Figure 8.8 – The portrait video is now back in a 9:16 aspect ratio

And that's it for creating a portrait export using iMovie. This workaround, along with the Keynote method mentioned previously, works for changing the aspect ratio of your exported video. However, if you need to change video information such as file formats, or create a version of your video export within a specific file size, you'll have to use a transcoder such as Handbrake.

How to install and run Handbrake

When we used Keynote, we changed the aspect ratio of our video by *encoding* a new video: Keynote rendered and exported a new video file. But there is another method for changing the aspect ratio: applications such as Handbrake *transcode* the original video, changing information about it. This section will show you how to install and get to grips with Handbrake.

In the *Technical requirements* section earlier in this chapter, we went through where to find Handbrake. After downloading the app, the first thing we need to do is make sure Handbrake is in the Applications folder. Here's how to make sure it is:

1. When you download Handbrake, you'll get a DMG file. Double-click the file and it will expand into a **Volume** (not as in loudness; a Volume is a simple storage device you can eject from your computer):

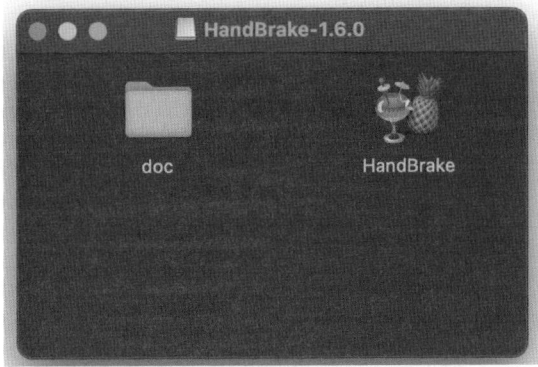

Figure 8.9 – The Handbrake Volume

2. The *HandBrake* icon on the right is the app itself. This needs to be moved to the Applications folder (the ⌘ + ⇧ + A shortcut). Drag the app into *Applications* and it will copy into there.

3. Once the copying is complete, it's time to clear up the download stuff. Close the Volume window, right-click on the Volume, and click **Eject**. You can also delete the DMG file.

4. In the Applications folder, find and double-click on HandBrake. Alternatively, search for the app using Spotlight (⌘ + *spacebar*) and press *Enter* when it comes up. The app will open, and the interface will look similar to *Figure 8.10*:

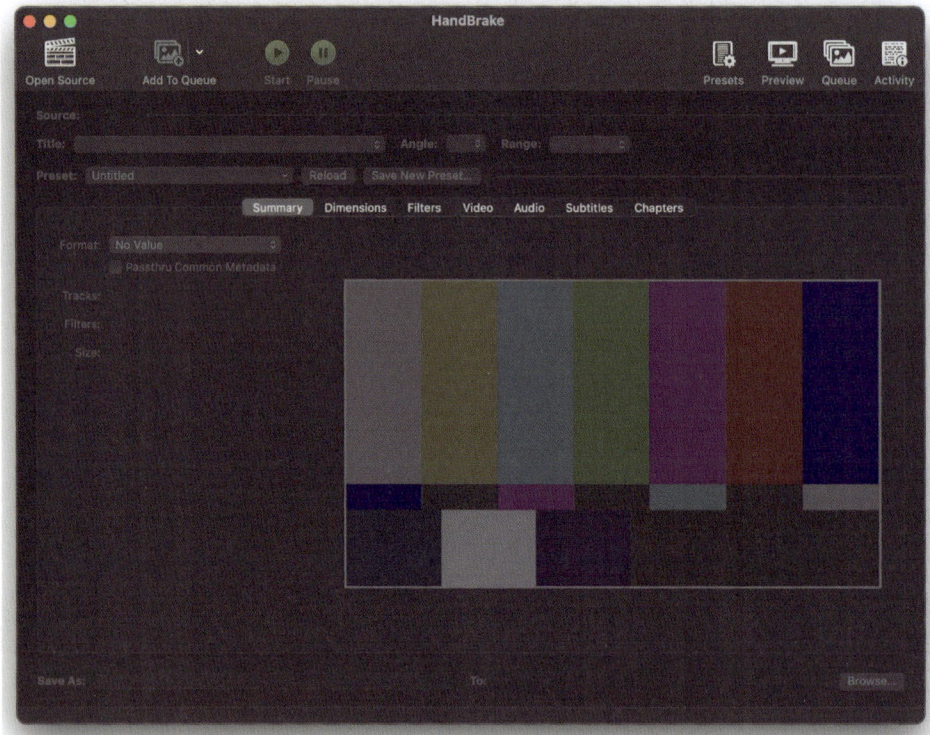

Figure 8.10 – The blank Handbrake interface

Adding a source to Handbrake

To be able to transcode, Handbrake needs a source video that it will apply changes to. That's your master export from iMovie. There are a couple of ways to add a source video to Handbrake:

- Choose a video file from the Finder window that comes up when you open the app.
- Click the **Open Source** button at the top left of the Handbrake window. That will open the Finder menu for choosing a file.

There's a lot to look at in the Handbrake interface, and it can be overwhelming at first, so we're going to start with just the bits we need. First, let's look at changing the aspect ratio of videos with the **Dimensions** tab.

Changing video cropping in Handbrake

Handbrake lets you crop pixels from each side of the video you add, allowing you to change your video's aspect ratio to anything you wish. After you've chosen your file for transcoding in Handbrake:

1. Look for a line of navigation tabs near the top of the window. These change what is shown on the interface, and let you change different aspects of the video. Click on **Dimensions**.

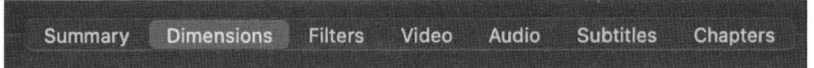

Figure 8.11 – Handbrake's navigation tabs

2. Next, look for some options on the left with the heading **Orientation and Cropping** (*Figure 8.12*). Under that, use the **Cropping** drop-down menu to change from **Automatic** to **Custom**.

3. Four boxes with different numbers should come into focus from being grayed out. These show, in numbers of pixels, how much cropping is happening at the top, right, bottom, and left of the video (reading them clockwise):

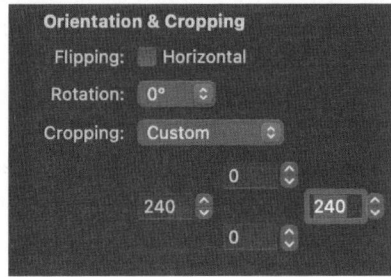

Figure 8.12 – Handbrake's custom cropping menu

4. Handbrake's automatic cropping may have put numbers into the boxes already (as in *Figure 8.12*). This automatic tool is very clever – it looks for blank parts of the video such as letterboxes and pillarboxes that can be cut out.

   Sometimes, this will work perfectly. However, if you want to make sure you're getting the intended aspect ratio, change all these values to 0 for now.

5. To get the cropping right for the aspect ratio, we need to work out how many pixels we need to crop from the top or sides. We can tell that from the difference between the two pixel dimensions. If we're changing a full HD 16:9 video to 4:3, we would be going from dimensions of 1920x1080 to 1440x1080. That means we're cropping:

   - 240 pixels off of each side (for a total of 480)
   - 0 pixels off the top and bottom

Custom Export Formats, ft. Handbrake

6. Hit *Enter* to save the cropping changes. Under the **Final Dimensions** heading near the bottom of the Handbrake window (*Figure 8.13*), the new storage size and aspect ratio of the video will be displayed:

Figure 8.13 – The final dimensions of the cropped video

It's useful to check this part of the Handbrake window because the **Aspect Ratio** reading will update with every crop change you make. If it's giving some strange number that isn't an aspect ratio you recognize, it's a good signal to go back and check the cropping.

Exporting from Handbrake

When the final dimensions are correct, it's time to choose a destination and transcode the video. Here's how to do that:

1. At the bottom of the Handbrake window is the **Save As** menu (*Figure 8.14*). Click on the box specifying the name of the file and choose an appropriate name that's different from the original, such as `file_transcoded.mp4`:

Figure 8.14 – The Save As menu in Handbrake

2. There will be a file path listed next to the filename showing where the transcoded file will be saved to. To change this, click the **Browse…** button and **Choose** a different save location in Finder.
3. To start the transcode, click the green **Start** button at the top of the Handbrake window. The app will give an estimated time for how long the transcode will take.

> **If your file doesn't end up where you expect**
>
> Sometimes, despite setting an export location, Handbrake doesn't put the transcoded files in the right place. If the files aren't where you expect them, you can use the **Queue** window, which is useful for keeping track of your encodes in any case:
>
> 1. Click **Queue** at the top of the Handbrake window.
>
> 2. From the left-hand list, click on the file you want to know the location of. The new name you gave for the transcoded file will be listed.
>
> 3. The panel on the right of the window tells you a lot of information about the transcoding job. Under **Summary**, the actual destination of the transcoded file is given.

When changing the aspect ratio of one video, Keynote is still probably your best bet – it's simpler, and the app is already part of macOS. Also, because you're using a video thumbnail and the visual reference of a slide, cropping and resizing the video is a more intuitive process. That doesn't mean you shouldn't ever use a transcoder though. One of the main use cases for transcoders is when you have multiple video files you want to make changes to.

Transcoding multiple files with Handbrake

Handbrake comes into its own if you have a whole series of files to transcode, even if each video needs different settings. To transcode multiple files, we need to create a queue. Here's how to do that:

1. Open Handbrake and use the Finder window to select the first file you want to transcode.
2. Change the relevant settings in the different Handbrake tabs, such as **Dimensions** for changing the aspect ratio.
3. Use the **Save As** menu to change the name and destination of the transcoded file.
4. Click **Add to Queue** on the Handbrake toolbar (*Figure 8.15*):

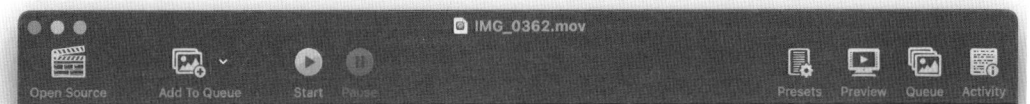

Figure 8.15 – The Handbrake toolbar

5. Click **Open Source** and select the second file you want to transcode, repeating *Steps 2 to 5* for as many files as you want to transcode.
6. When you've added all the sources you want, click **Start Queue**. Handbrake will run through the transcode for every video in the queue.

When transcoding multiple files, the **Queue** window (see *Figure 8.15*) is very helpful for monitoring the progress of the different transcodes and checking for any errors. If Handbrake can't transcode a file, it will give up on the transcode and move on to the next item in the queue. But this method we've looked at isn't the only way of adding multiple videos to a transcoding queue. You can also save settings in a preset and apply this to folders full of files.

Using presets in Handbrake

If you have a massive number of files that need changes, it might not be realistic to set the transcoder's settings for each file. Luckily, Handbrake has a **Preset** drop-down menu full of presets that change dimension, video, and sound quality settings depending on the platform and resolution you want to encode a video for. The default preset is **fast 1080p30** (1920x1080 resolution, 30 frames per second, fast encoder preset – more on that later). A couple of the platform-specific formats that you may want to try are:

- **Preset | Web | Discord Small 2 Minutes 360p30**
- **Preset | Web | Gmail Large 3 Minutes 720p30**

These presets can be very useful because they squeeze your video file inside the free file upload limits for Discord (8 MB) and Gmail (25 MB). Try selecting these and seeing what settings it changes in the different Handbrake menus. It's a useful learning experience for setting your own presets. Speaking of that…

Creating presets in Handbrake

Handbrake allows you to input settings and save them as a preset, which can then be applied to as many videos as you like. For example, I have a folder of old videos that are all 16:9 exports, but the original recording shown in them is from an iPad, which is a 4:3 screen. Therefore, I want a preset that will remove the pillarboxes at the side of the screen for all of them:

1. Open Handbrake and choose one of the relevant files from the Finder window.
2. Make sure the main **Preset** is set to the default, **Fast 1080p30**. It's a good foundation to build from; other presets can stop your encodes from working due to some of the custom conditions that Handbrake adds.
3. Click on the **Dimensions** tab.
4. Change **Cropping** to **Custom**, and crop 240 pixels from the left and right.
5. Press *Enter* to save the cropping changes – the aspect ratio will now be 4:3.
6. In the **Preset** menu, click **Save New Preset** (*Figure 8.16*):

Figure 8.16 – The Preset menu in Handbrake

A window will appear (*Figure 8.17*) that allows you to add some more information to the preset you're making:

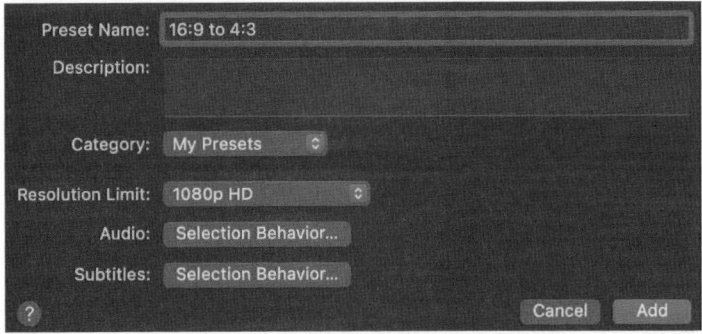

Figure 8.17 – The Save New Preset menu

7. The resolution limit of 1080p HD is important to keep because the cropping we've selected only works for 1920x1080 videos. Ignore the other settings for now.
8. Click **Add** to create the preset.
9. Now, in the **Preset** drop-down menu, hover over the **My Presets** option at the bottom. Your saved preset will be there to use whenever you like in the future.

Now that we have created a preset, we can apply it to a large number of videos that all need transcoding in the same way.

Batch-transcoding a folder of videos

We're now going to build on our use of our **Queue** from before by adding a whole series of videos to be transcoded using our preset:

1. Make sure all the files you want to transcode are in one folder in Finder.
2. Click on the Finder folder containing the videos and drag and drop it over the Handbrake window. Handbrake will scan in the source videos you added.
3. Select your preset from the **Preset** drop-down menu.
4. Choose a save location for all the new files using the **Browse…** menu. As you're transcoding multiple files in one go, it would be a good idea to create a **New Folder** for the transcoded files to go into.

Now that we've put the correct settings and destination in place, we can put the queue together:

1. Add all the videos to the queue. Go to **File | Add Titles to Queue…** or use the ⇧ + ⌘ + B keyboard shortcut.
2. All of the files in the folder will appear in a list with ticked checkboxes (*Figure 8.18*). You can remove a video from the queue at this point by clicking on its filename:

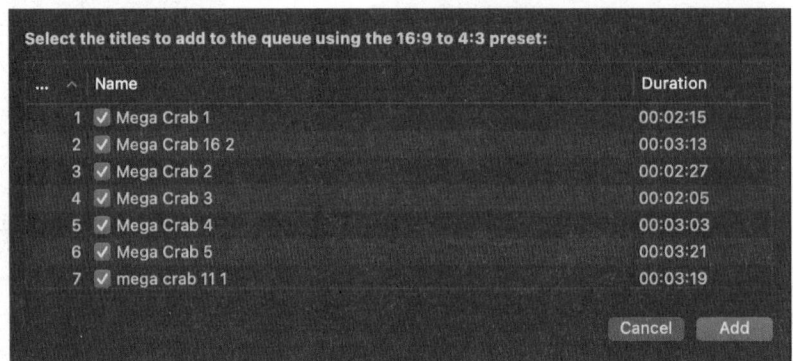

Figure 8.18 – The Add Titles to Queue menu

3. Click **Add** or hit *Enter* to add all the videos in the folder to the queue with the current transcoding settings.
4. Click **Start Queue** on the Handbrake toolbar:
   - It might be worth waiting before you do this – see if you can apply the compression suggestions mentioned in the next section to a new preset.

Now, we can batch transcode videos, which is useful if you're ever working with a huge number of files. But the aspect ratio isn't the only thing we can change with a transcoder. If you are using a transcoder, it's usually because you want to change multiple attributes of a video. Perhaps what transcoders are best known for is reducing file sizes, which will be important for sharing master copies of your videos in different places. If you need a certain aspect ratio and a smaller file size for your video, you can use different tabs within Handbrake to change both settings.

Using Handbrake to compress files

Compression is the process of taking something with a higher quality and reducing its size by getting rid of information. Why would we ever want to reduce our video's quality? Well, as you'll be keenly aware if you exported videos in ProRes from iMovie, master video copies are huge. Many websites (and other destinations – clients, for example), have file size limits that you'll need to stick to. Keeping a master copy means that if the file size isn't an issue, we can use the best copy of our video available. I promised I'd explain why ProRes files are so much larger, so here goes.

What is ProRes?

ProRes files are ginormous, and although we won't get deep into the weeds of video compression, it's useful to know why **Best Quality (ProRes)** video is so much larger than maxing out the video quality using iMovie's Custom slider on export. A disclaimer to video experts: this is a massively simplified explanation – but the important learning is still attached.

Almost every video in existence is compressed – they have to be. If videos were uncompressed, they would be so large that they would be impossible to store, stream, or even play. One type of compression, **inter-frame**, is done by skipping out frames and making guesses about what is going to happen in the skipped frames instead of storing the information. This is just like animating a path with keyframes (choosing start, middle, and end positions, and animating in between them), except the animated path in this case is the guesses the compression algorithm makes. It makes *guesses*, as it were, because they take up substantially less space than actual video information. Why? Well, to record and keep all the information about a frame, the encoder needs all the pixel information in that frame. Think how many pixels 1920x1080 is, and you probably get the picture.

Compression algorithms are extremely good at making guesses between keyframes, so much so that we often don't notice a loss of quality in the compressed videos we watch. Everything flows smoothly and naturally, as a video should. But ProRes is designed to not make these guesses. Although it does compress videos in other ways, it isn't messing with guessing, and there are two upshots of this:

- The video quality is almost lossless
- It's easier and faster to edit with

Wait. If ProRes files are much larger and hold much more information, how on Earth can they be less taxing on your computer? Well, that's because your NLE doesn't have to make guesses between keyframes. It has information about all the frames ready and waiting, which means it can get on with the job of importing, rendering, and exporting video more quickly. Don't believe me? Try exporting a video from iMovie in **High** quality, then **Best (ProRes)**. The ProRes export will be faster, especially if you have a Mac with an M-series chip, as these have parts of the chip dedicated to making ProRes work faster.

So, that's what ProRes is, and its almost-lossless quality makes it best to export the master copy of your video in it. But it's not just NLEs that benefit from ProRes. Transcoders such as Handbrake also have an easier time working with a ProRes master file because they can see all the frame information too. This allows them to skip out frames and make better guesses, more quickly.

Compressing video with Handbrake

There are more ways to reduce file size with a transcoder than you or I could ever hope to count, so we're going to focus on some sure-fire rules for effectively decreasing the size of your video:

- Use the H.265 codec
- Use Handbrake's suggested quality range
- Leave the audio alone

Let's go through each of these rules in turn.

Use the H.265 codec

The word **codec** is a compound of encode and decode. Codecs are a set of instructions to computers for how they should encode a video or audio file (how it's created) and decode the file (how it's eventually played).

The indisputable codec standard for video is H.264. It's been around since 2003, and it's everywhere. The standard was improved in 2013 with the introduction of H.265. You might be more familiar with this as HEVC on Apple devices, the codec we used to export Keynote animations, and one you might use for saving videos with QuickTime Player too. H.265 is a set of instructions that make computers do what H.264 does, but more efficiently. That means smaller file sizes for the same visual quality. The codec Handbrake uses can be changed by doing the following:

1. Open Handbrake and navigate to the **Video** tab.
2. Click on the **Video Encoder** drop-down menu and choose **H.265 (x265)**

Quality range in Handbrake

On the right of the **Video Encoder** menu in Handbrake is the **Quality** slider. For H.265, it uses a unit called RF. The lower the RF, the higher the quality of the output video, but the higher the file size. This is because it's using more information from the original video and making fewer guesses. The opposite is the case for a higher RF. Handbrake recommends using the following quality ranges, which vary based on the resolution of the video:

- RF 18-22 for 480p (Standard Definition)
- RF 19-23 for 720p (HD)
- RF 20-24 for 1080p (Full HD)
- RF 22-28 for 2160p (4K)

You can see from this scale that the higher the resolution of the video, the less of its data that you need to keep for the video to still have high visual quality. For a full HD video, for example, sticking to RF 20 allows you to reproduce the video with a very similar quality to the original, but with file size savings. The H.265 codec will make additional file size savings because of its improved efficiency.

Leave audio alone

This one is fairly self-explanatory. Don't bother reducing audio quality to save file size. There are two reasons for this:

- Audio takes up very little space in a file
- As humans, we notice (and dislike) a drop in sound quality more strongly than a drop in video quality

Because audio is such a small part of the video file, and we love good audio quality, don't fiddle with the audio settings. Any saving in file size will ruin the audience experience. Now that we've covered these individual factors, let's put them into practice by compressing one of your master files.

Creating a ProRes export from a mobile project

If you don't have a ProRes export already, let's quickly create one from your Berlin recap video from *Chapter 3*. The following steps describe how to export a project from iMovie for iOS/iPadOS, import that into iMovie for macOS, then export it as a master copy. So, firstly, on your mobile device:

1. Open the iMovie app.
2. Tap on your Berlin project to open the project view.
3. Tap the middle icon, **Share**.
4. Tap **Options** at the top of the **Share** window.
5. Change the **Type** to **Project** and tap **Back** to exit the menu.
6. Make sure Bluetooth is on and AirDrop is set to **receiving** on both your mobile device and your Mac:

    AirDrop settings can be found in the **Control Center** area at the top right of the screen. On mobile devices, you'll need to swipe down with one finger.

7. Back on your mobile device, tap **AirDrop** at the top of the **Share** menu. Then, under **Devices**, tap on your Mac when it comes up.

These first steps allow you to export everything involved with your video to your Mac, with the individual clips still in place so you can edit them again. Now, it's time to use the exported project file (`.iMovieMobile`) to open the Berlin project on your Mac, using the file you sent to yourself:

1. Open iMovie on your Mac.
2. Go to **File | Import iMovie iOS Projects…**.
3. Locate the `.iMovieMobile` file. Any other kind of file will be grayed out in Finder as iMovie can't use it. If you sent the file using AirDrop, it will be in **Downloads** (the ⌥ + ⌘ + L keyboard shortcut).
4. Select the file, then click **Import**. iMovie will create a new project with the timeline arranged exactly as you had it in the mobile app.
5. If you're happy with the video, go to **File | Share | File…**.
6. Set the resolution to the highest available (1080p for the Berlin project) and **Quality** to **Best (ProRes)**. Make sure **Compression** is set to **Better Quality**:

Figure 8.19 – A master copy of the Berlin video

We now have a ProRes export that we can compress into a more manageable size. So, let's get it into Handbrake and follow the three rules we set out previously.

Compressing a master video with Handbrake

The amount that you need to compress a file will be different depending on the requirements of the website you're using, or the client you're making a video for. But following the three compression rules mentioned previously will get you a very watchable but much smaller viewing copy of the video. Let's set about compressing our master export:

1. Open Handbrake and select your master export from the Finder window.
2. Go to the **Video** tab and use the **Video Encoder** drop-down menu to choose **H.265 (x265)**.

3. The default **Quality** rating, **RF22**, is within the advised range for a 1080p video, so let's keep that as it is.
4. The standard preset, **fast 1080p30**, doesn't do anything untoward to the sound but do check the **Sound** tab (*Figure 8.20*) to make sure that there is only one audio **Track** listed. If there are two, set the second to **None** using the drop-down menu. The second bar is for stereo audio (two different channels), which iMovie doesn't export in:

![Sound tab showing Track, Codec, Mixdown, Samplerate, Bitrate, Gain, and DRC columns]

Figure 8.20 – An example Sound tab; just keep an eye on the Track information

5. In the **Save As** menu, give the file a name you'll remember and set its save destination to an appropriate place.
6. Click **Start** in the toolbar to begin the transcoding process.

If Handbrake's estimate for the time the process will take (shown on the app icon) is excessively long, there's another setting we can change. To speed up the encoding process – at the expense of some efficiency, and therefore a larger file size – you can choose a faster **encoding preset**:

1. Click **Stop** on the Handbrake toolbar, then **Stop All** in the window that appears.
2. Go back to the **Video** tab: in **Encoder Options**, drag the **Preset** bar two spaces to the left to **veryfast** (as in *Figure 8.21*):

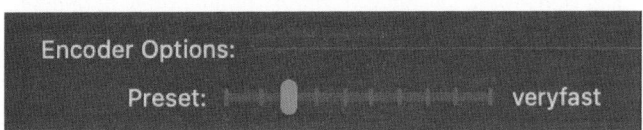

Figure 8.21 – The veryfast encoder preset can be a good sweet spot between file size and encoding speed

3. Click **Start** on the Handbrake toolbar again.
4. When the encoding is finished, open Finder to check the size of the new file against the master export to see if the file size has reduced.

My ProRes "Berlin" export went from 1.12 GB to 17.1 MB – over a 98% reduction in the file size. You should see a similar reduction if you compressed from a ProRes file. But what if we want to compress the file further? Let's say we wanted to fit the Berlin video into an 8 MB Discord attachment. We can use a more definite scale of quality to achieve this.

Compressing to a specific size with bitrate controls

The file size of your video isn't random – a lot of it is down to the relationship between its length and the **bitrate** of the video. The bitrate is the amount of information in the video per second, and we can change this to decide an exact file size for our video. This is the calculation for bitrate:

```
Bitrate [kbps] = File size [MB] / (file length [minutes] *
0.0075)
```

Let's run through an example. If I want my Berlin recap to fit within 8 MB, I also need to know the file length. It's 1 minute 15 seconds, which is 1.25 minutes. 0.0075 is a specific and constant number that's always in the calculation, so let's fill out the calculation for my Berlin video, calculating what's in the bracket first:

```
Bitrate [kbps] = 8 [MB] /(1.25 [minutes] *0.0075)
Bitrate = 8/0.009375
Bitrate = 853 kbps
```

So, my video needs a bitrate of 853 kbps to fit into 8 MB. Here's how to set that in Handbrake:

1. Navigate to the **Video** tab.
2. In the **Quality** section, click the circle for **Average Bitrate (kbps)** (as in *Figure 8.22*). The RF value doesn't matter now.
3. In the box, type the bitrate you calculated and hit *Enter*. Leave the checkboxes ticked:

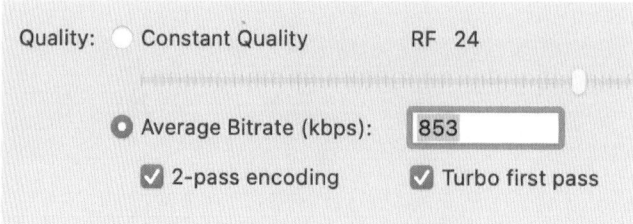

Figure 8.22 – Setting an average bitrate for the video

4. Make sure its **Dimensions** are still 1080p and that **Video Encoder** is still set to **H.265 (x265)**.
5. Click **Start** on the Handbrake toolbar.

When the encoding has finished, you may find that the file is slightly larger than you calculated it should be (nothing in editing is ever an exact science!). If you need to get the video under a certain size, reduce the average bitrate and try the encode again.

Disadvantages of using Average Bitrate

The **Average Bitrate** option is how you get a file to almost exactly the size of your choosing, but it's not the best method to use. Handbrake recommends using the **Constant Quality** option, and there are certainly disadvantages to encoding using **Average Bitrate**:

- Video quality is subjective, not mathematical – ensuring a constant quality will be better for the viewer than an average rate of information.
- Calculating the file size doesn't produce exact results because there are more factors at play than just the video length and size. This means that even with this method, it can still take a lot of trial and error to get a file to the intended size.
- Encoding with an average bitrate instead of constant quality takes longer, mostly because the transcoder needs to repeat the process (2-pass encoding) to make sure that bits of the video with more color changes and movement are given more data.
- Reducing the file size with bitrate can, if done too excessively, destroy video quality. Sometimes, it's better to save on space by reducing the resolution using the **Dimensions** menu.

With these disadvantages in mind, it's probably best to stick with Constant Quality where you can. But that covers things for the compression process. Hopefully, this section has enlightened you on how video compression works, and how you can effectively and simply reduce file sizes using Handbrake.

Summary

In this chapter, we looked at how you can take your exports from iMovie and customize their aspect ratio, and compress them to fit within file size limits. iMovie will only export in a 16:9 aspect ratio, but we learned that by changing the slide size in Keynote, or rotating our clips in iMovie and correcting them with QuickTime Player, we can create a video with just the aspect ratio we want.

You can also change a video's aspect ratio using transcoders such as Handbrake; they are best placed for changing multiple aspects of a video and applying preset changes to a large number of videos. Handbrake is probably best known for letting you use different codecs and quality settings to compress videos. We learned how to do this simply and effectively, as well as how to make a file close to a chosen size by calculating bitrate.

Now that your exports have been customized for their intended destination, it's up to your audience or clients to enjoy them. This book has hopefully been a useful and accurate guide for making the most of iMovie, but I can be sure that not everything went to plan when you were following along. In the next and final chapter, we're going to look at some of the problems that often occur in iMovie, and how to fix and prevent them.

9
Common iMovie Problems and Their Solutions

One thing the iMovie user guide won't point out is the program's shortcomings. There may be the occasional note of a bug being fixed in the updates, but the gremlins that continue to plague users don't get a mention, and this leads to us iMovie editors continuing to experience these problems.

In earlier chapters, as part of the extra tip boxes, we briefly touched on some areas that can catch you out when using iMovie. But this chapter aims to compile all the issues I've seen pop up repeatedly for people using this NLE. It won't be exhaustive, but it will hopefully help you to avoid some of the most common pitfalls.

There is, of course, a difference between a problem or bug in iMovie, and coming up against the way the app is designed. I've seen people struggle with the magnetic timeline and clip connections, and that is perfectly valid, but it's not something that can be avoided. If you're coming across an issue with iMovie that isn't documented in this chapter, ask yourself whether it could be part of the design philosophy of the app. If it isn't design-related, quit iMovie and restart it: I've had to do that a lot while writing this book. However, if the problem does persist and seems design-related, it may be that iMovie's take on the timeline paradigm goes against the way you like to edit. In that case, it might be worth switching to using a different NLE entirely. The main topics we'll cover in this chapter are as follows:

- Import and rendering problems
- Space and hard drive problems
- Export errors and codes

Technical requirements

What you need depends on what problems you're diagnosing and fixing. But across this chapter, we'll be looking at iMovie for iOS/iPadOS, as well as iMovie for macOS. The latest versions of these apps are recommended. For some of the issues, we'll be using Handbrake to sort out the problem, so you'll need a Mac for that, with at least version 1.4. Instructions on installing Handbrake can be found in the *Technical requirements* section of *Chapter 8*. For solving the most persistent of export errors, we'll be downloading a sound capture device: Blackhole 2ch. This is available at `https://github.com/ExistentialAudio/BlackHole`. It has one purpose, so the version number does not matter much – but for reference, I used version 0.4.0 to test out the fix in this chapter. Neither Blackhole nor Handbrake are the only programs that do what they do, so if you want to use an alternative, that's fine. As always, though, be diligent with your research and be careful what you download. With that, let's get into diagnosing and solving some iMovie problems.

Problem – iMovie won't accept your video format

Right from the start of an iMovie project, you may encounter issues where iMovie won't accept the files you've recorded, or won't play them properly. There are some limits to the import process that may be the cause of these problems, but sometimes, iMovie can just be a bit awkward with the videos you're trying to use. Firstly, let's look at file types and limits in iMovie. iMovie expresses its disapproval of certain files in a couple of different ways:

- If you drag and drop the video in, a no entry symbol will show, and the video won't appear in the timeline
- If you use the ⌘ + *I* menu to import a video, the video file will be grayed-out, and you won't be able to select it

Most video files that you use won't come across this problem, but there are certain video **containers** (the letters at the end of the filename) that iMovie just doesn't accept, even though YouTube uploads, programs such as *VLC Player*, and most NLEs are fine with them. The most common problem containers for iMovie are as follows:

- `.avi` (Audio Video Interleave – the original Windows video file container)
- `.mkv` (Matroska video)
- `.webm` (web media – this can be video or audio)

But containers aren't the whole story. Certain containers are attached to certain codecs (for example, MKV and the VP8/VP9/AV1 codecs), but different codecs can be interchanged with different containers. This means that for the containers that iMovie accepts (the full list is M4V, MOV, and MP4), the video file might have been encoded with a codec that iMovie doesn't like. In that case, it won't accept the video.

Solution – transcoding video that iMovie won't accept

There is such a vast range of codecs available that it would be impossible to keep track of what combinations work in iMovie. Therefore, the only real solution is to transcode videos when iMovie won't allow them to be imported. Because of its versatility, Handbrake is a good tool to use for this job. We looked at how to transcode files with Handbrake in *Chapter 8*, but here's a recap focusing on just changing the container and codec to something iMovie will accept:

1. Open Handbrake.
2. Select your video in the **Finder** window and click **Open**. In the **Summary** tab, the container for the transcoded file (under **Format**) will be set to MP4, which we'll keep because it's great for compatibility.
3. Handbrake will default to the **fast 1080p30** preset. If your video has a resolution higher than 1080p, go to the **Dimensions** tab and use the **Resolution Limit** drop-down menu to increase the limit to the size of the video you're using.
4. Similarly, if your video has a frame rate that's not 30 FPS, go to the **Video** tab and select its framerate from the **Famerate (FPS)** drop-down menu:

    - The **Same as Source** option would seem the sensible choice, but unfortunately, it's not particularly reliable, as it can often cause the encoding process to fail

5. Still in the **Video** tab, move the **Quality** slider to one of the following settings to maintain the visual quality of the original video:

    - **RF19** for a 720p video
    - **RF20** for a 1080p video
    - **RF22** for a 4K video

6. Choose a sensible export location and filename in the **Save As** section at the bottom of the Handbrake window.
7. Click **Start** to begin the transcoding process.

This process is useful when iMovie refuses to import a video, but it can also be a sensible failsafe process. If you don't know for a fact that both your video's container and codec are suitable for iMovie (they would be, for example, if you recorded footage on an iPhone or iPad), it can be a good idea to run your files through Handbrake before editing them. This usually eliminates any problems that might lie dormant but cause a lot more heartache later on in the edit. If you want a recap on how to transcode a bulk set of videos, have a look at the *Transcoding multiple files with Handbrake* section of *Chapter 8*.

Problem – clips don't play properly

Sometimes, there will be issues with videos that were imported seemingly fine before. That's why it's a useful failsafe to run videos through a transcoder first before importing them. But if you come across a problem where videos you've already imported are not playing, there are some techniques to run through that might help "remind" iMovie of the video it's supposed to be playing.

Solution – "reminding" iMovie of the clips in the project

Follow these steps:

1. Find the media that's not playing properly in Finder.
2. Click on the file and drag it, holding the file over the iMovie timeline (no need to drop it in). If iMovie has "forgotten" information about the file and isn't playing it properly, showing it the original file can get it working again.
3. Similarly, you can try re-importing the same media as before through the import menu (⌘ + *I*).

If that doesn't work, it might be worth copying the timeline into a new project:

1. Copy all the clips in the timeline with ⌘ + *A* and ⌘ + *C*.
2. Go back to the **Projects** menu by pressing *2* and create a new project with ⌘ + *N*.
3. Paste all the clips into the new project's timeline with ⌘ + *V*.

If that's still not working, some standard computer troubleshooting tips may come to your rescue:

- Quit iMovie and start it again
- Restart your computer

This whole issue highlights why it is so important to keep your original video files in Finder throughout the editing process and highlights the use of transcoding your media first before importing it. However, there is another common problem with clips – a very common one. The clip container and codec might be fine, and the import starts – but it inexplicably stops mid-way, with iMovie claiming that it is still trying to download videos from iCloud.

Problem – iCloud videos are still "downloading"

Many iMovie users are plagued by this issue, mostly on iMovie for iOS/iPadOS. You select media from the Media Browser to go into your project, but your clips don't end up there. The app explains that the media (videos, most often) is still being downloaded from iCloud, but nothing seems to happen – you're stuck with the files never in your timeline. There may be a few different reasons for this:

- You have no (or a slow) internet connection

- Your iCloud storage is full
- The footage that was being downloaded now can't be located

This problem is more likely to come up on mobile devices because more of the media we tend to use in projects come from iCloud libraries – specifically, the iCloud Photo Library. Any video or screen capture recorded on a mobile apple device heads to the Photos app, which for many users is backed up to iCloud. This is also more likely to cause headaches on the mobile app because iMovie doesn't make copies of video files on iOS and iPadOS like it does on Mac. As we learned in *Chapter 5*, the original media must be kept safely stored on the device – not doing so can cause issues such as this never-ending import.

Solution – tidy up your iCloud storage

When media is in the iCloud Photos Library, it's not stored on the device. That's why it needs to be downloaded to the device before it can be used in iMovie. You can try to fix the problem by:

- Ensuring you have a strong internet connection
- Deleting unnecessary files from your iCloud storage
- Checking the **Recently Deleted** folder in the Photos app to check you haven't removed footage you want to use in your project

With a strong internet connection, files shouldn't take more than a few minutes to download to your device. If the downloads are still stuck, the download has likely been stopped because of iCloud storage limits. Apple devices seem to delight in telling you your iCloud storage is full (even when they're a way off being full), in the hope of you paying them for more. If you get a storage warning, here's a quick guide to freeing up iCloud storage space:

1. Check what videos, music, and voice memos you can safely delete from iCloud storage, and delete them. By "safely," I mean avoiding deleting files associated with your video at all costs!
2. Go into the **Recently Deleted** folder for each app such as Photos or Voice Memos and – after double-checking you don't need them – permanently delete the files. You won't save any space until that's done.
3. In the **iCloud** section of your Settings app, check what apps are linked to iCloud and unlink them if you don't need them to sync. My favorites to untick? **Stocks** and **News**.
4. If you still need to free up space, select all the biggest files in your iCloud storage (this could be videos in your Photos library) and share them to your device's Files app (**On My iPhone/iPad**), or Finder on Mac. Then, delete the files from iCloud. That will ensure your files are still safe, and that a lot of storage is freed up.

Unfortunately, if you can't find the footage you planned to use and it's not in the **Recently Deleted** folder, it's likely that it has been deleted permanently, and can't be retrieved. In that case, you will sadly need to record something new.

There is a more general problem at play too. The iCloud downloading process is one that just doesn't tend to sync well with iMovie. It crops up all the time in iMovie forums, and it doesn't seem that it's being addressed in updates to iMovie. Therefore, the best solution to this problem is to avoid using iCloud for storing large files such as your **rushes** (recorded footage before editing).

Long-term solution – remove project media from iCloud libraries

Because the iCloud download problem stops you from getting media into the timeline in the first place, there is at least no need to take risky steps to rescue a project that's stopped working midway through the editing process. We can avoid the iCloud issue repeating itself by starting again and keeping our recording files in the device's storage. On mobile devices:

1. Go to your Photos app.
2. Find the recording and select it.
3. Tap the **Share** icon.
4. Tap **Save | Files**.
5. Give the file a name you'll remember and select the **On my iPhone/iPad** folder in your Files app. Tap **Save**.
6. Exit the menu and delete the video from Photos.

On a Mac, you might have experienced iCloud download issues if you used the integrated Photos library in iMovie's left-hand Libraries pane (we covered this in *The Photos Library* section in *Chapter 4*). Here's how to move your media away from being iCloud-dependent on a Mac:

1. Go to the Photos app and locate the media you want to use in your video.
2. Click on each video you want to use: there will be a tick next to each, which means they've been selected.
3. Drag all these videos outside of the Photos app – this creates copies that you can add to Finder.
4. Drop the media into a project folder for your video.
5. Return to the Photos app and delete the videos you just made copies of.

As we're not concerned about iCloud storage space in this example, it might be a good idea to leave those videos in the **Recently Deleted** folder while you edit. You won't get any downloading problems as you're not using iCloud, and the original videos will still be floating around in case anything goes wrong. Remember, it's always best to keep copies.

As a rule, it's also a good idea to keep at least 10% of your device storage free. Processes tend to slow down and weird things happen when device storage is at more than 90% capacity. That hopefully covers the iCloud downloading issue; with media properly imported into iMovie, let's go over some of the problems that may come up with the clips you're editing.

Problem – audio and video drift out of sync

If you've recorded video and audio separately – perhaps you have a dedicated camera and a separate microphone – you'll need to sync the two up in the timeline. If you're having trouble with that, check out the *Syncing multi-camera footage* section of *Chapter 6*. Otherwise, here's a recap on syncing video and audio:

1. Find a point in your video where there is a clear visual cue for a short, sharp sound (such as a clap or the sound of drums).
2. Mark that point in the video with a marker (*M*); then, find the start of the sound in the audio track, select the audio track, and mark that point too.
3. Drag the audio so that the two markers are in the same place. If you have Snapping toggled on (*N*), the markers will be drawn together when they're close.

But here's where the problem comes in: you may have the video and audio perfectly in sync at a marker at the start of the video, but by the end, they have drifted so the video is noticeably behind the audio, or vice versa. Why's that happening? When you record audio and video separately, the rate at which the data is recorded won't necessarily match up. It's almost inevitable and is most obvious the longer the video is. NLEs such as Final Cut Pro have automatic tools to fix this (which iMovie, supposedly being an NLE that "just works," should have too), but in iMovie, you have to make this fix manually by making a speed adjustment.

Solution – change the speed of the audio clip

When audio and video drift apart throughout the video, one of them needs to be sped up or slowed down to match the other. I would suggest changing the audio because it's lighter in terms of file size, which makes it quicker and easier to make changes to. So, here's how to solve the drifting problem and ensure that the audio and video are synced across the timeline:

1. Ensure the video and audio are synced at a marker point near the start of the video.
2. Find a sound with a clearly identifiable visual cue near the end of the video, marking the visual cue with *M*.
3. Mark the point where the sound starts on the audio file. Even though you synced the video and audio at the start of the project, the markers may be in a different place by the end.
4. With the audio selected, open the Speed Editor with ⌘ + R.

5. Drag the circle at the end of the audio clip so that the two markers match up. If you have snapping toggled on (*N*), the markers will snap together when they're close.

6. Zoom out of the timeline with ⇧ + Z and check that both sets of two markers at both sync points are still in line.

You don't need to worry about the change in audio speed having any adverse effects on the audience's experience. The typical drift in audio in a 20-minute video can be fixed with no more than a 1-2% speed change. You can always check the **Preserve Pitch** checkbox in the **Speed** toolbar menu to help smooth over the change too. And that covers the fix for audio drift.

If you're having other problems with clips while editing – especially if they're not doing what the steps in this book suggest they should – make sure you quit and restart iMovie. This should put most problems right. But even if your clips are behaving themselves, there may be some usability problems that creep up on you as you get deep into a more complex edit.

Problem – editing on iMovie is slow or choppy

Stuttery editing is a bit more of a nebulous problem – there could be all sorts of reasons why iMovie is slow. The next port of call if restarting iMovie doesn't help is to restart your Mac, but make sure you do so safely:

1. Wait for any current iMovie tasks to finish (look at the white circle in the top right of the iMovie window).
2. Quit iMovie with ⌘ + Q to make sure your progress has been saved.
3. Restart your Mac.
4. Reopen iMovie. If you have multiple iMovie Libraries, only open the one(s) you need for the project. This will put less strain on iMovie.

If a restart doesn't work, it's time to diagnose why iMovie might be struggling. The first step to working out the problem is asking yourself whether you're working on a particularly intensive project. Your Mac may be struggling to render all the clips in the timeline if:

- The project settings are set to 4K and/or a high framerate
- The project has lots of uncompounded effects (titles, green/blue screen, PiP keyframing)
- There are lots of clip speed changes (the more they are sped up, the more intensive this is)
- The project is long (over 20 minutes)

For the most part, we don't want to change any of these, because if the timeline is in a high resolution or has a lot of effects – and you have good reasons for doing this – you shouldn't have to sacrifice elements of the project to work on it. There are all sorts of potential solutions, ranging from more simple to more drastic – give the following a try, in order.

Solution 1 – change the project settings

If you're working in a timeline with a higher resolution and/or frame rate than you plan to export in, it's well worth fixing the project settings so that both you and iMovie have an easier time. To do so:

1. Create a new project (⌘ + N) and add the correct project format clip (see the *Beginning your assembly edit in iMovie* section of *Chapter 5*) to the timeline.
2. Press *2* to go back to the **Projects** screen, then double-click on the original project.
3. Copy the whole timeline of your original project (⌘ + A, ⌘ + C).
4. Go to the new project and paste the clips in after the project format clip (⌘ + V).
5. Delete the project format clip and start editing again.

The editing process should now be smoother, considering that a 1080p project has a quarter of the number of pixels to process relative to a 4K project! If things aren't improving, it might be that the effects in the project are still making things slower.

Solution 2 – compound your effects

Effects in iMovie are especially taxing on your Mac's graphics capabilities, but they still have to be rendered like all other clips. Therefore, playing through an effects-heavy or significantly sped-up section is likely to slow things down as your Mac struggles to process everything in real time. This can be avoided if iMovie doesn't recognize the effects as effects – in other words, if the effects are normal clips.

To turn a PiP, overlay, green screen, animated title, and more into a single clip, the process is the same. You just need to export the clips, combining them into one compound effect that you can re-import:

1. Copy the clips involved in your effect into a new project.
2. Preview, evaluate, edit, repeat: when you're sure you're happy with the effect, go to **File | Share | File…**.
3. Export the effect in the resolution of the wider project, making sure – especially as you'll be editing the clip again – that you've chosen **Best (ProRes)** from the **Quality** drop-down menu.
4. When the export is complete, import the compounded effect into your original project, replacing the separate clips that made up the effect before.

Compounding the effects helps reduce the graphics workload for your Mac, and keeping the project you pasted the effect into lets you come back and tinker with the original effect if and when you need to. However, if your original project is still working slowly, you might have to break it up into smaller parts.

Solution 3 – split the project into multiple timelines

When a project is longer than 20 minutes, you may find that iMovie slows down a lot. This is just the combined effect of more and more clips needing to be rendered. If work on the timeline is too stuttery to continue, it might be beneficial to find breaks in your video where you can split it into different projects. Here are some rules for splitting up the project:

- For **narrative**: Split at the end of a thought, sentence, or (preferably) scene
- For **visuals**: Split after transitioning to black, white, or any other full-frame color
- For **audio**: Split when all sound has faded out completely

Why the need to think so hard about where we split the project? This method uses QuickTime Player to stitch the separate parts of your project back together because exporting all your projects from one timeline would take an unacceptably long time. As we know from *Chapter 1*, combining videos in QuickTime Player is inordinately quicker than rendering and exporting from an NLE.

However, because we're using QuickTime Player, we need to split our timelines up, knowing that we can't smooth over audio and visuals later. Avoiding areas with audio means that you won't have a sudden jump in the sound, and ending each project on a block color screen means that it's easy to keep visual continuity. Keeping each project to a scene of your video – instead of splitting purely by project length – means that if you edit one project in a different style to the next, there's a plausible narrative reason for it. It's never ideal to split up a project like this, but with these considerations in mind, we can lessen the impact and still create the video we want.

Make sure that between the end of one project and the start of the next, there's not more than a couple of seconds of dead air. You could do this by dissolving to a color background exactly 0.5 seconds long at the end of one project. You would then start the next project with the reverse: 0.5 seconds of the same color background that dissolves into the start of the next scene.

When you're happy with each project, export it to a file as normal, in the highest quality you have space for (considering you have multiple projects). When you've done this with all the sections of your video, it's time to employ QuickTime Player to bring the video together. For a more detailed explanation of QuickTime editing, check out the *In-file editing with QuickTime Player on macOS* section of *Chapter 1*:

1. Open the first section's export file in QuickTime Player.
2. Use the ⌘ + *E* shortcut to open Clips mode.
3. Drag the second section's exported file over the QuickTime Player window and drop it so that it sits after the first section.

4. Repeat this for all the sections in the video, clicking **Done** in the QuickTime Player window when the last export section has gone in.
5. Click **File** | **Export** to save the whole project as one video.

Splitting up the project can be done as many times as necessary to stop iMovie from slowing down, but remember that each time you do it, the video won't transition as smoothly and will seem more disjointed. Make as few different sections as iMovie's performance will still let you get away with. If things are still going slowly, it might be that your Mac has run into the problem of having less than 10% of its storage space left. iMovie may be largely responsible for this, too.

Problem – iMovie constantly fills hard drive space

You may find that when editing in iMovie – even without bringing in any new clips – your hard drive starts to fill up. When you check what's eating at the storage (**Apple Menu** | **About This Mac** | **Storage** | **Manage…**), you find that the iMovie Library is taking up way more space than the videos you put there in the first place.

You'll remember that iMovie for macOS makes a copy of every video file you import. This means that when you're considering storage requirements for your project, you need to double up: a 20 GB video file will ultimately take up as much as 40 GB on your Mac when you start editing with it. But this isn't what continually fills up space on your Mac. What does is the creation of render files.

Render files make it easier to play your timeline without things juddering to a halt. This rendering process is iMovie doing some export work while you're editing. Other NLEs give you the choice to render as you go along, and if you don't, export times will be much longer. However, the problem is that with the automatic creation of render files, the iMovie Library constantly gets larger, and all in the background.

Solution – delete render files

If your iMovie Library balloons to an unreasonable size, fortunately, you can easily delete the render files that have been created:

1. Go to **iMovie** | **iMovie Preferences** (⌘ + ,).
2. Click the **Delete** button next to **Render Files**.
3. Leave iMovie alone, open, for a few minutes while it recreates the minimum necessary render files to be able to edit smoothly.

It is as simple as that. Deleting render files doesn't delete any of the media you've imported, nor any clip on any timeline. The only possible disadvantage is that exports will take a lot longer. For that reason, if you're about to export a project and you have the space to do so, it's best to wait until after you've exported before deleting render files.

Step 3 is an important one to remember – if you try to edit immediately after deleting render files, the whole process will be jumpy and very slow. Deleting render files should be seen in the same way as defragmenting a drive. What I mean by that is it's not something you need to do constantly – pressing the **Delete** button begins a process that cleans up any big and unintended problems that are slowing down the use of your computer. The hard drive that's fragmented – or render files in the case of iMovie – isn't the enemy to start with. The purpose of render files is to help make editing smoother, so don't constantly try to delete them.

Hopefully, the problem/solution notes provided so far cover most of the unexpected problems that might come up while you're editing in iMovie. Now, we're going to be moving on to problems you might come across when exporting.

Problem – iMovie export has failed

Export errors are pretty scary. They stop your video from becoming a reality, so they can't be ignored. They're also pretty confusing – but luckily, there's a way to decode them. Export errors occur when iMovie can't find the footage that makes up clips in the timeline, or when the footage is corrupt. Most of the time, this problem won't present itself until the export, which means that transcoding your footage and editing it again might not be a practical solution.

When an iMovie export fails, a banner notification will come up saying the export has failed. Make sure to click on this as it holds the information you need to diagnose the problem. Whatever else is in the message will end with a number – it's this number that matters.

Solution 1 – find and delete the problem frame

The number the explanatory message gives is the first frame at which iMovie ran into an error. If your export failed quickly, the problem frame is likely to be near the start. If it failed right before the progress circle in the top right of the iMovie window closed, the problem frame is likely to be near the end. The number in the iMovie error message gives us the exact frame, but it's often in the thousands, so how do we work that out? Well, the only calculation we need to do is:

```
Problem frame number / frame rate of project
```

Let's imagine a scenario where your error occurred at frame 10,085, and your project is at 60 FPS:

1. Divide the frame number by the frame rate (10,085/60 = 168.0833…).
2. For now, ignore anything after the decimal point: the whole number is the number of seconds into your project the problem frame is:

    - Our problem frame is in the 168th second, or 2 minutes, 48 seconds into the project

3. Move the playhead to that second of the video – we're looking for a **dropped frame**, which will often show itself in the Viewer as the screen goes black for one frame. If you can see the dropped frame, place the playhead on it and skip to *step 7*.
4. If the problem isn't visible, we can calculate the exact frame to cut out. Multiply the remainder from the calculation by the frame rate of the project (0.0833*60 = 4.988).
5. Round the number up or down to the nearest whole number. In this example, 5 is the nearest whole number, and that's our number of frames within the second. Therefore, the problem will be at the timecode 02:48;05 – the 5th frame of the 168th second of the video.
6. To get to the fifth frame of the second, use the arrow key method discussed in the *Checking the project frame rate – counting frames* section of *Chapter 5*.
7. Trim the problem frame out. To do so, split the project at the playhead position (⌘ + B) then press , (comma) to trim back one frame:

    - This will make no difference to the viewing experience of the video but should allow you to export

8. Try the export process again. If there's a new error, this one should give a frame later on in the project. Repeat these steps one more time with any new error, but if you get another after that, try the next solution.

This is another iMovie issue that demonstrates why it's useful to transcode your footage first: it can help to avoid dropped frames, along with all the other benefits, such as reducing file size and ensuring compatibility. But if you're in this situation, it may be that even after cutting problem frames out twice, they just seem to keep cropping up. In that case, the art of the botch is required. It's time to cheat the export process.

Solution 2 – screen-record the project

Sometimes, however hard you try, iMovie will put up constant barriers to stop you from exporting your project. In that case, you'll need to use a different method to turn your timeline into a video. The longer and more complex the project, the more likely this problem is to occur. It happens in other NLEs too – the 40-plus minute YouTube documentary *Cost of Concordia* (edited in paid NLE Adobe Premiere Pro) ran into a series of impassable export errors and had to be screen-recorded several times, stitched together, and uploaded.

To be able to screen-record a project, we also need to capture the sound coming from the timeline. Macs have inbuilt screen recorders, but no native way to record the sound coming from your computer. This is where Blackhole 2ch comes in. It's a virtual audio driver that lets you choose your Mac as a sound source once it's installed. The link to its GitHub page is in the *Technical requirements* section at the start of this chapter. To get it working for screen-recording a project once it's installed, see the following:

1. Go to **Apple Menu | System Settings | Sound**:

    If you're using macOS 12 (Monterey) or previous, **System Settings** will be listed as **System Preferences**.

2. In the **Output** tab, select **Blackhole 2ch**:

    If the Blackhole device isn't listed, the installation hasn't gone correctly; you'll need to try installing it again. For a different installation method that's pretty handy, but outside the scope of this book, try the package manager HomeBrew at `https://brew.sh/`.

With the computer sound set to output to our sound capture device, we can get the screen recording set up:

1. Open the macOS **Screenshot and Recording Options** menu with the ⌘ + ⇧ + 5 shortcut.
2. Click the **Record Entire Screen** option (as in *Figure 9.1*).
3. In the **Options** drop-down menu, make sure **Microphone** is set to **BlackHole 2ch**:

Figure 9.1 - The screenshot and recording options menu bar

4. Press the *Esc* key to close the menu bar.
5. Open iMovie and go to the project you need to screen-record.
6. Click on the timeline to place the playhead at the 00:00 timecode.
7. Bring up the recording options bar again with ⌘ + ⇧ + 5 and click **Record**.
8. Wait a couple of seconds, then start the project playing full-screen with the ⇧ + ⌘ + *F* shortcut.
9. When the video has finished, wait a couple of seconds again. Press ⌘ + ⇧ + 5 again and click the button in the center to stop recording.

The recording will save to wherever was selected under **Options** for the screenshot and recording options menu – most likely the desktop. Now, all that needs to be done is to tidy up the recording:

1. Double-click on the recording to open it in QuickTime Player.
2. Use the ⌘ + *T* shortcut to enter Trim mode.
3. Trim out the parts of the recording before the video starts and after it ends so that there's no dead air in the final video. Click **Trim**.
4. Go to **File | Export As**. Depending on the resolution of your Mac's screen, QuickTime Player might offer a 4K export; only export in the resolution the project was set to in iMovie.

With that, you should have a version of your video that can be uploaded or shared. However, be aware that screen-recording a project should only be a last resort. If your computer isn't high-powered enough, the screen recording will look jumpy and frames will be lost as your Mac tries to keep up with playing the project while running the screen recording at the same time. Ultimately, this can make the video not worth watching anyway.

The way to get around this is to screen-record small portions of the video at a time and stitch it together afterward. However, as we outlined in the *Solution 3 – split the project into multiple timelines* section, ironing out the cuts between recordings is very time-consuming and fiddly when there are sound and complex visuals to match up. For that reason, it's best to keep your screen recording as a safe copy of the video and keep trying to export the original – if you can bear it. An exported, rendered file is always the best outcome. Finally, let's look at some processes to go through if you come across an issue that's not listed in this chapter.

What if my editing issue isn't listed here?

Many of the issues that come up during editing are a result of the way iMovie or other Apple apps are designed. That's not an excuse, but it does mean that it's a matter of process and workflow rather than *fixing* an issue, so it takes a bit of a different approach. Do take a look back at earlier chapters if you can't find the issue here. For example, for setting your project to a certain resolution, see the *Determining project format* section of *Chapter 5*. If the audio is behaving weirdly or getting cut off early on your iPhone or iPad, hopefully, the *Editing audio in Movie mode* section of *Chapter 3* will help. If you can't find anything in this book about what you're experiencing, firstly I apologize. Secondly, take a look at the next section.

General solutions for general problems

If you come across a problem with iMovie that this book hasn't given a specific fix for, try the following steps in order and see whether they can help. You might find yourself trying the first couple of steps many times when editing:

1. Go back to the **Projects** screen by pressing *2* and double-click to go back into your project:

    - Alternatively, click on the timeline. It sounds a bit weird, but where your cursor sits can sometimes make editing clunky because its focus gets trapped in the Media Browser.

2. Quit and restart iMovie.

3. Check iMovie Preferences (⌘ + ,) are at their defaults (as in *Figure 9.2*):

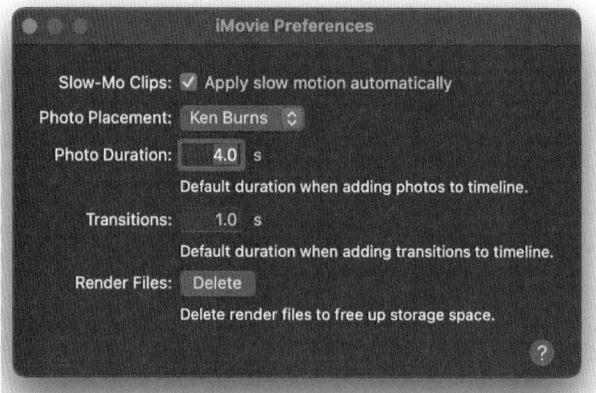

Figure 9.2 - iMovie Preferences' default settings

4. Restart your Mac.
5. Copy your project files into a new timeline.
6. Download and install a minor update (for example, version 12.4 to 12.5) or patch update (for example, 12.6.1 to 12.6.2) for macOS if there's an update available.
7. Search for the problem online and ask in help forums if you can't find a solution:

   - There's a community iMovie forum on the Apple website (`https://discussions.apple.com/community/ilife/imovie`), while on Reddit, there is r/iMovie (`https://www.reddit.com/r/iMovie`). At the time of publication, both are active support communities.

If the collective wisdom of the internet can't help, it might be time for some more drastic fixes. But you need to exercise caution with these and be prepared. Export any unfinished projects, then make sure to back up all of your rushes, other project media, and finally your iMovie Library to an external drive or online storage:

1. Delete the iMovie app before reinstalling it from the Mac App Store. To do this, open Launchpad (it should be on the Dock, but it will be in the Applications folder if not) and right-click on the iMovie icon. Click the **x** icon (*Figure 9.2*) to delete the app:

Figure 9.3 – iMovie in Launchpad

Finally, you should back up your Mac entirely on an external drive before trying these steps. If these changes make the experience of using your Mac worse in general, you're going to want to go back to how things were; these changes can't be rolled back without a backup. Make sure you read up on creating a backup using macOS' Time Machine in **System Settings** before you try any of these:

1. Download and install a major update for macOS (for example, macOS Monterey to Ventura) if there's an update available.
2. Delete and reinstall macOS itself, to start afresh.

Reinstalling macOS, in terms of removing absolutely everything from your hard drive, is a catch-all way to destroy whatever was causing problems in iMovie – apps, settings, preferences, the lot. As the problem could ultimately be coming from system-level files that you should never mess with, a technique like this can solve problems that you wouldn't have been able to.

Just remember, whatever the problem, the solution is rarely to go out and buy a new Mac. Apple has a responsibility to make sure its apps work on its computers, as intended. If a fresh install of macOS isn't solving things, and your Mac isn't a decades-old antique, then it's their responsibility to try and find a solution for you, warranty or not.

Summary

In this chapter, we looked at some of iMovie's most common problems, whether importing clips, editing in the timeline, or exporting a video file. Common troubleshooting tips such as quitting and restarting, copying clips to a new project, and transcoding footage before use should be applied liberally to avoid or quickly remedy any issue that crops up in iMovie. Hopefully, this chapter has armed you with tools to deal with iMovie problems and helped you understand that things will always go wrong when editing. It's never just you.

And that brings us to the end of this book about iMovie. Believe me, there's still more to discover, more to try, and more to achieve. But that's up to you now as an editor. Don't let people tell you iMovie isn't good enough – it's your skill, creativity, and flexibility that make iMovie a match for paid or industry-standard NLEs, and ultimately what helps you edit like a pro.

Index

A

actions
  editing, in Movie mode 54, 55
alpha channel 179
animated titles
  creating, in Keynote 186-188
  exporting, from Keynote 188, 189
animations
  building out 192-195
  with Dynamic Backgrounds 206-208
aspect ratio 51
  examples 211
  modifying, with Keynote 212-215
  sideways, exporting from iMovie 215-218
  working with 210-212
assembly edit 6, 108
  Clip Trimmer, using 110, 111
  Precision Editor, using 109
assembly editing 49
  in Movie mode 49
audio
  background audio, limitations 65
  editing, in Movie mode 64, 65
  fading 67, 68
  smooth audio transitions, making with J- and L-cuts 68-70
  sounds, layering in Movie mode 66, 67
audio ducking 39

audio keyframes
  creating, on Mac 168, 169
  using 168-170
Audio & Video tab
  music choice 114
  using 111-113
automatic editing
  cons 19
  pros 19
Average Bitrate
  using, disadvantages 233

B

background audio 64
  in iMovie, for macOS 92, 93
  limitations 65
backtiming 90
bitrate controls
  used, for compressing video to specific size 232
blue/green screen effect 157
  using 160-162
Build Order
  used, for creating multi-stage animations 189-192
Build Out animation 192-195

C

chroma keying 160
clip connection 89
clips
 rearranging, in Movie mode 50
clips, customizing in Movie mode 55
 audio volume 57
 filters 59
 Speed editor 55, 56
 titles 57-59
 voiceover and record 60
Clips mode
 audio, adding 11-14
 clips, splitting 10, 11
 using 9, 10
 video, adding 11-14
Clip Trimmer
 using 110, 111
codec 228
compound clips
 creating 172-174
 creating, in iMovie 172
compression 226
connected audio
 working with 91, 92
connected media 88
 working with 90, 91
crop to fill 51
cross-dissolve transitions 170
crossfading effect 68
custom titles
 creating, with Keynote 180-183
custom transitions
 overlays, using 204
cutaways
 used, for multi-camera editing 151, 152

cutaways, types
 B-Roll 147
 reaction shot 147
 take 148
cuts 60
 graphic match 61
 jump cut 60
 match on action 61
 montage 61
 rhythm cutting 61
 using 60, 61

D

double-exposure effect 150
Dynamic Backgrounds
 animation with 206-208

E

editing
 coherence 6
 conciseness 7
 meaning, adding 7, 8
 principles 5
 purposes 5
editing, process
 need for 4
Edit menu, Magic Movie
 Edit 26
 Music 29, 30
 Replace 31
 Speed 31
 Text 27, 28
 Titles 27
 using 25, 26
 Voiceover button 30, 31

edits
  QuickTime Player, selecting to make 14
encoder 210
events
  creating, in iMovie Library 78
  using 79
exporting 70, 71

F

fade handle 67
fade-to-black 61
files
  compressing, with Handbrake 226
fine cut 111
finished video
  saving 14
folder of videos
  batch-transcoding 225, 226
foreground audio 64
frame 10
frame rate 106
freesound
  URL 66

H

H.265 codec
  using 228
Handbrake
  audio quality 229
  bitrate controls, used for compressing video to specific size 232
  exporting from 222
  folder of videos, batch-transcoding 225, 226
  H.265 codec, using 228
  installing 219
  presets, creating 224, 225

  presets, using 223
  ProRes export, creating from mobile project 229, 230
  quality range 228, 229
  running 219
  source, adding to 220
  used, for compressing videos 228
  used, for transcoding multiple files 223
  using, to compress files 226
  using, to compress master video 230, 231
  video cropping, modifying 221
High-Efficiency Video Coding (HEVC) 189

I

iCloud Drive 100
images and transparency 184
iMovie 5, 17, 76
  background audio 92, 93
  cutaways, using to hide jump cuts 147
  editing issues 249
  events 77
  fade transitions, adding to 148-150
  filters 25
  for macOS 76
  importing, from devices 96
  import menu, customizing 98-100
  import menu, using 98-100
  Keynote files, importing into 185, 186
  libraries 76
  media, adding from Photos library 80
  media as favorited, marking 101, 102
  media as rejected, marking 101, 102
  Media Browser settings, customization 102-104
  media for editing, preparing 95, 96
  multiple iMovie Libraries, creating 78
  opacity effect, creating 150, 151

overlay 146
overlay type 147
Picture in Picture (PiP), using 162-164
risks of importing 97, 98
sideways, exporting from 215-218
solution 249-251

iMovie for macOS 95

iMovie Library 77
events, creating 78, 79
events, using 79

iMovie media
Audio & Video tab, using 111-113
backgrounds, using 119, 120
maps, using 117-119
titles, adding 115, 116
transitions, using 120-122
using 111

iMovie navigation, with keyboard shortcuts 81
editing tools 84-86
file and project actions 81
timeline and menu navigation 82, 83

iMovie, problem
audio and video, drift out of sync 241
export, unsuccessful 246
hard drive space, filling up 245
iCloud videos stuck for download 238, 239
imported videos, not playing 238
stuttery editing 242, 243
video format, disapproval 236

iMovie project settings 104
frame rate, checking 106
frame rate, selecting 106-108
process 105
rules 104

iMovie, solution
audio clip speed, modifying 241, 242
effects, compounding 243

iCloud storage space, freeing up 239, 240
problem frame, deleting 246, 247
project media, removing from iCloud libraries 240
project, screen-recording 247-249
project settings, modifying 243
project, splitting into multiple timelines 244, 245
render files, deleting 245
video files, storing in Finder 238
videos, transcoding 237

in-file editing
with QuickTime Player on macOS 8

inter-frame 227

intertitles 45

iOS 15, 16
keyboard shortcuts, using 49

iPadOS 15, 16
keyboard shortcuts, using 49

J

J- and L-cuts
used, for making smooth audio transitions 68-70

K

Ken Burns animation 23
Ken Burns effect 51-53
keyboard shortcuts
using, on iOS 49
using, on iPadOS 49

keyframe animations
audio keyframes, using 168-170
transition effects, using 171
using, on macOS 166-168

Keynote
   animated titles, creating 186-188
   animated titles, exporting from 188, 189
   files, importing, into iMovie 185, 186
   titles, exporting 183, 184
   used, for creating custom titles 180-183
   used, for creating path animations 196-201
   used, for modifying aspect ratio 212-215

Kuleshov effect 19

L

layering 66

M

macOS
   keyframe animations, using 166-168

Magic Move
   used, for creating transitions 204, 205

Magic Move animations
   using 202-204

Magic Movie 18, 19
   Edit menu, using 25, 26
   exporting 33
   graphics styles, customizing with
      Styles menu 24, 25
   limitations 39
   movie, creating 20-22
   music, customizing 25
   photos, adding 23, 24
   videos, adding 23, 24
   videos, combining with 31-33

magnetic timeline 89, 90

master file 143
   exporting 142, 143

media for editing
   preparing, in iMovie 95, 96

mobile project
   ProRes export, creating 229, 230

motion blur 107

Movie mode 42
   actions, editing 54, 55
   assembly editing 49
   audio, editing 64, 65
   clips, customizing 55
   clips, rearranging 50
   creating 42
   need for 42
   photos, editing 51
   project, creating 42-44
   project, settings 46-49
   setting up 42
   sounds, layering 66, 67
   transitions, editing 61, 62
   video, adding 46
   videos, editing 53

Movie mode interface 44

Movie mode Media Browser
   using 45, 46

multi-camera editing 151
   multi-camera footage, editing 156, 157
   multi-camera footage, syncing 153-155
   with cutaways 151, 152
   with opacity effect 151, 152

multi-camera footage
   editing 156, 157
   syncing 153-155

multi-stage animations
   adjusting 195, 196
   creating, with Build Order 189-192
   exporting 195, 196
   importing 195, 196

multi-stage Magic Move animations
   exporting 205, 206
   importing 205, 206

N

non-linear editing (NLE) programs 7

O

opacity effect
   creating 150, 151
   used, for multi-camera editing 151, 152
Open Broadcast Software (OBS) 210
overlays 53
   used, for custom transitions 204
   used, for displaying whole photo 53

P

path animations
   creating, with Keynote 196-201
peak loudness 30
photo animations
   using 51-53
photos
   adding, in Magic Movie 23, 24
   editing, in Movie mode 51
Photos library
   media, adding from 80
Picture in Picture (PiP) 162, 179
   Swap transitions, using 164-166
   using, in iMovie 162-164
   Zoom transitions, using 164-166
picture lock 64
playhead 6
post-production process 4
Precision Editor
   using 62-64, 109
presets
   creating, in Handbrake 224, 225
   using, in Handbrake 223

project files 71
Project Media tab
   using 80
ProRes 227
ProRes export
   creating, from mobile project 229, 230

Q

quality control 70, 71
QuickTime Player
   selecting, to make edits 14
QuickTime Player, on macOS
   in-file editing with 8

R

ramping 170
room tone 70, 170

S

shot/reverse-shot 147
slip edit 63, 110
sound-bridging 121
split screen effect 157
   adding, to iMovie for macOS 159
   creating, on iOS 157, 158
Storyboard editing menu
   using 36, 37
Storyboard Edit mode
   using 38
Storyboard mode 18
   limitations 39
   project, creating 34-36
   using 33, 34
Swap transitions 166
   using, in Picture in Picture (PiP) 164-166

T

timecode 6
timelapse 171
timeline 6
   magnetic timeline 89, 90
   tracks, versus connections 87, 88
timeline paradigm 6, 18
toolbar, editing tools 122
   color balance 122-124
   color correction 124, 125
   copy and paste 141, 142
   crop 125-127
   crop actions 132-134
   enhance 140, 141
   equalizer 136-139
   filters and audio effects 139, 140
   information 140, 141
   Ken Burns animation, creating 128-132
   noise reduction 136-139
   Reset All 141
   speed 139
   stabilization 134, 135
   volume 136-139
track 87
Trailer mode 33
transcoder 210
transition effects
   using 170, 171
transitions
   creating, with Magic Move 204, 205
   editing, in Movie mode 61, 62
   using 60, 61
transparency
   exporting, in video 189

Trim mode
   using 8, 9
trim to playhead 26

V

video
   compressing, with Handbrake 228
   transparency, exporting 189
video cropping
   modifying, in Handbrake 221
videos
   adding, in Magic Movie 23, 24
   adding, in Movie mode 46
   combining, with Magic Movie 31-33
   editing, in Movie mode 53

W

whip-pan 135

Z

Zoom tool
   using 104
Zoom transitions
   using, in Picture in Picture (PiP) 164-166

Packtpub.com

Subscribe to our online digital library for full access to over 7,000 books and videos, as well as industry leading tools to help you plan your personal development and advance your career. For more information, please visit our website.

Why subscribe?

- Spend less time learning and more time coding with practical eBooks and Videos from over 4,000 industry professionals
- Improve your learning with Skill Plans built especially for you
- Get a free eBook or video every month
- Fully searchable for easy access to vital information
- Copy and paste, print, and bookmark content

Did you know that Packt offers eBook versions of every book published, with PDF and ePub files available? You can upgrade to the eBook version at `packtpub.com` and as a print book customer, you are entitled to a discount on the eBook copy. Get in touch with us at `customercare@packtpub.com` for more details.

At www.packtpub.com, you can also read a collection of free technical articles, sign up for a range of free newsletters, and receive exclusive discounts and offers on Packt books and eBooks.

Other Books You May Enjoy

If you enjoyed this book, you may be interested in these other books by Packt:

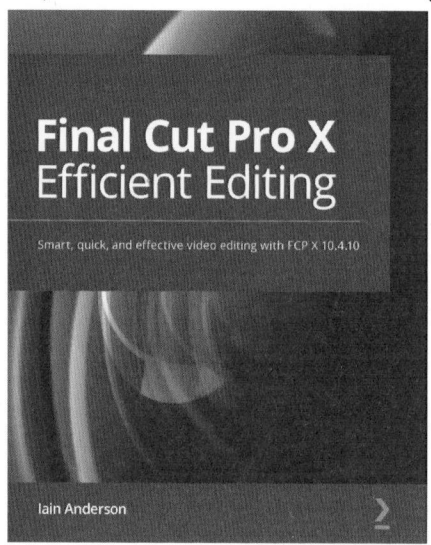

Final Cut Pro Efficient Editing

Iain Anderson

ISBN: 9781839213243

Understand the media import process and delve into media management.

Effectively organize your footage so you can find the right shot quickly.

Discover how to assemble a rough cut edit.

Enhance an edit with color correction, effects, transitions, titles, captions, and much more.

Sweeten the audio by controlling volume, using compression, and adding effects.

Filmora Efficient Editing

Alexander Zacharias

ISBN: 9781801814201

- Navigate Filmora's interface with ease
- Add and manipulate audio using audio tracks
- Create high-quality professional videos with advanced features in Filmora
- Use split screens and Chroma keys to create movie magic
- Create a gaming video and add humor to it

Packt is searching for authors like you

If you're interested in becoming an author for Packt, please visit `authors.packtpub.com` and apply today. We have worked with thousands of developers and tech professionals, just like you, to help them share their insight with the global tech community. You can make a general application, apply for a specific hot topic that we are recruiting an author for, or submit your own idea.

Share Your Thoughts

Now you've finished *Edit Like a Pro with iMovie*, we'd love to hear your thoughts! Scan the QR code below to go straight to the Amazon review page for this book and share your feedback or leave a review on the site that you purchased it from.

`https://packt.link/r/1-803-23890-9`

Your review is important to us and the tech community and will help us make sure we're delivering excellent quality content.

Download a free PDF copy of this book

Thanks for purchasing this book!

Do you like to read on the go but are unable to carry your print books everywhere?

Is your eBook purchase not compatible with the device of your choice?

Don't worry, now with every Packt book you get a DRM-free PDF version of that book at no cost.

Read anywhere, any place, on any device. Search, copy, and paste code from your favorite technical books directly into your application.

The perks don't stop there, you can get exclusive access to discounts, newsletters, and great free content in your inbox daily

Follow these simple steps to get the benefits:

1. Scan the QR code or visit the link below

https://packt.link/free-ebook/9781803238906

2. Submit your proof of purchase
3. That's it! We'll send your free PDF and other benefits to your email directly

Printed in Great Britain
by Amazon